PRAISE FOR PAUL MONES'S
WHEN ^CHILD KILLS

"Not since the highly publicized '60 Minutes' interview of Richard Jahnke, who at age 16 killed his father in their Wyoming home, and Alan Predergast's ensuing book, have we glimpsed the stark reality of parricide. Mones . . . the leading authority in defending these cases . . . humanely conveys the plight of children caught in the web of child abuse and/or neglect. With compassionate insight, he documents the cases of eight children and presents interviews with twelve more, chronicling the years of abuse that led to their desperate actions. . . . In an informative but casual writing style, he presents a strong case for compassion toward those trapped in a justice system unwilling or unable to cope with family violence. HIGHLY RECOMMENDED." —*Library Journal*

"In an impressive, well-documented study of juvenile crime and parental sadism, L.A. attorney Mones, writing with sensitivity, eloquently defends brutalized teenage parricides."
—*Publishers Weekly*

"This book is the most compelling indictment of the consequences of child abuse that I have ever read. *WHEN A CHILD KILLS* is an excellent book that I highly recommend." —Alvin F. Poussaint, M.D.
Psychiatrist, Harvard Medical School

A LITERARY GUILD ALTERNATE SELECTION

A DOUBLEDAY BOOK CLUB ALTERNATE SELECTION

WHEN A CHILD KILLS

Abused Children Who Kill Their Parents

PAUL MONES

POCKET STAR BOOKS

New York   London   Toronto   Sydney   Tokyo   Singapore

A Pocket Star Book published by
POCKET BOOKS, a division of Simon & Schuster Inc.
1230 Avenue of the Americas, New York, NY 10020

ISBN: 0-671-67421-8

First Pocket Books paperback printing September 1992

10 9 8 7 6 5 4 3 2 1

POCKET STAR BOOKS and colophon are registered
trademarks of Simon & Schuster Inc.

Cover photos by Jim Galante Studio

Printed in the U.S.A.

PERMISSIONS

TO ALL THE CHILDREN
WHO SUFFER SILENTLY AT
THE HANDS OF THEIR PARENTS

ACKNOWLEDGMENTS

I am privileged to have lived a life so full of high-minded, compassionate people.

To the late Paul Davidoff, my mentor and dear friend, I am indebted for instilling within me the will to fight the good fight until the end.

This book is the direct result of my work as a children's rights advocate. I first began in early 1980 as the director of Juvenile Advocates, a program designed to assist incarcerated children in West Virginia. The following attorneys not only gave me critical support in carrying out a difficult job, they inspired and motivated me through their own work, teaching me that true justice is not a given in our country but something that must be fought for every day. To Dan Hedges, Charles "Skip" Garten, Lee Adler, Circuit Court judge Larry Starcher, and Darrell McGraw, former justice of the West Virginia Supreme Court of Appeals, I shall always be indebted.

I want to give special thanks to the following people, who provided critical assistance throughout the writing of this book. To psychiatrists Dr. Dorothy Otnow Lewis of New York University and Dr. Shervert Frazier of McLean's Hospital in Boston, psychologist Dr. Ronald Ebert, also of McLean's Hospital, and sociologist Dr. Murray Straus of the University of New Hampshire, I am immensely grateful. All freely gave of their time and patiently answered my questions. I would also like to thank Jerry Miller, director of the National Center for Institutions and Alternatives, for his insights and the critical casework support he has given me over the last ten years. I am also indebted to Dr. Eli Newberger of Children's Hospital in Boston, whose early support of my interest in parricide gave me the confidence to persevere.

I would also like to acknowledge with deep appreciation the assistance of other colleagues in the family-violence area: Kirk Williams of the University of Colorado at Boulder, David Finkelhor of the University of New Hampshire, and Anne Cohn Donnelly of the National Committee for the Prevention of Child Abuse and Neglect for statistical assistance and input. I am also grateful to the FBI's Uniform Crime Report division for their research assistance, and to Los Angeles County deputy district attorney Scott Gordon for his helpful insights.

To my literary agent and attorney, Susan Grode, I remain eternally grateful for making a dream become reality. A person of immense loyalty, she has created a new life for me, opening up the whole new crazy and thoroughly satisfying world of writing.

I am forever indebted to Bill Grose, senior vice-president of Pocket Books, for his willingness to take a chance on a first-time author and for his enormous support throughout the writing.

I am also very grateful to all of the staff at Pocket Books and Simon & Schuster who helped make this book what it is. For the critical changes that were made I am very thankful to Elaine Pfefferblit, who was crucial in helping to shape my original vision; Michael Sanders, who gave the book coherency and put it to bed; and to Claire Zion, for her support in making the final touches.

The understanding, immense devotion, and moral and emotional support my friends Eben Rawls, Skip Reeder, Richard Saul, and David Burke gave me during the last three years has provided the fuel it took to finish this book. I want to thank especially my dear friend Don Dutton, who, wearing his professor-of-psychology hat, provided critical editorial assistance, especially in framing the psychological analyses in the book.

I learned how to be an attorney in law school, but the foundation for my dedication to creating a more just and equal society was laid by my parents, Ray and Gwen. They instilled in me at an early age that we enrich ourselves not by saying "me first," but by helping those less fortunate. Their contribution to this book, along with that of my sister, Lesli, who provided unconditional support and encouragement to what I once thought a pipe dream, is inestimable.

The words on this page would never even have existed if my wife, Niki, had not instilled in me the confidence to put pen to paper and write the initial proposal, nor would it have been completed without her selfless, tireless emotional and editorial support at every stage. Through helping me with that one paragraph I had been obsessed with for a week to my panicked phone calls telling her I had to stay late, she shared the struggle of the writing, and can now share the joy in its completion.

CONTENTS

CONTENTS

AUTHOR'S NOTE

I shall be forever grateful to the children who permitted me to include their stories in this book, for quite literally, it would not have been possible without them. Though the interviews were particularly excruciating for some of them, all willingly did it because they believed it necessary to prevent another child from killing his or her parents. I am especially thankful to those who will be reading these words from the confines of their dimly lit cells. The cooperation of all their family members, friends, and neighbors, as well as their defense attorneys, is sincerely and deeply appreciated. I would also like to thank the prosecutors, judges, and detectives who gave me their time.

Though this book contains the stories of eight children who killed their parents, I interviewed fifteen others who, though their accounts do not appear here, helped me immensely. I deeply thank them, their families, and their attorneys, for they gave me critical insight. This book is, in fact, as much about them as it is about the eight I chose to include.

The names and identities of all the people in this book, especially the children's, have been significantly altered in order to protect their confidentiality. To insure this, in certain cases I also developed composite characters. Dates, locations, and certain other facts have been changed for a similar reason.

The material in this book comes from trial notes; court

transcripts; depositions; personal interviews conducted with the children, and their family members, friends, neighbors, and others before, during, and after trial; police and coroners' reports; interviews with defense attorneys, detectives, prosecutors, and judges; and press reports.

Persuade me to the murther of your lordship,
But that I told him, the revengive gods
'Gainst parricide did all the thunder bend,
Spoke, with how manifold and strong bond
The child was bound to the father.

—*King Lear*, II, i, 1144—48

WHEN A CHILD KILLS

Introduction

Founded in 1895, the West Virginia Industrial School for Girls sits at the end of a winding one-lane road. While its name conjures up benign images of sober young women working tirelessly to better themselves, one look at the massive limestone edifices and barred windows immediately reveals its actual mission. It is a reform school, a prison for children.

In the spring of 1980, I became the director of Juvenile Advocates, a West Virginia–based children's rights organization funded by the United States Department of Justice. Our primary aim was to prevent the illegal and unnecessary incarceration of youth in the state, to this day a critical problem not only in West Virginia but throughout our nation. It is a dark irony that children who break the law routinely receive not only miserable legal assistance, but are locked up in substandard and oftentimes dangerous jails and detention facilities.

It was my responsibility to provide legal help to the juveniles held in West Virginia's reform schools, youth detention centers, county jails, and mental hospitals. Since the kids could not come to me, I spent most of my time on the road, setting up makeshift offices at institutions such as the Industrial School for Girls. When I wasn't interviewing teenagers, I was usually in court, seeking to change an institution's practices or to obtain the release of a child. I never did make many friends in the legal establishment, since the people I challenged were judges, prosecutors, jail administrators, and inept defense attorneys.

I had taken the job primarily to escape the drudgery of Legal Aid. Though preventing evictions and protecting clients from unscrupulous businessmen who prey on low-income people was important work, after two years it seemed as if I were only rearranging deck chairs on the *Titanic*. Even though I was completely ignorant about the juvenile justice system, I was sure the job would be rewarding. The last contact I had had with kids who broke the law had been at the corner candy store near my home in New York. Back in the late 1950s and early 1960s we called these kids "j.d.'s" or hoods. They sported black motorcycle jackets, pointy-toed shoes, and Brylcreem pompadours, while the girls wore toreador pants so tight they looked painted on, along with the dramatically dark eye makeup that seemed to end at their ears. When the j.d.'s weren't lounging against some souped-up '58 Chevy smoking nonfilter cigarettes, they were usually sitting in the last row of the "slow learner" class.

It was common knowledge on the street that, each time these kids were arrested, the cops would give them "j.d. cards." If you accumulated three, off you went to reform school. When my friends and I talked about j.d.'s, our conversation inevitably turned to guessing how many j.d. cards a particular kid had.

Micky Donnelly was a j.d.'s j.d. He was short, with these deep-set chestnut eyes and overhanging, heavy, dark-brown eyebrows that said "Don't screw with me." And nobody ever did. My most vivid memory of him was when Mr. Dortmunder, my tyrannical and rotund seventh-grade industrial-arts teacher, smacked Micky in the head for talking in class. Obviously Mr. D. didn't know about Micky's reputation, for, the next moment, Dortmunder was lying on his back next to a table saw. Neither I nor any of my other thirteen-year-old classmates were going to pull Micky off our esteemed educator. Dortmunder survived the attack, but the word around school the next day was that the incident qualified Micky for his third j.d. card. I never saw him again.

Before I joined Juvenile Advocates, I imagined the reform schools filled with clones of Micky Donnelly. Several visits to the various institutions, however, were enough to open my eyes. While the penal facilities had their share of Mickys, kids who had committed violent crimes against others, almost 90 percent had been arrested for property-related offenses—grand theft auto, breaking and entering, vandalism. Proportionately few, I found out, ever assaulted anyone.

At the time of my first visit to the Industrial School for Girls in the summer of 1980, the original four-story, dark-red limestone structure had long been closed down. Across a deep ravine several hundred yards away, the Department of Corrections had constructed a rather innocuous two-story building purposely designed to look more like a college dorm than a penitentiary.

About once every six weeks, I visited the reformatory, setting up an office in one of the empty classrooms in the school across from the main residential building. During each visit, anywhere from five to fifteen "residents" would relate their problems and complaints, all the way from having an incompetent lawyer to being forced to wear ill-fitting sneakers.

Most, I noticed, had difficulty expressing themselves and suffered from learning disabilities. Rebecca, whom I met about a year after I began my visits, was the exception.

She was the last of twelve teenage girls I saw that day. Like almost every other inmate, she had a pasty complexion from the lack of outdoor activity, but the contrast of her long, jet-black hair brushing across her forehead made her face seem even paler than the others. She was tall and uncharacteristically slim for someone forced to subsist on a diet rich in fat and starch. Before I even introduced myself, the winsome fifteen-year-old strode up to me like a soldier reporting to her commanding officer and declared, "I shouldn't be here. I didn't do anything wrong." Though it was a familiar refrain, she spoke with real conviction, forcing me to pay close attention to the words that then spilled out.

Originally charged with theft and illegal possession of a .32-caliber handgun, Rebecca had been in the institution for about eight months. As part of a plea bargain, she had pled guilty to the theft, and the state dropped the gun charge. Oddly, she had no other criminal record, though she did have a long history of running away from home.

Before I could say a word, Rebecca had launched into a rapid-fire speech about being "set up."

"Set up? By whom?" I asked skeptically.

"Everybody, just everybody," she replied, indignant.

"Before we get into what other people did to you, tell me one thing. At the time the cop stopped you, did you have a gun in your purse?"

She nodded, then shot back, "But you gotta understand, it's much, much more complicated than that."

It almost always is.

Rebecca came from a tiny mining town in northern West Virginia, a place where coal dust coats everything from the lungs to the light bulbs. She had lived with her mother and her mother's boyfriend in a cramped two-bedroom trailer since her parents' divorce about seven years earlier. Her father worked odd jobs out of state and only occasionally made it back to see his daughter for Christmas or Thanksgiving. In fact, she had not even heard from him for two years until he called one evening just after her fourteenth birthday. He told her he was back in town for a while and wanted to see his "little girl."

Rebecca jumped at the chance to go stay with him. It was not just because she missed him; she desperately wanted to get away from her mother. She and her mother battled constantly, and everything seemed to produce an argument, from what to have for breakfast to what time Rebecca had to be home after school. "The only thing Mama and me could agree on was the color of the sky," Rebecca told me.

Things with her father went well for a few days, until one rainy Saturday morning when she woke up to find him straddling her chest trying to stick his penis in her mouth. They struggled fiercely, and she managed to push him off. Furious, she ran back to her house, and once inside, headed straight to the nightstand in her mother's room. She took out an ivory-handled .32-caliber revolver, stuffed it in her purse, and ran out the door.

Her mother screamed for her to come back with the gun, but Rebecca kept on walking. "I had one thought," she said to me. "Blow the son of a bitch away."

As she trudged along the side of the road with tears streaming down her face, she was boiling with anger and at the same time was overwhelmed by depression. "My own dad," she thought, "how could he do this to me?"

Just before reaching her father's house, she decided to turn around. "He just wasn't worth it," she told me. Within minutes a county sheriff called by her mother screeched up beside her. She was handcuffed and thrown in the back seat.

Rebecca told her mom and appointed lawyer that her father tried to rape her, but her attorney urged her to plead guilty to a lesser charge, saying the judge would not believe her story. Reluctantly, she agreed.

Before meeting Rebecca, I had interviewed numerous reform-school residents who had been abused by their parents in ways far worse than she. And yet it had simply not seemed significant to me at the time that not one of them had ever lashed out against his or her abusive parent. Their crimes, from simple assault to murder, from shoplifting to armed robbery, were perpetrated against friends, neighbors, teachers, and strangers—all innocent bystanders.

I drove away from the reform school that afternoon knowing I had been profoundly affected by Rebecca, but not yet comprehending exactly how. Her halfhearted attempt to kill her father seemed both totally reasonable and yet completely appalling.

Rebecca's attorney refused to answer my phone calls or letters. When I spoke to her probation officer a week after the interview, I was surprised to learn that this had not been the first incident of sexual abuse. Rebecca's father had probably sexually abused her when she was seven years old, but no formal charges had been brought against him.

With a calm I did not feel, I asked the probation officer why Rebecca's charges of sodomy and sexual abuse were not considered by the court.

"I don't know if you know it, Mr. Mones," she said disdainfully, "but Rebecca is, ah, well, ah . . . a very loose girl, and you know . . ."

"What this girl may do with a fifteen-year-old boy on a Friday night in the back seat of a car is one thing," I retorted angrily. "But in this state, when a father has sex or even tries to have sex with his fourteen-year-old daughter, it is a crime."

"If you think she shouldn't be there, you have your remedies," she coldly replied, then slammed down the phone.

Though I was immensely sympathetic to Rebecca's plight, I had seventy-five other cases that demanded my attention. By the time I had finished preparing Rebecca's case for appeal, she had completed her sentence and had been released from the Industrial School. My legal obligation to Rebecca was ended, but my journey into the world of those who live on the outer shores of humanity had just begun.

In researching potential defenses for Rebecca, I was amazed to discover how little had been written about the subject of parricide, children who kill their parents. Only a few court decisions dealt with patricide or matricide, and none dealt with the family dynamics underlying the killings. All the cases portrayed the parents as normal, righteous people cut down by their deranged or wicked children. Typical of these decisions was the 1954 New Jersey matricide case of State v. Beard. After upholding the first-degree murder conviction of the son, the New Jersey Supreme Court felt compelled to comment, "The killing of one's own mother has horror written in its very thought." Similarly, I could not find one legal-journal article on the subject.

The scant professional research that I could locate was mostly contained in psychiatric journals, the articles primarily written from a traditional psychiatric (usually psychoanalytical) perspective, the homicide analyzed solely in terms of the child's own intrinsic mental processes. Though several articles discussed parricide as the child's reaction to a brutal and sadistic parent, the majority seemed to ignore completely the child's relationship with his family and greater social environment. According to these theories, the child himself was not even aware of the motive for the homicide, since that was locked deep in his subconscious. Though they had the support of the mainstream mental-health community, I found most of these theories eminently unsatisfactory, for experience told me that they explained only part of the story, ignoring the fact that there was a real and unquestionable motivation present—the parents' abusive actions—which had nothing to do with unconscious processes.

What disturbed me even more was that, though the dearth of information on the subject might have suggested that parricide was almost unknown in our society, the crime statistics said otherwise. Since 1976, when the FBI began to tabulate homicides according to the relationship between victim and offender, patricide and matricide have accounted for between 1.5 to 2.5 percent of all homicides, which means three to four hundred cases each year in the United States. Though these are comparatively insignificant numbers statistically, they are profoundly distressing in human terms.

Parricide seems largely to have escaped the attention of lawyers, psychologists, psychiatrists, social workers, and sociologists, yet it has long been firmly established as a tragic myth in popular culture and literature. From my first high-school lit courses, I had known that parricide was an age-old phenomenon and definitely not some social disease attributable to drugs, rock and roll, or the moral disintegration of late twentieth-century American society.

The ancient Greeks, we learned, were well versed in parent killing. The great dramatist Sophocles told the story of Oedipus, the mythic king of Thebes, who killed his father, Laius, and later married his mother, Jocasta. Euripides and Aeschylus, two other Greek dramatists, wrote about Orestes and Electra—the children of the warrior Agamemnon—who killed their mother, Clytemnestra.

Patricide and matricide are also prominent themes in the writings of Shakespeare (*Hamlet* and *King Lear*); Dostoevsky (*Crime and Punishment* and *The Brothers Karamazov*); Eugene O'Neill (*Mourning Becomes Electra*) and Albert Camus (*The Stranger*). Without a doubt, the most famous parricide story in American culture is that of Lizzie Borden.

Though Lizzie Borden was a real person who was arrested for the ax murder of her parents, Andrew and Abby Borden, in Fall River, Massachusetts, in 1892, I use the word *story* because the case has taken on such mythic proportions. At least two dramas, a musical, and numerous books and essays have been written about the case. And then of course there is the school-yard rhyme:

> Lizzie Borden took an ax
> And gave her mother forty whacks;
> When she saw what she had done,
> She gave her father forty-one.

Contrary to the voluminous folklore that has grown up around the Borden case, Lizzie was found *not* guilty. And it was not because she was adjudged to be insane or acting in self-defense. Lizzie Borden was found not guilty because, as Ann Jones points out in *Women Who Kill,* the crime was simply beyond the comprehension of the community; they could not bring themselves to believe, even with very convincing evidence, that prim and proper Lizzie could have done such a thing.

Parricide, prosecutor Hosea Knowlton said in his closing argument, is "the most horrible word that the English language knows." Similarly, Lizzie's defense attorney, George Robinson, rested his case by telling the jury: "It is not impossible that a good person may go wrong. One heretofore good may go wrong and a reputation be blasted by a wrongful act, but our human experience teaches us that if a daughter grows up in one of our homes . . . [is] educated in our schools, walks our streets, associates with the best people, and is devoted to the service of God and man . . . it is not within the human experience to find her suddenly come out into the rankest and baldest of murderesses. That would be a condition of things so contrary to all that our human life has taught us that our hearts and feelings revolt at the conception." The words ring as true today as they did almost one hundred years ago; most of us have a difficult time accepting that any child, for any reason, could kill his mother or father. As you will read, denial and shock permeate the fabric of these cases, in the child's family, in the courtroom, and throughout the community.

Always the most profound of taboos in ours and every other society, parricide directly contravenes a universal religious and cultural principle—children must venerate their parents. The familiar biblical exhortation to "honor thy mother and father" is in fact relatively moderate when compared to the Chinese Confucian tenet of "filial piety." In feudal Chinese society, parents not only arranged marriages and directed their children's educations and careers, but every action a person contemplated was first considered in light of its effect on parental well-being and family honor.

Parricide is so singularly distressing to us, too, because it goes beyond religious principles and challenges the very structure of society; it is truly the definitive act of rebellion against the society's rules and order. In contemporary culture, our family loyalty and honor is but a smaller reflection of loyalty to the larger group, our country, and one's obedience to parents is therefore equated with loyalty to one's country. In fact, *Webster's Third New International Dictionary* defines the word *parricide,* after a primary definition of killing mother, father, or close relative, as "one that commits the crime of treason against his country."

This concept is deeply rooted in our language as well. *Patriot* and *parricide* are derived from the same Latin root *patr,* meaning father, and in the throes of nationalistic fervor we refer to our country not by name, but by using the political words of endearment *motherland* or *fatherland.*

In pre–World War II Imperial Japan, loyalty to the father was *literally* equated with loyalty and respect for the emperor. Ancient Japanese custom dictated that the child had an unquestionable obligation to "repay parental favor and kindness" with absolute obedience. Thus, the most blasphemous crime a Japanese citizen could commit next to killing the emperor was *akugyaku.*

Akugyaku, "villainy," meant taking the life of a father or lineal male ascendant, a form of treason. *Akugyaku* and *muhon* (the murder of the emperor) were the two most serious offenses and thus carried the most stringent of punishments— death or life in prison. All other homicides, for example, killing a mother, friend, or storekeeper, were considered "ordinary murder" and carried a penalty of three years to life. While parent-killing drew the most serious punishment, infanticide was considered the least grave form of murder, carrying a penalty of less than three years.

In my further research, I also discovered that newspaper and magazine coverage of parricide was minimal, even in our time. What little reporting there was focused almost exclusively on the lurid details of the homicide or the parent's good reputation. The child murderer was portrayed as insane or utterly malevolent. It did not seem possible that there was *anything* a parent could do to trigger his or her own demise. To even think otherwise would have been sacrilegious.

In 1979, an article entitled "Murder Strikes at Home" appeared in the magazine the *National Review.* In discussing the motivations of a young man who killed both his parents, the author (a close friend of the deceased couple) wrote, "What had driven the boy who called me uncle to this mad act of violence? An inherent mental instability? Had the anti-war hysteria and counter-culture somehow dissolved his personality? Or, more likely, drugs? For certain individuals a single dose of LSD is enough to upset the mental balance permanently."

In the media coverage of these cases, in the consciousness of the community, and in the attitudes of the legal and mental-health professions, historically one crucial element was glaringly absent—an awareness and understanding of child abuse. Why didn't this hidden motive come to light sooner? The fact is that, until child abuse entered the national consciousness in the late 1970s, it was as if it had never existed before. Children never spoke about their physical, sexual, and emotional battering; friends and neighbors never admitted they saw any mistreatment; and no doctor, lawyer, or judge ever bothered asking about it. This aspect of parricidal killings only began to be treated seriously after a seemingly inexplicable murder on the evening of November 16, 1982.

Sixteen-year-old Richard Jahnke lived with his father, mother, and sister in an upper-middle-class neighborhood in Cheyenne, Wyoming. Mr. Jahnke, a criminal investigator for the IRS, was known to the community as a strict disciplinarian who often beat his children severely if they chewed food with their mouths open or brushed their teeth improperly. Richard was not a troublemaker; on the contrary he was a responsible teenager who did well in school and was a member of the local ROTC.

Before going out for dinner one night, the elder Jahnke, in one of his typical tirades, shoved his son, saying, "I'm disgusted with the shit you turned out to be. I don't want you to be here when I get back." As soon as his father pulled out of the driveway, Richard raced around the house collecting all his father's weapons. He armed himself with a .38-caliber pistol, a combat knife, and a twelve-gauge shotgun. He gave his sister a .30-caliber carbine and told her to wait in the living room. She would be his backup in case their father made it into the house. Richard then went to the garage and waited.

Several hours later, as Mr. Jahnke was getting out of the family car, Richard ended his namesake's life.

Soon after Richard was arrested and charged with first-degree murder, he told the police, "I just couldn't handle it anymore." This became the first parricide to attract intense national attention since Lizzie Borden because Richard claimed he was acting in self-defense. In painstaking detail, Richard and other witnesses told the jury how he had been brutalized since he was two years old, how Mr. Jahnke had sexually and physically battered Mrs. Jahnke and Richard's sister, Deborah. Though the jury was moved by Richard's plight, they found him guilty of manslaughter. The judge had no such mercy and sentenced him to five to fifteen years in the state pen. The Wyoming Supreme Court upheld the verdict and the sentence in 1984, but the public outcry was so intense that the following year Gov. Ed Herschler commuted Richard's sentence and he was released.

Two years and about 420 reform-school interviews later, I found myself working on my first actual parricide case. There was nothing remarkable about seventeen-year-old Donald. Known as a shy boy, he played clarinet in the high school marching band, attended Bible classes on Wednesday nights, and had never been arrested. He lived on a small farm in the West Virginia panhandle with his father, a brick mason. Much like Richard Jahnke, Donald had been mercilessly beaten and verbally belittled since he was a young boy. As his dad watched a game show one evening, the short boy with braces and Coke-bottle eyeglasses snuck up from behind and shot his father three times in the head. He calmly put the .38 pistol back in the living room closet and called the police. It was Jahnke and Rebecca all over again.

I resumed the research I had begun on Rebecca's behalf, but much more exhaustively this time. Nothing had changed. Though the Jahnke case had thrust the abuse/parricide issue into the harsh light of day, I quickly discovered that attorneys and judges still had an unenlightened view of parricide and refused to acknowledge the motivations involved. Though the feminist legal community had, in the late 1970s, embraced the similar issue of battered women who killed their husbands, a cogent framework for the defense of patricide and matricide cases was still lacking. Even among my colleagues in the children's rights arena, I found few who had any interest, much less experience, in the area.

Despite my efforts, Donald was ultimately convicted of first-degree murder and sentenced to ten years to life. His case taught me a simple but critical lesson: the heart of a parricide defense is the child abuse prosecution of the dead parent. The parent must be held accountable in death for the abuse she visited against her child in life. Putting on such a defense demands that the attorney reconstruct in painstaking detail the relationship between child and parent, a process that is both difficult and emotionally draining.

In the conventional homicide case, an attorney need only concern herself with events on the day of the killing or perhaps two or three days prior to it. In parricides, an incident that occurred twelve years before the killing is as important as what took place twelve hours before it. This reconstruction is frequently frustrated not only by faded memories and missing documents, but by our collective aversion to saying anything bad about the dead, regardless of how dreadfully the person acted in life.

Since meeting Rebecca in 1981, I have worked on about one hundred cases in thirty states. While I have represented a number of these children by myself, early on I decided to work primarily as a consultant to local attorneys in order to provide expertise and advice to as many children as possible. If I defended the entire case alone, I could handle no more than three or four cases a year. As an attorney's expert, however, I work regularly on six to eight cases at any one time in as many states. My involvement ranges from simple strategizing with the attorney over the phone to delivering a closing argument to the twelve strangers charged with deciding the fate of a frightened sixteen-year-old.

As with most criminal matters, the vast majority of parricide cases are handled by plea bargain and not presented to a jury. As a result, about three-quarters of my work involves planning and preparing for plea bargain negotiations. This does not change the fact, however, that all cases must be approached as if they are going to trial.

Gathering together the strands of my research, experience, and numerous case records, I have developed a comprehensive manual that guides other lawyers in preparing and trying parricide cases. Among other things, the packet includes a protocol for identifying witnesses and readying them for testimony; suggestions for uncovering "hidden" clues of abuse; a "how to" on picking the jury; and sample opening and closing arguments. All my knowledge and experience, however, cannot prepare any lawyer for the emotional element of these cases.

As lawyers, we are taught to regard our cases with cold objectivity. There is no right or wrong, just winning or losing. This credo rings loudest in criminal law, where the rules are more important than the game itself, and the experienced practitioner savors his wins with the enthusiasm of a gunfighter of the Old West. Yet maintaining this armor of aloofness in patricides and matricides is virtually impossible.

Parricides are nasty, draining cases for everybody—judge, jury, prosecutor, and especially for the defense attorney, with the death of the parent signaling the onset of an emotional civil war. Each case unfolds like a Greek drama, with one chorus tearfully lamenting that they should have done something to prevent the tragedy, and the other stoically maintaining that the parent or child brought the situation upon themselves.

Almost three-fourths of my cases involve boys who kill their fathers, a figure that approximates the overall statistical breakdown of the killings, and for this reason it is by far the longest part of the book. On the opposite end of the spectrum are matricides committed by girls, cases I rarely see. In between the two extremes are boys who kill their mothers; girls who kill their fathers; sibling conspiracies to kill parents; children who kill their entire nuclear family; and children who hire third parties, usually relatives or friends, to kill one or both parents. Regardless of the scenario, however, parricides are so similar that, given just a few sketchy facts about the homicide, the psychological and behavioral profile of the child and the pattern of abuse are fairly predictable, as are the actual events which triggered the killing.

The disproportionate majority of these cases involve white middle-class or upper-middle-class boys between the ages of sixteen and eighteen who have never been arrested—even for jaywalking. If they have a record, it is usually for victimless crimes such as vandalism, shoplifting, or playing hooky. These are *definitely* not teenagers like Micky Donnelly who are in trouble with the law so frequently that the local juvenile detention center is like a second home. Nor are they like those gang members who every so often drive by the hamburger stand near my home and let loose a burst of automatic weapons fire because someone standing in front is wearing the "wrong" colored shirt. My clients tend to be mediocre or above-average students, and most are loners, anxious to please their peers and overly polite to adults.

Their peaceful, submissive facades, however, hide the life of pure pain they live, for they are raised in homes where chaos and persecution are the order of the day. These children exist on the extreme end of the child abuse spectrum, most being victims of what I call "poly-abuse." Not only have they typically been physically, mentally, and often sexually abused since they were very young (oftentimes since infancy), but they have witnessed the repeated abuse of other family members as well.

Abuse is actually the wrong word, for it sugarcoats what these children are forced to endure. *Torture* far more accurately describes when a mother ties her two-year-old daughter to a chair, then locks her in a dark closet for eight hours a day. And it is torture, not abuse, when a father, while raping his ten-year-old daughter, threatens to kill her—or her mother or siblings—if she tells anybody.

Who are the parents of these children? For the most part they are successful wage earners, regarded by their peers as honest, hardworking people who have a reputation for perfectionism both on and off the job. Though some have domineering, intimidating personalities, they are like their children in that they have rarely run afoul of the law. They are usually very private people, and most do not have alcohol or drug abuse problems. In sum, they are generally indistinguishable from the rest of us, except for the way they treat their sons and daughters.

These parents and children have relationships marked by extreme emotion—colossal expressions of love and devotion running side by side with a tremendous undercurrent of hate and resentment. "These cases are a psychoanalyst's nightmare. They [often] combine an aggressive violent streak with a seductive . . . loving streak," says Dr. Jerome Miller, former

Massachusetts commissioner of Youth Services and now director of the National Center for Institutions and Alternatives, who has treated many of these children. Ironically, to the outside world such parents and children often appear to have unusually close relationships. They are in each other's company much more than the average parent and child; and the child is almost always immensely respectful, to the point of being obsequious. These parents exploit not only their authority, but also the trust their children place in them. They do not want their children to "honor" them, they want their children to worship them as gods. And they do.

Most of these parents recognize no boundary between themselves and their children—for them their son or daughter is an extra limb or just another object that belongs to them, like a piece of furniture. They perceive the act of conception as granting them absolute, unfettered control over the life they have created. Their child exists solely to satisfy their needs and desires and thus is raised to have no independent identity.

A psychiatrist friend once described the primary difference between what, for lack of a better term, might be called the "typical" physically or verbally abusive parent and the parent who dies by the hand of his child. The former beats or belittles her child because she has an honest, albeit misguided, belief that it is the appropriate way to reform or control the child's behavior; the second parent doesn't care about reforming the child's behavior—instead he is addicted to his power over the child and the pleasure derived from exercising it.

Despite the passivity that has marked these children's lives, the parricides are frequently carried out in a brutal, calculating manner. The homicides typically occur when the parent is in his least defensible position, thus increasing the child's chance of success. The circumstances of the killing, in fact, often suggest an ambush, with the parent sleeping, coming in the front door, watching TV, or cooking dinner with their back turned when attacked. Rarely is the parent ever killed while beating, or for that matter, yelling at the child. The vast majority of perpetrators concoct some plan and often discuss their intentions with friends days or weeks before the actual killing. A particularly disturbing characteristic of these homicides is what police refer to as the "overkill factor." Only rarely is the parent killed with a single clean shot; most often the child will shoot, club, or stab the parent numerous times.

Having said the above, certain caveats are in order. First, not all perpetrators of parricide are teenagers. (To the best of my knowledge the youngest was three years old, a Detroit child who shot his father in June 1988 because the father was beating his mother. No charges were filed.) However, in cases where the "child" is over twenty-one, severe and debilitating mental illness or greed is infinitely more likely to have motivated the killer rather than abuse. What is unique about adolescents, moreover, is that, more than any other single age group, they are particularly susceptible to lashing out against abuse.

Adolescence is unquestionably an exhilarating time in one's life. But it is also a period of tremendous anxiety and bewilderment. And even in the best of normal, well-adjusted families, it can be a time of tremendous upheaval. The teenager is going through a complex process of seeking independence, learning that she or he has an identity beyond the life of the family. For parents, the process is moving in reverse—they must begin to let go. The result is a fairly constant power struggle over almost everything imaginable, from curfew to cleaning the bedroom.

At the same time, the child's reasoning process undergoes a fundamental transformation. To paraphrase what Mark Twain observed as an elderly man: When I was fourteen, I thought my father was a darn fool, but by the time I was twenty-one I was amazed how much he'd learned. Teens make a transition from a stage where decisions are made without significant reflection to one in their early twenties, where decisions are made based primarily upon experience. Many young people in this in-between period lack the ability to perceive fully the consequences of their actions—examples of this are seen every day in the news: teens using drugs and alcohol to life-threatening excess; having sex without concern for pregnancy or disease; or dropping out of school with little thought for the future. When abuse is added to this mix, it exacerbates an already confused, complicated period, thus making a violent reaction much more likely.

Of course, not all teenagers who kill their parents are victims of abuse. Some parents are high-minded, utterly innocent, virtuous human beings, "Ozzie and Harriet" types, good people who are slain because their child is acutely psychotic, hearing voices that command her to kill the two enemy agents from another planet sleeping in the upstairs bedroom. Others—and this is an infinitesimal few—are murdered because their child is a dissolute being, hell-bent on prematurely wrenching the family fortune from Mom and Dad.

This book concerns itself with teenagers who kill their parents, but is not about the malevolent, greedy kid or the sick, delusional kid who kills the good and righteous parent. Such parricides in my opinion represent an insignificant fraction of the total. Not all those who work with parricidal adolescents agree with me, though. Most notably, Wayne State University psychiatry professor Dr. Emanuel Tanay believes that the majority of adolescents he sees are not reacting to abuse, but "suffer from a temporary or chronic break with reality." He attributes only a small number to sustained, debilitating abuse—"reactive parricide."

Nor do I mean to imply that the young people you will meet in this book are all virtuous souls, free from all behavioral or mental problems. All have been devastated to one degree or another by their experiences, and indeed, it would be virtually impossible for anybody to come through such childhood trauma completely unscathed. Nor do I want to convey that all of their parents are thoroughly evil, uncaring souls. They are not, and their children will tell you so.

Ironically, despite the meteoric rise of child abuse as a national issue since 1980, the problem continues to be shrouded in ignorance and is usually met with silence, rather than with recognition and open discussion. Sadly, even in our times, child abuse continues to be treated as it always has—as a family affair. Children are silent because they are fearful or embarrassed to speak out just as the perpetrator is silent for fear of being discovered. Relatives, friends, and others keep silent out of deference to, or fear of, the abuser, or because they are unaware of the mistreatment. When the system does finally intervene on the child's behalf, this brings more silence still.

Once the abuse is reported, the system closes in around the family, shielding them from exposure. Most of us have little knowledge of the process of investigating and removing

17

a child from the home, usually the first step when a credible charge of serious child abuse is lodged against a parent. Even the neighbor who reports an incident of abuse has no legal right to know the disposition of the complaint. Under penalty of law, the child, parent, social worker, and other participants are prohibited from discussing the case with any outsider. Similarly, the public and media are prohibited from sitting in on any proceedings, and all records are sealed.

Most public discussion (and for that matter, research) about child abuse focuses on the child in the present as a helpless victim. We lament the cruel treatment and ask how we can help this unfortunate child, what we can do to protect her in the future. Yet most of us have only a generalized notion of how physically and psychologically devastating child abuse actually is.

Two circumstances, however, usually compel relatives, friends, neighbors, and the public to confront the tragic realities of this grievous social evil. The first is when the parent "abuses" the child to death, when the child becomes the ultimate victim, silenced forever. The child's story of torture is starkly painted in criminal court by police officers, social workers, and medical examiners. The second circumstance is when a child kills his parent, and then we see the truly dark side of child abuse, the victim transformed into perpetrator, the violence coming full circle.

The most difficult thing for me about these cases is the moral ambiguities that they present, with guilt and innocence never clearly defined. Yes, these kids have taken their parents' lives, often in a ruthless, seemingly pre-meditated fashion. But, my mind says, was theirs the only finger on the trigger? Are the parents not in part responsible for their own demise because of the abuse they visited upon their children? Or are the parents even more tragic victims than their children, probably having themselves been victimized by their own parents? And what of the family, friends, neighbors, church leaders, and teachers who saw the beatings, heard the screams, or at least knew something was "wrong"? Do any of them bear some responsibility?

While I feel profound sorrow and compassion for these children, I am, on some level, bewildered by their actions. Despite the fact that I have represented numerous children throughout the nation, am thoroughly familiar with the dynamics of parricide and the psychological research on abuse, and can satisfy myself as to the facts that led to a particular homicide, I still struggle with the simple question of why *this* child did not remain passive like almost every other abused child.

My first reaction to the dead parent is commonly disdain and hostility. But as the facts unfold, and my understanding of child and parent increases, my anger diminishes and is replaced by pity. For all the depravity they visited on their children, they are tortured, afflicted souls who often consciously and sometimes unconsciously helped to bring about their own demise.

These cases present profound and complex questions because they expose the fundamental contradictions, prejudices, and double standards endemic in our attitudes toward the role of parents, the treatment of children, and the individual's and society's obligation to families. No one involved in these cases comes away unscathed, something even you, the reader, will soon realize. Before you begin to read, ask yourself how you would react if Lisa Steinberg, Jessica Cortez (a five-year-old beaten to death by her mother and mother's boyfriend in New York in 1988), Matthew Eli Creekmore (a three-year-old battered to death by his father in Seattle in 1986), or any of the other estimated five thousand children killed every year by their parents had not died, but after enduring years of mistreatment, had instead killed their parents? This book looks at young kids who did just that, and what kind of justice and compassion we show them.

But these are much more than stories about kids who kill their parents. They are stories about how loved ones, friends, neighbors, and the system deal every day with the ravages of family violence. It is my fervent hope that this book will help us all to better understand and confront child abuse and family violence, because the battering and exploitation of our children is eroding the very foundation of society.

The Legacy of Child Abuse

Something like this can happen anywhere. And it did, in fact—the emergency dispatcher took this call at 1:58 A.M. on April 16, 1985. It was made from a modest three-bedroom, gray-shingled house on a quiet street in a picturesque New England town.

"Nine one one."
"Ah, can I have an ambulance and a police car, please?"
"Sure, what's the address?"
"Um . . ."
"Calm down. What's the address?"
"Forty-three Lantern Road."
"Okay. What's the problem there?"
"Um, um . . . I was sleeping and someone shot someone."
"Someone what? Shot something?"
"Yeah."
"Did you get hit?"
"No. Almost."
"Then what do you need an ambulance for?"
"Because my dad, my dad . . ."
"All right, calm down. What's the problem with your dad?"
"He's been shot."
"Did he shoot himself?"
"No, someone shot . . ."

21

"Someone shot him?"

"Yeah."

The first police car roared up to the house exactly two minutes and twenty-one seconds later. It was followed by an invasion of blaring sirens and flashing lights that brought all the neighbors out into a frigid night. Murder was a rare event in the town, especially in this middle-class neighborhood, and nobody wanted to miss out on the action.

In the living room Tim, a slight, auburn-haired boy, wearing only his underwear, sat on the sofa, tears streaming down his face, his body shaking uncontrollably. Though he had just turned eighteen, his round cheeks and hairless face made him look several years younger. In the darkened bedroom, the detectives found Clyde, Tim's forty-eight-year-old father, lying on his side beneath the covers of his bed. His long, curly, salt-and-pepper hair was matted with blood that oozed from bullet holes in the back of his head. The mattress was soaked with blood and bits of bone and brain matter. On the floor at the entrance to the bedroom lay several spent cartridges from a .22-caliber rifle and Clyde's empty wallet.

"Dad and I spoke before he went to sleep," Tim said, clutching his dog's shaggy mane.

"He was in good spirits, and no, we didn't argue about anything. My dad went to sleep and then I watched a little more television. Then I turned off all the lights and went to bed. . . . I was awakened by the sounds of gunshots coming from Dad's room. Five or six shots, I'm not sure. When I heard them, I tried to roll onto the floor. Just then this person slammed open the door to my room, pointed a rifle in my direction, and fired two shots."

"Can you describe the killer's face?" an officer asked.

"No, it was too dark, but I got a quick look at him from the muzzle-flash of the rifle," Tim replied. He described the classic intruder—the man we all fear will enter our house in the stillness of the night, a tall stranger wearing a ski mask and dark clothing. Tim told the officers that he heard the man escape through the sliding door in the living room.

As one of the cops later noted in his report, "during the entire encounter Tim was polite and courteous to the officers." Despite his cooperation and demeanor, however, it was glaringly obvious to the investigators that he was lying. Though a stranger had supposedly invaded the house there were no windows broken, no locks jimmied. After inspecting the molding around the sliding glass door, the crime-scene investigators determined from the way the cobwebs were torn from the frame that the door had been opened by someone *inside* the house. Just as puzzling, the ground had been covered with snow, yet the police found no footprints in the house or evidence that anyone had recently been in the backyard. Two highly trained canine units were brought to the scene, but the dogs failed to pick up a scent.

And then there was the most damning physical evidence—the tiny splatterings of blood that covered Tim's body. The blood on his undershorts, he explained, was from pimples he'd squeezed on the inside of his thigh. He also told the officers that there were no guns in the house, but they noticed two dark patches like powder burns on his right hand and a scrape in the hollow of his right shoulder where the butt of a rifle would rest.

While searching Tim's bedroom, a typical teenage boy's room with rock posters on the walls and a hockey stick leaning in a corner, they uncovered a trapdoor under a pile of clothing. In the crawl space below, they found Clyde's driver's license and several of his credit cards next to a .22-caliber rifle that had been fired no more than an hour before the police arrived.

With so much evidence implicating the boy, the officers again asked Tim about his relationship with his dad. He had been living with his father, a foreman at the local sawmill, since his parents' divorce some ten years earlier, he said. His younger brother, Rusty, lived with his mother, Doreen, on the other side of town. In Tim's words Clyde emerged as a generous provider solicitous of his children's, and even his ex-wife's, needs.

"Are you sure there were absolutely no problems between you and your dad?" queried one of the detectives.

"I told you," Tim protested vehemently, "there were no hostilities between us . . . I loved my dad very much." At this point Tim realized that his story was unraveling and told the officers that he didn't want to answer any more questions without an attorney present.

Two and a half hours after he dialed 911, Tim was read his rights and arrested on suspicion of first-degree murder. An officer led him to his bedroom to dress before being taken to the station. As he sat on his bed tying his sneakers, he gazed vacantly into the crawl space.

The front page of the small-town newspaper reported the tragic loss of one of its own, the photo under the headline showing a smiling Clyde at the mill's last July Fourth picnic. He was a short man, but powerfully built, with bulky shoulders and huge forearms.

Since the Waylens were a large, well-established family in the region, the odds were that many who read the paper over supper that evening knew some member of the clan. Though he was not one of the town notables, most people thought Clyde a reliable, industrious person. He had gone to the local high school and from there to work in one of the mills just outside town. He belonged to the Kiwanis Club and drank beer every Friday night at the White Owl Bar and Grill.

He was a "happy, likable, easygoing guy who didn't bother anybody," townspeople said. "He did more for others than they did for him. It's a total surprise to us that something like that can even happen. A person like that just doesn't have those sorts of enemies."

VICTIM'S SON TO BE CHARGED screamed the headline the next morning. In the accompanying photo Tim wore an ill-fitting, drab-gray jail smock, and his hair was disheveled. With a beefy deputy at each elbow, he stared at his hands, which were cuffed to a heavy waist chain. He looked small, young, lost.

Tim's mother, brother, and his assorted uncles, aunts, cousins, and second cousins were astounded, but so was everybody who had ever met Tim or his dad. They were all flabbergasted because Tim was just like his dad—a "regular guy." He attended the same high school his father had, and he held a responsible after-school job at the local pizza parlor. No one who knew him would have said he was a tough kid, a troublemaker; not a soul could remember when they had last seen him in an argument. He didn't have a mean streak, nor was he violent. Nothing about Tim would lead anyone to think him capable of killing anyone, especially his dad.

Doreen had just spoken to her son and ex-husband the very evening of the killing. Around dinnertime, she had had a pleasant discussion with Tim, who was excited because Clyde had promised to get him a job at the mill over the summer. Later, about three hours before the killing, Clyde had called to make plans to see Rusty over the weekend. By all accounts it was a normal conversation. Like everybody else, Doreen insisted that there had been no problems between Tim and her ex-husband.

The family consensus was summed up by an aunt: "Of course they had problems—what family doesn't? But there is no way that Tim shot his father. It's just not possible." Friends echoed the sentiment. As one of Tim's closest friends said, "they had a good father-son relationship. Clyde was very supportive of Tim, and Tim was real proud of his dad."

Initially, the police theorized, with some pretty convincing evidence, that drugs were involved. Several weeks before the murder, Tim was supposedly "fronted" some marijuana. Instead of selling the drugs, he ended up smoking it all, and the dealer wanted his $200. Tim was broke, had to come up with the $200 quickly, so he asked his dad. Understandably, Clyde was infuriated, and there was even a blowup between father and son in front of one of Tim's friends. Despite his displeasure, Clyde gave his son half the money, a surprising thing for any father to do, to say the least.

The investigators were, however, not sure how drugs played into the homicide. Did Tim kill Clyde because he was angry that Clyde wouldn't give him the rest of the money? Or did Tim kill Clyde because of some more involved criminal conspiracy as yet unknown to them?

Even after the police established an airtight case against Tim, friends and relatives still couldn't believe he had actually killed his father. Several family members had their own theory: the drug dealer to whom Tim owed money had entered the house that night planning to kill Tim and mistakenly shot Clyde. After two weeks, though, even the family became convinced that the police were right.

It was difficult enough to accept the fact that Tim had killed his father, but the motive that eventually emerged was even more horrifying. Tim's answer to the "why" crashed over them like a merciless thunderstorm, leaving them disbelieving and angry, confused and fearful.

Tim's case, discussed in detail in Part I, was a classic parricide. Like the others in this book, it is killing of a kind most of us find difficult to accept, much less understand. It is so much easier to believe that strangers—crazed dope dealers or desperate burglars—kill the Clydes of this world, rather than their own flesh and blood.

When we think of homicide, we imagine the dark, seamy streets of a big city stalked by cold, calculating, and remorseless individuals. The perpetrator is a faceless, soulless stranger who lies in wait to mutilate a young schoolgirl. Without the slightest provocation, this incarnation of evil will execute the hardworking 7-Eleven clerk for $9.34, or the rookie patrolman with a wife and three kids who has just pulled him over for speeding. You surely don't know him. And of course he doesn't live in your neighborhood, certainly not next door to you.

Each night millions of Americans listen to an endless barrage of news reports that confirm these perceptions—"Today in Stockton, California, six children were gunned down as they played in a school yard"; "Last night, in Detroit, three persons were slain in a drive-by shooting." Though we are knee-deep in this murder and mayhem, we refuse to acknowledge the indisputable truth: we are infinitely more likely to be killed or assaulted by someone we know, *not* by a stranger. The odds are that the elementary school child you heard about on the six-o'clock news was killed not by some pervert in a stained raincoat who drives a beat-up '67 Chevy, but by her mother, father, uncle, or a friend of the family's.

Though national crime statistics are generally unreliable—much crime, especially property offenses and sexual assaults, goes unreported—some of the most reliable violent-crime records are those compiled by the FBI. No doubt this is due to the obvious significance of murder to the public and law enforcement alike. According to the FBI's "Crime Clock," in 1990, one person was killed in the United States about every half hour. Since 1976, the United States has had a yearly average of 20,000 homicides. This figure varies considerably from year to year: for example, in 1980 a high of 23,040 was reported, compared with a 1984 low of 18,690.

Contrary to public perceptions fueled by the news and entertainment media, drive-by gang shootings, robbery-related deaths, and other homicides perpetrated on innocent people by strangers account in any one year for a little less than 20 percent of all murders. About four of every five homicide victims are related to or acquainted with their assailants. Murders among family members account for about one-fifth of all killings, the largest single group being husbands killing wives, followed by parents who kill their children. Homicides perpetrated by friends, coworkers, neighbors, and the all-important categories of boyfriends and girlfriends account for another 60 percent of the total.

Another prevalent perception is that teenagers are excessively violent and commit more homicides than adults; in actuality, while those under eighteen represent about 19 percent of the population, they commit only 9 percent of all the homicides. Homicide graphed against age follows a bell-shaped curve, steadily increasing from the teenage years into the late twenties and decreasing thereafter. Seventeen-year-olds, for example, commit *five times* as many homicides as those in the thirteen- to fourteen-year-old group; those between twenty-five and twenty-nine, however, are the most violent group, committing four times the number of killings as their seventeen-year-old counterparts.

Except for the category of brothers killing sisters, parent killing is the rarest form of intrafamily homicide. In every year since 1976 there have been more than 300 parricides. Yet this does not include the upward adjustment for unsolved murders. For example, in 1984 the reported number was 374. Still, according to University of New Hampshire sociologist Murray Straus, one of the country's leading family-violence researchers, the actual number was probably closer to 500.

In 1989, a statistically representative year, 21,500 homicides were committed, 1.6 percent or 344 of them patricides (194) and matricides (150). Sons commit about 90 percent of all these offenses, the majority being patricides, while the rarest cases involve daughters who kill their mothers.

There is one widely held stereotype about homicide that is fairly accurate. Regardless of the relationship between victim and perpetrator or the age of the killer, the murder weapon is most likely to be a rifle or handgun. It should come as no surprise that when a parent is shot by his child, the weapon was typically purchased by the parent.

Just as people are surprised to learn that most homicides are not perpetrated by strangers but by assailants well known, if not related, to their victims, we are unaware of the extent to which assault, attempted murder, and other nonhomicidal violent crime occurs in the home. After studying murder facts, it does not take much to figure out that tens of thousands more people come close to being homicide statistics in their homes each day.

Statistics concerning the prevalence of family violence— child abuse, spousal abuse, elder abuse, sibling abuse—are not as accurate as those on homicide because of the average person's overwhelming reluctance to discuss, let alone report, abuse. Despite this, though, researchers have determined that there are literally millions of people who are beaten and maimed by their loved ones every year.

In 1980, sociologists Murray Straus, Richard Gelles, and Susan Steinmetz published what remains to this day the definitive text on family violence, *Behind Closed Doors: Violence in American Families*. In this first national study, the authors found that one out of every six couples (about 8.6 million couples) experienced an incident involving a physical assault during the previous year. Though the majority of these assaults were what the researchers called "minor"—pushing, slapping, shoving, or throwing objects—one-third were severe, involving kicking, punching, and choking.

Most violence in the family, however, is perpetrated by parents against their children. The researchers identified three basic categories of violence against children. "Ordinary" violence, hitting and slapping, was by far the largest category— approximately 97 percent of all children are struck at least once a year. Secondly, 8.8 million children between the ages of three and seventeen were victims of "severe" violence, "assaultive acts which go beyond pushing, slapping, and throwing things, and which therefore carry a high risk of causing injury serious enough to require medical attention, [i.e.] kicking, punching, beating up, stabbing, and shooting."

Finally, 2.2 million of our little citizens were the victims of "very serious" violence.

Tragically, domestic violence takes not only the lives of fathers, mothers, sons, and daughters. As Straus and Gelles point out in their book, *Intimate Violence*, "between 1972 and 1984 there were 69 officers killed in [responding to] domestic disturbances. . . . This number is less than the 210 officers who died answering robbery calls, yet even this number is high when one considers the assumption that the streets pose much greater danger than the home."

In spite of the darker reality, we persist in our idealization of the family as an island of peace in a savage, chaotic world. Incidents of family violence are drastically underreported, while accounts of violence perpetrated by strangers continually find their way to banner headlines. Nowhere, however, is our myopia more pronounced than on television. In every family-oriented show, from "Leave It to Beaver" to "The Cosby Show," the family is depicted as a place where tranquillity reigns and parents resolve problems with Solomonic wisdom. One would be hard-pressed to find a single family television series in the last thirty-five years where a father or mother even spanked or slapped their child in anger, much less the all-too-common harsher punishments.

Though society's refusal to acknowledge and begin to deal with the gruesome reality of family violence seems perplexing on the surface, it is not difficult to understand given the family's sacrosanct importance to society. The family, in fact, is arguably our single most important institution, biologically perpetuating society and nurturing the individual. And although other institutions such as the church and school provide social, ethical, and moral training, it is generally accepted that mores and values are most effectively transmitted from one generation to the next by the family. All of this leads family-violence expert Murray Straus to remark, "We don't like to say blasphemous things about a sacred institution. The family is an absolutely central institution that fulfills very important functions, and so there's a natural hesitancy to bad-mouth it."

Historically, it has been our collective wisdom that these critical functions (reproduction and transmission of values) could best be carried out if the government simply left families and in particular, parents, alone. And that is exactly what has happened.

Western and Eastern cultures alike have traditionally given parents, specifically fathers, unfettered authority over the lives of their children.

In the landmark text *The Battered Child*, Samuel Radbill writes, "In ancient times, when might was right, the infant had no rights until the right to live was ritually bestowed. Until then, the infant was a nonentity and could be disposed of with as little compunction as for an aborted fetus. The newborn had to be acknowledged by the father; what the father produced was his to do with as he wished."

In ancient Rome, for instance, as sociologists Russell and Rachel Dobash discovered, a healthy birth did not mean a child would live, for that decision was solely vested with the father. Similarly, in Asian cultures parents have until very recently had extensive power over their children's lives; in Chinese society female infanticide, as a response to economic pressure, can be traced back millennia. There are reports that the practice has recently resurfaced as a result of the strict one-child policy and the traditional Chinese family's reliance on male children to support aging parents.

In Western society, unbridled parental domination is an enduring tradition whose roots are seen in the Old Testament. The Ten Commandments not only ordered children to "honor thy father and mother," they sanctioned the directive with the ultimate punishment for those who violated it: Exodus 21:15—"Whoever strikes his father or mother shall be put to death," and Exodus 21:17—"Whoever curses his father or mother shall be put to death."

Later generations took this biblical command quite literally. Under the old English common law, children were regarded as the property of their fathers. Parents could require their children to work for them or place them in indentured servitude in return for payment. Absolute obedience was not an issue, for children who attempted to rebel were whipped and beaten or placed in workhouses. In their book *The Legal Rights of Children*, Davidson and Horowitz state that the harsh treatment of children went hand in hand with prevailing moral and religious beliefs that "childhood was an inherently evil state." This tradition carried over to our own shores where, in 1646 in the Massachusetts Bay Colony, newly arrived citizens (ironically, escaping repression) enacted the Massachusetts Stubborn Child Law. Parents who claimed that their children were "stubborn and rebellious" and "disobedient of voice" could seek one of several "state reprimands," including execution. Obviously, democracy and due process were not things the Pilgrims wanted in their homes.

Though records indicate that no disobedient children were put to death, all other forms of punishment have historically been used to enforce the parental prerogative. Today most parents limit their physical punishment to slapping and pushing, yet significant numbers do still whip, paddle, punch, tie up, and withhold food and water to discipline their kids. In fact, it is only in our own times that we have begun to acknowledge that excessive punishment happens, and that it damages a child's body and mind.

The adage "spare the rod and spoil the child" reflects a genuinely held and still widely practiced belief that physical punishment is somehow "good" for children. Indeed, many people discuss physical punishment in therapeutic terms, as if children "need a good lickin' once in a while" like they need to eat spinach or wash behind their ears. Murray Straus points to another misguided motive—punishment as symbolic and religious cleansing—reflected in the oft-used phrase "beat the devil out of the child."

"At one time the phrase had a theological meaning," Straus said in an interview. "In the book *The Changing American Parent* by Miller and Swanson, the authors reprinted some of the letters between John Wesley, the founder of the Methodist Church, and his mother, Suzanna. Suzanna was a model mother . . . utterly devoted. . . . Wesley wrote her and said, in effect, 'What did you do that made all of us turn out so well?' She wrote back that she beat the devil out of them. Her objective was to send the children to bed whimpering." Like many parents of her day, Suzanna Wesley believed that the devil was physically present in a child.

No one doubts that the exercise of strong parental authority, especially in a child's formative years, is essential to healthy, normal development. Consequently, however, parents wield an unparalleled degree of influence and power over their children, who are completely dependent upon them. In this respect, the parent-child relationship is unique, the *only* social union not based on choice. As New York psychiatrist Albert Shengold writes in his insightful book on the long-term effects of child abuse, *Soul Murder,* "the child's almost complete physical and emotional dependence on adults easily makes possible tyranny and therefore child abuse." And tragically, for reasons ranging from ignorance and immaturity to emotional illness and sadism (and the fact that they themselves were mistreated by their parents), tens of thousands of parents *do* abuse their immense power, brutalizing their children with their fists, words, and sexual desires.

Only in very recent history has society openly admitted that some parents abuse the sacred power entrusted to them. In fact, it has only been in the last one hundred years that we have recognized through laws and social practices that children are independent beings, entitled to protection from the excesses of their parents. The first invasion of the parental prerogative occurred in 1874, in New York City, under somewhat ironic circumstances. A young girl named Mary Ellen was found starving and chained to her bed in her tenement apartment. No child-protection agency existed; instead the action to remove her from the home was carried out by the Society for the Prevention of Cruelty to Animals. This incident was the impetus for the formation of the New York City Society for the Prevention of Cruelty to Children, which still exists today.

The last quarter of the nineteenth century saw the emergence of child protection groups in big cities, yet the efforts of these private, charitable organizations were not directly focused on child abuse, but on the protection of youngsters, especially newly arrived immigrants, from the ravages of poverty, through child labor laws, for example. By the turn of the century, state legislatures began to realize that there was a real and urgent need for new laws to prevent children from being abused and neglected in the home by parents and relatives.

Despite the passage of these early child-abuse laws, enforcement was ineffective. Then as today, enforcement was hampered by our chronic reluctance to disclose family problems publicly. A further obstacle at that time was the lack of an adequate legal framework for reporting and investigating abuse. Complicating these problems, no one in the law-enforcement, social-work, or medical professions was able, without an eyewitness, to ascribe a particular injury to parental abuse. This situation did not change for over a half century.

As Samuel Radbill wrote in *The Battered Child* on the history of child abuse:

> Medicine was oblivious to child abuse until concern about [it] grew out of Dr. John Caffey's perturbation of mind about curious X-ray manifestations in some children. . . . Radiologists, like pathologists, were essentially "back room boys," and rarely went to the bedside. Caffey, however, was trained as a pediatrician [and] was able to relate these unexplained X-ray findings to clinical pictures. While he soon recognized that multiple fractures were due to trauma (and not as had been thought to rickets or scurvy), he was unable to convince his colleagues that parents might be the instrument of this trauma. In 1946, Caffey published a paper entitled "Multiple Fractures in the Long Bones of Infants Suffering from Chronic Subdural Hematoma." This attracted attention of pediatricians to the ramifications of child abuse, [but] the issue smoldered for years.

Throughout the 1950s, radiologists and pediatricians conducted follow-up research, with formal recognition of child abuse as a medically diagnosable syndrome finally emerging in a landmark article published by the *Journal of the American Medical Association* in 1962. In that article, Denver pediatrician C. Henry Kempe described how physicians could medically identify a physically abused child. He termed the phenomenon the "battered child syndrome":

> The battered child syndrome . . . characterize[s] a clinical condition in young children who have received serious physical abuse, generally from a parent or foster parent. The condition has been described as unrecognized trauma by radiologists, orthopedists, pediatricians, and social workers. It is a significant cause of childhood disability and death. Unfortunately, it is frequently not rec-

ognized or, if diagnosed, is inadequately handled by the physician because of hesitation to bring the case to the proper authorities.

Kempe's findings were critically important because they gave physicians, for the first time, specific clinical procedures to distinguish between accidental and intentional injuries. Though repeated blows to an infant's arms or legs might not, for example, actually result in a broken or dislocated bone, they do create hairline-thin or green-twig fractures, visible on X rays six months and more after the bruise has disappeared. In addition to the diagnostic breakthrough, Kempe's work produced two important results. First, though focused primarily on physical abuse, his efforts launched a complementary body of research on all aspects of sexual and psychological abuse. Second, his work proved conclusively and scientifically that child abuse was a critical and pervasive problem. Kempe's findings proved so dramatic that they inspired the AMA to write an editorial that stated, "It is likely that [the battered child syndrome] will be found to be a more frequent cause of death than such well-recognized and thoroughly studied diseases as leukemia, cystic fibrosis, and muscular dystrophy." As Straus and Gelles observed in *Intimate Violence*, "[s]oon after the publication of the editorial, politicians, journalists, and social activists began to quote it. First the qualification 'it is likely' was dropped, then the quote was transformed to read that child abuse was the fifth most common killer of young children."

This ground swell of recognition led in the late 1960s and early 1970s to the revamping and updating of child abuse laws. Across the country, state legislatures acted to fund and establish a comprehensive child abuse reporting system. Each state's social services department also developed comprehensive plans for identifying and processing reports of child abuse.

Despite the dramatic research findings and the legislative action creating new agencies, the nation's Norman Rockwell image of the idyllic American family did not really begin to reflect the grim reality until over twenty years after Kempe's publication. Our consciousness about sexual abuse was first rudely awakened in 1984 by two events: the airing of an ABC television movie, *Something About Amelia*, about the sexual abuse of a teenage girl by her father; and Florida senator Paula Hawkins's announcement in her keynote address to the Third National Conference on the Sexual Victimization of Children that she had been sexually abused as a young child. Both events generated substantial increases in reports of sexual abuse and a proliferation of news stories about the problem.

Coincidentally, it was also not until 1984 that the federal government formally recognized family violence as a critical social problem by creating the Attorney General's Task Force on Family Violence. After eight months of hearings throughout the country, the commission acknowledged that its work was just beginning. As the chairperson, Assistant U.S. Attorney General Lois Herrington remarked, "Family violence is an enormous problem, but we have no idea how enormous. . . . What we know is that we don't know anything."

Notwithstanding these strides in recognition and changes in policy, the parental prerogative remains protected in many ways, a distinct double standard for judging victims and perpetrators of child abuse that still exists throughout society. This double standard is evident in our social attitudes, in the legal system; and it is visible in every case in this book.

The most blatant example of our hypocrisy turns up in our language. Researchers, doctors, legislators, and lawyers have developed a whole vocabulary that sanitizes the truly insidious nature of these acts of brutality. *Abuse* is too nice a word to describe what some parents do to their children.

This sanitized vocabulary enables us to discuss such acts comfortably without actually visualizing what took place, the leading edge of a blunt institutional response to the problem. *Child abuse* may sound like dirty words, but they cannot convey the ugliness of the acts themselves. If an adult female is vaginally and anally penetrated by a man against her will, the perpetrator is charged with rape and sodomy. But if a father violates his two-year-old daughter in the same despicable manner, it goes down on the books as sexual abuse. It is not rape because there is an irrefutable legal presumption that force was not used. And if John Senior beats his drinking buddy to a bloody pulp with a two-by-four, he's arrested for attempted murder; but if he beats Johnny Junior within an inch of his life, we call it "child endangerment" because there is a legal presumption that the father did not intend to kill his child, only to discipline him.

Our discomfort in even talking about child abuse is but one difficulty among many encountered in dealing with every aspect of this tragedy, from reporting to prosecuting the perpetrator. Remember, these are usually young victims caught up in circumstances that don't conform to the orderly particulars of the law.

FBI records show, for example, that approximately five hundred to six hundred children are killed by their parents every year, yet this is probably the most inaccurate of all FBI homicide statistics because of the huge number of abuse-related deaths covered up as accidental. According to the Chicago-based National Committee for the Prevention of Child Abuse and Neglect, it is more likely that *five thousand* children (fifteen times the number of patricides and matricides), most under three years of age, are killed by their parents or custodians every year. (The United States is not the only country with such a high infanticide rate; in West Germany in 1989, almost one thousand children died from beatings.)

Despite these numbers, infanticides are the most difficult homicides to prove. Across the nation, the primary problem prosecutors face in infanticide cases is that it is virtually impossible to demonstrate the parent intended, or acted with malice, to kill their child even if the child was subjected to continual beatings and torture. Because parents are frequently the only witnesses and routinely plead that they merely intended to punish the child, convictions for first- or second-degree murder, both crimes that presume intentionality and carry severe sentences, are rare. Moreover, regardless of the severity of abuse resulting in the child's death, jurors seem reluctant to accept that parents can and do have the ability to kill their children. Knowing these circumstances, prosecutors often accept a plea of involuntary manslaughter rather than pushing for a conviction of first- or second-degree murder, which can carry terms of ten years to life. In many such cases, the parent receives a minimum sentence of only two to six years.

A small article I read in *The New York Times* in September of 1989 brought home to me how little some things have changed since little Mary Ellen was removed from her home over one hundred years earlier.

> Muskogee, Okla. (AP)—The grandparents of a 4-year-old boy have been charged with keeping the child in a caged pen during the day outside the motor home vehicle in which they lived. He had no toilet and only a bottle of water. . . . [They] said they built the pen to keep the boy from roaming out onto a nearby highway. . . . The grandparents face a misdemeanor charge, usually filed in cases of failure to pay child support. It calls for a year in jail or a five hundred–dollar fine upon conviction. [The prosecutor] said it was the only charge available. "We looked at the child abuse statutes very carefully," he said, "and our feeling is it requires an injury or maiming of the child, which is not present in this case."

Just as society is chronically unable to gauge accurately the extent and severity of child abuse, it also chronically fails to recognize the degree to which children are vulnerable and unable to protect themselves. In human terms, this means that many of the people within the system whom one might expect to intervene—social workers, teachers, cops, judges, and juries, even, at times, doctors and psychologists—consistently overestimate the victim's ability to reveal the abuse and ask for help. Too often, intervention, when it does come at all, is too late for both children and their parents, when a parent has already seriously harmed a child or a child has struck back.

To us as adults, it is hard to believe that a child would endure any abuse without telling an outsider and asking for help. Indeed, in my experience, once severe abuse has led to a parricide, everyone immediately asks the question, "Why didn't the child get help?" Yet there are compelling psychological reasons that make seeking and getting help the rare exception, not the norm.

First, children have no choice, psychologically, but to attach themselves to and identify with those who care for them. As Harvard Medical School psychiatrist Bessel Van der Kolk, an expert in the treatment of abused children, explains in *Psychological Trauma:*

The emotional development of children is intimately connected with the safety and nurturance provided by their environment. Children universally attach themselves to their caregivers. This is a survival mechanism necessary to provide the needs that a child is unable to satisfy alone. Certainty of the presence of a "safe base" allows for normal emotional and cognitive development. . . . In the absence of such a safe base, as in cases of child abuse and neglect, a child goes through a variety of psychological maneuvers to preserve maximum protection. Abused and neglected children often become fearfully and hungrily attached to their caregivers, with timid obedience, and an apparent preoccupation with the anticipation and prevention of abandonment.

Though seemingly inconceivable to the average person, when caregivers abuse children, the attachment can actually become even stronger. It is perhaps the most insidious aspect of child abuse that, as Dr. Van der Kolk noted, the abused child seeks protection from abuse in the abusive parent. A child's dependency on his parent is so profound and all encompassing that the parent remains the primary source of nurturance even in the face of draconian treatment.

Second, this overpowering urge to maintain and strengthen the attachment to a caregiver, even an abusive caregiver, is complicated by feelings of confusion and guilt after an abusive episode. "When the child recovers from the attack," Dr. Albert Shengold writes (quoting psychiatrist Sandor Ferenczi) in *Soul Murder*, "he feels enormously confused, in fact, split—innocent and culpable at the same time—and the confidence in the testimony of his own senses is broken."

To survive this ordeal, Shengold continues, the child has to register the "bad . . . as good. This is a mind-splitting or mind-fragmenting operation. . . . [S]uch children must keep in some compartment of their minds the delusion of good parents and the delusive promise that all terror, pain, and hate will be transformed into love." And rather than alienating their parents by challenging or condemning them, abused children often resort to self-blame.

When I worked as a court-appointed attorney in juvenile court, these points were made frighteningly clear to me. Following my work at Juvenile Advocates, I represented abused children, most of whom had been removed from their homes by the state. During my years providing help to incarcerated kids, I had come to the realization that my work was very much like that of an emergency-room doctor in a large city who worked only on Friday and Saturday nights. Not only did I see the most tragic cases, but my resources were woefully insufficient to meet the immense demand. Representing abused children, though, especially very young ones, I quickly discovered, was much more mentally exhausting than my earlier work in the reform schools and juvenile detention centers. I still felt like a doctor, but I had gone from an overcrowded, ill-equipped emergency room straight to doing trauma surgery on a battlefield.

My initial meeting with the children always took place at the courthouse, since abused children don't usually make office visits. Because of skyrocketing abuse reports in the early 1980s, courthouses were always stretched for space. As a result, I was often forced, along with dozens of other attorneys, to do the preliminary interview with the child in the corridor outside the courtrooms. With children running screaming through the halls, parents crying over the removal of their child or protesting innocence to their attorneys, cops jawboning with each other, and bailiffs screaming out case numbers, it was not the most conducive environment to speak with the scared, confused child.

Sometimes, however, I got lucky and was able to use one of the so-called interview rooms. One interview I remember particularly. The room was the size of a broom closet and had originally been used for holding adult prisoners. The room's past, however, had not completely been erased. Most of the chairs still had the short link of chain that was used to handcuff a prisoner, and in spots, obscene graffiti could still be seen through the pale-blue paint. The picture of the teddy bear picnic painted on the wall was a sensitive touch, but did little to comfort any of the children.

I had arrived at eight that morning to make sure I got a room and had just started sipping the first of my six cups of vending-machine coffee (which always had the flavor of chicken broth) when the social worker—Gladys Felder, a hardened foot soldier in the dirty war against child abuse—

led a very reluctant pudgy little boy into the room. Ricky was a brown-haired child of eight who had a Snoopy Band-Aid over his left eye and week-old black-and-blue marks on his neck and all over his tiny arms. His oversize Superman T-shirt added a touch of forlorn irony to his appearance.

In his right hand, he clenched his only possession, a neatly attired G.I. Joe doll, as if he were afraid someone would grab it from him. Ricky had been taken into custody by the police three days earlier after they received complaints about screaming coming from his apartment and discovered him lying on the floor in a dazed state. His mother told the police she beat him because he refused to go to sleep. Ricky was rushed to a hospital where he remained overnight and had spent the next two evenings at a church-run shelter for battered children.

As Felder gently ushered him toward me, yet another interrogator, she said, "His mother," and then stopped abruptly. "She b-e-a-t t-h-e s-h-i-t o-u-t o-f h-i-m w-i-t-h a w-o-o-d-e-n s-p-o-o-n f-o-r t-h-r-e-e h-o-u-r-s a-n-d h-e s-t-i-l-l w-a-n-t-s t-o g-o"—her voice tightened—"h-o-m-e." One look into his large, anxious hazel eyes, however, told me he knew everything she was saying. Felder then turned quickly and left the room with a stack of files filled with other disasters under her arm.

"Hi, I'm Paul. Great G.I. Joe you got there."

He wasn't interested in small talk. Still clutching his doll, he put both elbows on the table, looked me square in the eye, and said in a lost voice, "I want my mom. Where is she? I want her now. Please, mister."

I had done scores of these interviews and always got a lump in my throat when the child demanded to see his mother or father. It is simply heartbreaking to realize that there is nothing you can do to make a young abused child understand that he was taken away from Mommy and Daddy for his own good.

"You can't see her just right now."

"When, then?" he said, his tone slightly indignant.

"Later." I tried to sound comforting, but he was not convinced.

"When later?" he demanded, now kicking the chair with his heel.

"Just later." I knew, and he knew, that I couldn't give him a good answer.

He started kicking the chair more fiercely, and then came the words I always dreaded to hear. Tears streamed down his cheeks and he looked at the floor. "I was bad, wasn't I?"

"No, you weren't bad. You did nothing wrong." I reached to comfort him, but he batted my hand away.

"Then why can't I see her?" he said. Before I could respond, he began crying hysterically and slamming his G.I. Joe against the table. "I want my mommy, I want my mommy. I want her!" he screamed at the top of his lungs.

Ricky was eventually placed in a long-term foster-care home and reunited with his mother and stepfather about fourteen months later. No further reports of abuse were received.

Beyond the almost universal urge to remain attached to the abusive parent by assuming the blame for the abuse, many victims must also struggle with overt threats from the abuser. Abusers often warn children that if they ever tell anyone, they will be beaten, maimed, or killed, or worse, that the abuser will harm another member of the family beloved by the child, a sibling or the other parent. Going against a parent is difficult for even a normal, well-adjusted child. When the vow of silence is reinforced by threats from someone whose violence they have felt, it becomes virtually impossible for the child to risk speaking out.

Even assuming the abused child has the Herculean emotional strength to overcome these barriers, there is the very real probability that no one will believe his story. All children learn early on that the words of adults carry far more weight than their own. And when confronted, adults who abuse their children will commonly deny their behavior. If the child has in the past ended up in a hospital or been interviewed by a social worker, he or she has already heard their parents' stories and excuses: "He fell down the stairs"; "He accidentally tipped a pan of boiling water over himself"; "She continually scratches her vagina." A child who has heard her parents' lies accepted even once knows her fate is sealed; hope that anyone will rescue her is extinguished.

Abused children, like other oppressed peoples, learn to adapt to their environment. They rarely complain to their parents and ironically, spend considerable time trying to please them. Many learn to cope by figuring out the pattern of their mistreatment: they learn when abuse comes, and when it stops. As one of my young clients once said of his father:

"He'd be real calm and just tell me to go get the ruler. It was a yardstick made out of sheet metal. Then I'd give it to him and he'd begin whipping me. First on the rear, then on the legs and the arms. And then he'd start breathin' heavy. And after about twenty minutes I guess, he'd stop. He was pooped out. He'd just throw the ruler down and sit in his big green chair. Then he'd fall asleep."

Most children, never having known any other life, genuinely do not recognize themselves as abused. Though we tend to assume that the abusive parent-child relationship is always violent and unhappy, there are often periods of love, even immense demonstrations of caring; these parents do not abuse their children twenty-four hours a day. And it is upon these good, even great, times that abused children hang their illusive hope that things will change for the better.

Others survive by shutting themselves off from all feeling. For many, it's the only way to cope when the penis is being shoved into their mouths, the fist slammed into their faces, or brutal criticism hurled at them.

Jimmy, a fifteen-year-old, stabbed his father to death. He was a particularly difficult kid to represent because he refused to talk about any aspect of his relationship with his dad. Mostly he either nodded his head or shrugged his shoulders. During our interviews he would pace around the room or fiddle with a pencil, anything to avoid focusing on my questions.

Early on he had admitted that he was forced to suck his father's penis, but for months that's all he would say. Each time we spoke, I told him that he was going to have to tell the jury how he felt when it was happening to him.

About four months after the homicide, I went to visit him one evening at the juvenile detention center. Throughout most of the interview he played with an empty soda can, spinning it round and round on the Formica table. About halfway through the interview he interrupted me as I was discussing potential witnesses.

"You wanna know how he made me feel, right?" he said, his voice dull and mechanical.

I nodded and he stopped spinning the can. "Well, I just go away. Far, far away in my brain. I mean, I leave. As he was doing it to me, I just put everything on hold and sent my feelings out the window. That's how I did it."

As a result of being forced to squash all feelings, the personalities of these children are seriously compromised. Some researchers such as Shengold go so far as to call it soul murder. "Soul murder," he writes, "is neither a diagnosis or a condition. It is the deliberate attempt to eradicate or compromise the separate identity of another person. The victims of soul murder remain in large part possessed by another, their souls in bondage to someone else. . . . Torture and deprivation under conditions of complete dependency have elicited a terrible and terrifying combination of helplessness and rage—unbearable feelings that must be suppressed for the victim to survive."

Survival is a relative term for these children because the psychological and behavioral consequences of abuse can be much more debilitating than just cutting off feelings. While it is still a very new area of research, experts believe a child's short- and long-term reaction depends on such factors as the nature, duration, and gravity of the abuse, and the individual's emotional makeup. Some abuse victims are able to lead functional lives while still coping with the common problems of intense rage, low self-esteem, anxiety, and depression. With respect to sexual abuse, for example, David Finkelhor, one of the nation's leading child abuse researchers, says that women are more likely to suffer from depression whereas men are more disposed to react aggressively. Others, however, are crippled for life, suffering from drug and alcohol dependency or developing a range of chronic psychiatric disorders including dissociation, post-traumatic stress, borderline personality, and multiple personality.

The most insidious effect of abuse is that it dramatically increases the likelihood that the victim-child will become a victim-spouse or worse, a child abuser. The trauma of abuse so distorts a child's conception of family that the abnormal supplants the normal, establishing abusive parenting as appropriate. "Parents who have been exploited as children," Van der Kolk observed, "feel entitled to gratification and caretaking from their own children. If the child is ungratifying or does not meet developmentally inappropriate demands, parental rage is unleashed with little or no remorse."

Not all abused children become abusers. Despite their scars, with good doses of insight, help from caring people, and luck, abused children can go on to lead fulfilling lives and become good parents. But the odds are against them.

The psychological factors which make it likely that an abused child will become an abusive parent are also responsible for making abuse victims, particularly men who were severely physically and sexually brutalized, more susceptible to acting out aggressively and violently against those outside their families. And this aggression is not simply the product of rage. The pernicious lesson of child abuse is that confrontation and violence are acceptable ways to solve problems. Moreover, because they were treated as virtual nonentities by their parents, the ability of many of these victims to empathize and sympathize with strangers is profoundly diminished. Because years of mistreatment forced them to deaden their own pain, they cannot feel the hurt they inflict on others.

Though the relationship between abuse and violent crime only began to be examined in the mid-1980s, several studies have revealed some disturbing trends. One recent study found that 90 percent of the Folsom prison death-row inmates had been severely abused as children. Similarly, a study of fourteen juveniles on death row, conducted in 1988 by Dr. Dorothy Lewis of the New York University Medical Center, one of the nation's leading psychiatric experts on children who kill, found that "twelve of the [teenagers] had been brutally physically and sexually abused, and five had been sodomized by older male relatives."

Given the realities of parental control and the devastating psychological effects of abuse, what options are *realistically* open to our abused children? Most, regardless of their age, take the path of least resistance, learning to adapt to their environment and accepting the violence inflicted on them as their lot in life. Discussing their situation with friends or reporting it to authorities is simply out of the question.

In spite of these tremendous impediments, however, more

than 1.5 million reports of child abuse and neglect are filed each year. Some are reported by those rare children who possess the fortitude to seek help on their own, but most cases come to the attention of authorities because of outsiders—teachers, doctors, friends, and neighbors.

Of all these reported cases, however, the majority involve younger children, usually under ten years old, though there is no reason to assume adolescent abuse occurs less often. Why do fewer abused older children get help from people outside the family? We tend to believe that, once a person passes his twelfth or thirteenth birthday, he is a young adult, accountable for his own life circumstances, an individual who ought to be able to fend for himself.

Young children, so obviously helpless, engender more sympathy, for people understand that for a young child to seek outside help is next to impossible. To a four-year-old, the world is his parents, while to a fourteen-year-old the world includes his friends, his school, his soccer team, perhaps his after-school job. Many people thus assume that a fourteen-year-old can evaluate an abusive situation on his own and freely seek assistance, a false and harmful assumption. While an adolescent's survival skills are undeniably superior to a younger child's, an adolescent is not an adult. Most adolescents remain as paralyzed by the threats and intimidation as younger children.

And what happens if a report is made? For some children, the child protective services system works well. Children are dealt with in a compassionate, therapeutic fashion while their parents receive reparative counseling, and the home situation is well monitored. The process is long and arduous, but ultimately the family benefits. Unfortunately, this rosy scenario is the exception rather than the rule.

For the already traumatized child, being placed in the average county child protective services system is like throwing him or her from the frying pan into the fire. In most jurisdictions, the entire child abuse process has been criminalized so that the child is re-victimized by the system from the moment the report is received. First, the child, illogically, is yanked from the family while the abuser remains in the home. A social worker, often accompanied by a police officer, usually collects the child from the home, taking him or her to the hospital or a children's shelter. It is also the case, however, that the child's first stop is a police station. Until 1986 in Long Beach, California, for example, these children were brought into the police station through the main booking area and locked, for up to three days, in a holding pen on the same floor as female adult offenders.

Thereafter, an army of specialists—social workers, doctors, lawyers, judges, therapists—poke and pull the child at every turn. The child is interviewed, tested, observed, and then reinterviewed, re-tested, and re-observed by "professionals" who are often overworked, underpaid, and undertrained. Some children and their families manage to come through this process intact. Sadly, however, many children become forever lost in the netherworld of foster care, where they are bounced around from home to home throughout their childhood and adolescence.

"If the abuse was that bad, and she was afraid to tell anybody, why didn't she run away?" is another knee-jerk reaction of adults. Simply, most don't run away for the same reasons they don't tell anyone that they're being abused: they are trapped by the fear of punishment if caught; the fear Mom will take it out on a little brother or that Dad will rape a little sister; they don't want to abandon friends and family, the only world they know; they are also economically dependent on their parents.

The reality of running away, moreover, like our ideal of the American family, has been hopelessly romanticized. Yes, a few kids who run do go on to repair their lives, but those who work with runaway children know that this is the exception. Most do not survive well at all; from victims in the home, they go on to become victims and victimizers on the street. And while some cities have runaway programs, it is much more likely that a kid's first offer of help will come from a street hustler, not a social worker. Life on Hollywood Boulevard or in Times Square among the pimps and drug dealers is thousands of miles removed from Huck Finn's lazy afternoons on the Mississippi. We know now that children do not run away seeking thrills or adventure, but are most likely escaping abuse. Lois Lee, director of the Hollywood, California–based Children of the Night, one of the nation's leading programs for runaways, told me in 1990 that fully 100 percent of the children she reaches out to are victims of abuse. This is not to say, however, that kids never leave good, secure, supportive homes—they do, rarely.

There is one class of abused children who do not quietly endure their abuse, yet who also do not report their parents or run away. They refuse to remain silent, shattering the silence cloaking the family's terrible secret with the report of a gun. My clients and the subject of this book—they are the children who kill their parents.

PART I

BOYS WHO KILL
THEIR FATHERS

Introduction

One doesn't have to be an expert in human behavior to know that violence has historically played a prominent role in relationships between men. Much more so than women, men have traditionally turned to violence to solve any problem from political conflict to personal disagreement. In fact, the history of violence in America is largely the history of violence by men toward men. Men perpetrate 90 percent of the homicides and make up 90 percent of its victims, while men and boys as a group commit 90 percent of all violent crime. Fully 98 percent of the approximately 16,000 persons executed in the history of the United States were men.

From birth, most males are socialized by cultural attitudes and norms to perceive violence as both an acceptable way to solve a conflict and as a method for asserting authority. Not only do boys receive the brunt of physical punishment, but many fathers find it only appropriate that they should "give as good as they got." As Straus and Gelles point out in *Intimate Violence,* the U.S. Commission on the Causes and Prevention of Violence found that seven out of ten people thought it was important for a boy to have a few fistfights while he was growing up.

Perhaps the most famous case of a son's killing his father is that of Oedipus, the mythical king of Thebes who killed his father, Laius, and later married his mother, Jocasta. Allegedly, he did not know that the man he killed was his dad—or so he told the authorities. After he learned the truth, he was so racked with guilt that he gouged out his eyes. For the last 2,500 years or so philosophers and playwrights have tried to explain his motives.

Sigmund Freud was so fascinated by the case that it became a cornerstone of his theory of psychoanalysis. He theorized that, as a young boy, Oedipus was unconsciously sexually attracted to his mother, but was deathly afraid that if his father discovered his amorous desires, the old king would castrate him. All young boys, Freud reasoned, experience Oedipus' conflict, but the healthy ones (luckily, the overwhelming majority) repress these feelings so they can live normal lives. At about five years of age, the boy's fear of castration overcomes attraction to his mother, and he renounces the sexual love, coming to identify with his father.

Classic Freudian psychoanalytic theory holds that at the heart of patricide is the son's internal conflict caused by his overattachment to his father. This overattachment has pronounced homosexual overtones to it. The son kills the father because he perceives it as the only way to be free of him.

Though these two explanations are handy, diffusing the issues of guilt and innocence of son and father by blaming on one hand society, or on the other, a deeply rooted psychological impulse common to all men, they do not really help us to understand the impact and meaning of the act and do not come close to capturing the horror of the circumstances that lead to it.

Patricide by sons is by far the most common form of parricide, accounting for almost 70 percent of all parent killings. And of this figure, the clear majority involve boys who have been both severely physically and psychologically abused. Cases of purely emotional or sexual abuse exist, but they, too, often have a history of early physical abuse. I believe, however, as more research is done in these two areas, particularly the issue of male incest, sexual abuse will emerge as being a much more salient factor in these cases than anyone previously thought.

Tim

Tim Waylens, introduced in The Legacy of Child Abuse, did not earn enough money making pizzas at his after-school job to retain a private attorney, so the job of representing him fell to the county public defender's office. The first person to interview Tim was not an attorney, however, but Larry Steele, the only case investigator in the eight-person office.

Unlike most investigators who work for defense attorneys collecting evidence and tracking down witnesses, Steele is not a retired cop. In fact, before he became a licensed private eye, the fifty-five-year-old Steele had been a lobsterman. Though in his previous experience he had negotiated the slippery decks of boats in the harsh waters of the Atlantic rather than walking a beat, Steele quickly became as good an investigator as there is. He can get anybody, even the most ornery witness, to open up, a rare and valuable gift in his business. He seldom has to raise his voice, and it's not just because he's as big as a pro-football lineman, though that helps. Perhaps it is his gentle blue eyes and disarming smile. Years on the open ocean have carved deep lines in his cheeks, making his wide grin appear even wider between his bushy sideburns.

Tim had been locked up for two days in the hundred-year-old county jail before Steele went over to do an initial interview. Steele had never worked on a patricide case, but he was fairly experienced at judging human character and expected to find a distraught, angry young man, racked with guilt. Instead, as he later told me, Tim was "a polite, real soft-spoken kid, but there was very little emotion from him. After introducing myself, I asked him, 'Tim, what the hell happened here?' He didn't tell me anything. He just kept repeating, 'Something happened, something just happened.' "

Try as he might that morning, Steele couldn't get Tim to talk about why he shot Clyde. He gave up and moved on to other subjects and was amazed that Tim quickly relaxed, talking more freely about himself than the grave situation at hand. After a half hour discussing motorbikes and fast cars, Steele shifted back to the night of the murder. Tim was impervious, so Steele pushed a little harder.

"We're going to have some real problems with what you are telling me," he said to Tim, "because the police found the gun, your dad's wallet, and his other personal effects under the crawl space in *your* closet. You are in a world of trouble right now. Your story just doesn't hold up."

But the veiled threats didn't work. Steele had met his match. The choirboy wasn't talking. When Steele left the jail that day, he thought Tim was just a "self-centered little punk."

Tim's defense fell into the hands of the most experienced attorney in the public defender's office, Bill Latham. Most public defenders (p.d.'s) stay at their job three or four years, then move on to the more lucrative and prestigious world of private practice. Not Latham—he's been addicted to his job for fifteen years. Ever since his days as a high-school football tackle, he has loved a good fight against a worthy opponent. And nothing satisfies that need better than defending the underdog.

With dark, wavy hair and deep-set, black eyes, his calm appearance belies the ferocity with which he attacks each case in court. Yet like cops and prosecutors who spend most of their lives working in the foul trenches of the criminal justice system, he cannot help but be thoroughly cynical. When I later asked him to describe the job he loves, he said, "It's always an uphill battle with few positive rewards. Most of the time your client doesn't give you a lot to work with. . . .

Going to court is like being in a fight with your hands tied behind your back. You get the shit kicked out of you for a week, then the jury convicts your client, and you wonder why the hell you tried the case in the first place."

After Latham spoke to Steele, Tim's case appeared no different from all the others.

Latham knew something was wrong with Tim, but he couldn't put his finger on it. "Maybe the kid's a psychopath. Maybe he ate LSD and turned into some crazed killer for all I know," Latham told Steele. Realizing that they could not crack Tim, Latham brought in a local psychologist whom they'd often used to evaluate their clients.

Dr. Stevenson called Latham after the evaluation. "Bill, there's not a damn thing wrong with this kid. I think he knew what he was doing. I don't know what the hell your defense is going to be. Good luck."

"He's a young man who is emotionally self-centered," Stevenson wrote in his report, "who is quite naive about the situation in which he finds himself. He does not even emotionally comprehend that he is being charged with murder. . . . All he could talk about was how difficult it will be when he gets out of prison."

In his typically sardonic fashion, Latham later said, "I had a happy, well-adjusted homicidal juvenile on my hands."

Steele and Latham had more than a hunch that Tim was hiding something, for the police had found more than just the murder weapon and Clyde's wallet in the crawl space. A dildo and a bunch of hard- and soft-core porno magazines—items that the police had conveniently never mentioned in their newspaper interviews—had also turned up. In the course of his own inspection of the house, Steele noticed on the nightstand next to Clyde's bed what he described as an "industrial-sized" jar of Vaseline brimming with pubic hairs.

"Sexual abuse crossed our minds, but I don't think anybody really focused on it," Latham told me. And even when they considered the sexual-abuse angle, they did not think of Tim as the victim; rather, they reasoned Clyde was killed because he had possibly sexually abused Tim's girlfriend or a female relative.

After interviewing Tim's relatives, high-school pals, girlfriend, teachers, coworkers, and neighbors, Steele and Latham had come up with the same thing as the police—zilch. Zilch was good for the cops, who didn't care why Tim killed his father; but it was very bad for Tim's case. "His dad was Fred MacMurray on 'My Three Sons,'" Latham said dryly. "You couldn't meet a nicer guy."

Their gut feeling was that Tim's mother, Doreen, could shed some light on the investigation. After all, Tim was her son. Through broken sobs, the tired-looking forty-year-old woman repeatedly maintained that her son had nothing to do with Clyde's death. She was convinced that Tim and Clyde had a "loving relationship." When Doreen and Clyde had divorced some ten years earlier, their agreement was that ten-year-old Tim would reside with his dad while Rusty, five years younger than Tim, would live with her. According to Doreen, Clyde had always been closer to his older son and was adamant about retaining custody of Tim.

Though it was unusual for a father to demand custody of one child, Doreen welcomed Clyde's taking such an active role in his children's lives. Since their divorce, in fact, Clyde had proved to be a devoted father who tried to accommodate his children's every need. Unlike other divorced fathers, Clyde regularly saw Rusty and brought him over to his house to spend time with Tim. Up to the last conversation she'd had with Clyde the evening of the murder, all had seemed normal, Doreen insisted. A detailed interview with little Rusty supported all of Doreen's claims: Clyde was a loving, supportive dad. Rusty loved his daddy and had no idea why *anyone,* least of all his brother, would want to kill him.

The last person to see Clyde alive was his longtime friend and bowling partner Stu, who had dinner with Clyde that night then dropped him off at home about eleven-fifteen P.M. "There were no obvious problems between them . . . just common father-son talk about cleaning up and the like." If Clyde had had problems with his son, though, it would be unlikely that even Stu would know about them because, as Stu recalled, "Clyde was a very private person."

Steele remained unconvinced that Clyde was an untainted soul. Maybe relatives, friends, and co-workers had nothing to say, but he suspected that a review of the court files would reveal something. His suspicion was correct—well, almost. Though Clyde had an absolutely clean record, Millard Waylens, Clyde's father, had a criminal record and had even done time—for "carnally abusing a female under the age of eighteen," not a stranger, but his own daughter. The "carnal knowledge"—one of those antiseptic euphemisms for rape and sexual assault—had produced a baby, and Grandpa Waylens had served a couple of years in prison. At last, Steele felt that the door had just been opened, albeit a crack.

Checking back with Tim, Steele found that all he could remember was his parents' going to visit Grandpa in prison. Nobody had ever mentioned why Grandpa was there.

Grandpa Waylens's conviction lent further credence to their theory that sexual abuse was perhaps Tim's motive for taking his dad's life. Though not experts in child abuse, they were correct in assuming that incest tends to be transmitted from generation to generation. Not *all* incest victims and their siblings, of course, go on to abuse their children; yet a history of victimization is common to almost all perpetrators of abuse. The discovery of the family skeleton gave further support to Steele and Latham's theory that Tim killed his dad to stop the sexual abuse of a girlfriend or relative, but they had no other concrete evidence. The trial was six months away, but desperation was beginning to set in.

They had already reviewed all the evidence and made their own inspection of the house. Though they still needed to talk to numerous friends and relatives, the interviews they had already completed had revealed nothing unusual. Most troubling was that Tim wouldn't elaborate on his claim that "something just happened." Because of Steele's talents at persuasion, the job of prying Tim open was left to him.

Steele visited Tim two to three times a week, each time pushing a little harder, then backing off. He spoke with Tim, he said, "candidly."

"Tim, do you know what your future is going to hold for you? Let me tell you what it's going to be like. We have nothing to work with. Put yourself in the position of the jurors who are going to be sitting on your case. Think about how they will see the act you committed. Think of how it's all going to sound when it comes out on the stand. In my experience, it's not going to take them very long to convict you." Tim would just sit there passively, his eyes downcast, unresponsive.

Steele knew what he was talking about. He was born and bred in the tiny town. "Around eighteen percent of the national population is over sixty-five, but here it's over thirty percent," he told me. "It's an old, extremely conservative, very religious community. There are places in town that *literally* have a church on every block. The community thought, here's another wild kid probably on dope and alcohol who just flipped out."

After going through the trial scenario, Steele talked to Tim about prison. "Tim wasn't effeminate, but many things about him were *real* soft. I told him he would be eaten up."

"Tim," Steele told him forcefully, "you won't even make it into the general population. We will have to request that you be put into protective custody immediately. Otherwise you'll be sold for a couple of cartons of cigarettes. You'll be passed around and become somebody's wife in no time at all."

Latham accompanied Steele on several visits, playing the tough guy. "I told him flat out that going to prison would be a death sentence." But Tim held his silence. No matter what they said, he simply stared dispassionately off into space.

Though the picture looked bleak, Steele and Latham were obsessed and put all their other cases and investigations on hold. As Latham later remarked, this was not the typical murder case where "you get some guy who is all screwed up on cocaine who shoots his girlfriend." Tim was not a hardened delinquent, but a decent kid who for some unexplained reason had been driven to kill his dad. The case presented one of those rare opportunities to "do justice," and Latham refused to let it slip away.

Even at home Steele couldn't stop thinking about this strange crime. "I would sit with my baby," Steele would later say, "and I just kept thinking what the hell would it take for me to do to my little daughter to get her to blow me away?"

Less than a month before trial, and no further along, Steele and Latham were at wits' end. "We had no motive," Latham later said. "No reason. No defense." Four days before trial, Steele went to see Tim to try one last time to pry him open.

"When I went over to see Tim that day," Steele later told me, "I said, 'Do you realize what's coming up? In four days we are going to be in court and picking a jury. The jury is going to be watching you. They are going to be saying to themselves, "Sure, I'll say I could be impartial and fair and listen to all the evidence, but why the hell would this kid kill his father?" What the hell are we going to do? Your life is at stake. If there is anything that happened between you and your dad, you better tell me now because *we're running out of time*.' Tears welled up in Tim's eyes. He got emotional in a way I'd never seen before."

He sobbed for several minutes before he could say a word. Then he haltingly began to confess his father's sins.

My dad took sexual favors from me. After my mom and dad got divorced when I was ten, I started sleeping in the same bed with my dad for protection. I always had my mom and dad there, and now my mom was gone. I needed more protection. . . . About six months after the divorce my dad called me into his bedroom. He was masturbating. He showed me how to do it to him and I did. . . . Then he masturbated me. I got a hard-on but I didn't ejaculate. When it was over, he said, "This was just between us, okay?" That's how it started. In the beginning he never said nothing about telling anyone about it, but as I got older, he started in with the threats. "Don't tell anybody or you'll get beat."

Tim was sketchy with details, only saying that his father's demands had progressed to oral and anal sex when Tim was about fourteen. For the first few years, Clyde simply forced himself on his son, but as Tim matured, the pattern changed. His dad would use sex to punish him—if his room was not clean, the dishes dirty, or he was late in coming home.

As Tim got older, the sex got rougher. Clyde not only used the dildo on his son, but as Tim shamefully told Steele, "He tied me down to the bed or chair and had oral and anal sex with me. Towards the end he would hit me while he was having sex with me."

On the day of the murder, his father was angry because the school had called that day to say that Tim was playing hooky. His dad had just come home from his bowling league. Ironically, Tim spent the early part of the evening reading superhero comics before he went to sleep.

He was sitting up in bed when his dad came into his room. "I knew what he was leading up to when he started talking about the school problems. He wanted to have sex with me. I said, 'No!' My dad left, but he said, 'Well, you know it's going to happen sooner or later.' I sat in my room thinking, 'I'm never gonna get away. Never.' "

It was a little past midnight. Tim stared at the rifle that stood propped up in the corner of his room. He could have gotten up and walked right past the rifle and out of the house. He could have just gone to sleep. Instead, he got up, took the gun, and walked down the darkened hallway to his dad's room. He brought the barrel to within a foot of Clyde's head, closed his eyes and fired until there were no more bullets.

When he heard the story, Latham's first thought was, "Is this kid telling the truth, or is he trying to save his ass?" Latham sent Tim back to Dr. Stevenson.

Tim told Stevenson the same story, but he gave much more detail. Despite the psychologist's original conclusion, Stevenson was convinced Tim was telling the truth. In this second clinical evaluation he concluded, "During a recounting of [the homicide], Tim showed emotion for the first time. . . . His previous descriptions of his father were in unemotional terms. In tears he cried, 'My dad fucked me in the ass.' " Latham got the court to give him a continuance based upon "newly" disclosed evidence, twelve precious weeks to start afresh proving his young client's claims were true.

Though there were arguably some hints early on in the investigation that Tim had been sexually abused—his obscure silence about his motive, the jar of Vaseline, Clyde's demand to retain custody of Tim, and Grandpa Waylens's conviction—Steele and Latham would probably not have focused on incest had Tim not broken down and admitted to it. This is not a criticism of Steele and Latham or for that matter Dr. Stevenson, but rather an indication of how deeply hidden and misunderstood is the problem of male incest. As skilled, experienced, and dedicated as Steele and Latham were, the fact that Clyde could sexually abuse his son was simply outside their consideration.

Despite the momentary reprieve, Latham still had two problems. First, he was downright cynical about the truth of Tim's "new story." "Most clients accused of murder are smart enough to figure out that they don't want to do life without parole so they'd better come up with a defense," Latham told me. And he had another problem. Even if he could establish that Tim was abused, he was unsure how to tie the abuse to a viable defense.

Coincidentally, the day after the continuance was granted, Steele's wife was watching the "Oprah Winfrey Show," the topic: children who kill their parents. Not only had the show featured two teens who had killed their parents, but she told her husband that there had also been a lawyer who specialized in defending patricides and matricides.

I had appeared on that program with Nick, who at sixteen killed his sexually and physically abusive stepfather, and with Carla, a nineteen-year-old who killed her sexually abusive father. I received about twenty-five phone calls in the days after that show, most from adults who said they sympathized with Nick and Carla. As abused children themselves, they told me, they had often thought about killing one of their parents. Two more calls came from prisoners who had killed a parent and wanted my help; and then there was the call from Bill Latham.

As soon as I said, "Good afternoon," Latham said abruptly, "Hey! Are you the guy that specializes in defending kids who kill their parents?"

"Yes," I responded warily.

"Well, my name is Bill Latham. I'm an attorney, and I got one of 'em. I know I got a defense here, but I can't seem to put my finger on how to put it together. What can you do for me?"

I could help with everything from selecting the jury through closing argument, I said. "We want you to help on the whole nine yards. This case is too important. When do we start?" he asked excitedly.

First I had to see all the police reports and other evidence. "I'll tell you what. Instead of sending it, I'll fly out with the stuff myself," Latham suggested. A week later he was in my office.

The most critical service I perform for attorneys is organizing the defense to prove two key points: that the parent abused the child, and that the motivation for the murder was the abuse. Though it appears straightforward, establishing these two elements is complicated because they require the defense attorney to wear two hats. The former requires the defense attorney to temporarily become a prosecutor, in essence trying the dead for their abusive crimes against their children in life. Once the abuse is accepted, the defense attorney must switch back to the traditional role to prove that, but for the abuse, the killing would not have occurred.

Defending parricide cases involving allegations of sexual abuse is especially difficult because the crime of abuse is one whose evidence is, at best, transitory. Physical evidence such as pregnancy or a sexually transmitted disease in the victim is rare. Moreover, because of the nature of the acts themselves—the ultimate taboo, hidden, shameful, taking place when the parent is alone with the child—the only eyewitness is the victim.

After reviewing all the evidence and consulting with Latham, it was obvious that we were going to have to start almost from scratch. The first priority was to go back over all the physical evidence at the scene searching for proof of Tim's allegations. Second, in light of Tim's recent disclosures, we had to reinterview family members, friends, teachers, and others. Finally, it was imperative to get experts in adolescent sexual abuse and teenage violence to evaluate Tim.

Except for the dildo and the Vaseline, there was, not surprisingly, little physical evidence. Steele needed to go back to the house and take away both mattresses, every sheet and blanket, and Tim's and Clyde's underwear, all of which could bear semen stains and pubic hair. If any of Tim's pubic hairs could be found on his father's bed or in his father's underwear or vice versa, it would lend substantial credence to Tim's story. Getting solid evidence of semen would be trickier, for after so much time (six months since the shooting) they would be difficult, perhaps even impossible, to identify and type. Unfortunately, because sexual abuse had not even been suspected, the medical examiner did not test for the presence of semen on the victim's body. I also recommended that we retrieve all of the photo albums, diaries, and anything else that could shed light on Clyde and the relationship he had with his son.

When Steele went back to the house, he was shocked to find it virtually empty. We were dismayed to discover that

Clyde's family had destroyed everything. As Steele told me later, "they burned all of Clyde's stuff, all his underwear, all his clothing. A lot of Tim's clothes were also destroyed. Even the jar of Vaseline was thrown away." All we were left with was the dildo and the porno magazines that the police had recovered.

Lacking physical evidence, we desperately needed to find witnesses to shed some light on Tim's relationship with his dad. I knew we weren't going to find anyone who witnessed any sexual act, but maybe some friend or neighbor could help us bring into serious question the perception that father and son had "a great relationship."

Clyde's family steadfastly refused to accept any part of Tim's story. They didn't know why he killed his father, but it could not have been because of sexual abuse. Tim's mother, his aunt Madge, and several other relatives believed he was telling the truth, but none of them had seen or heard anything directly, nor did they possess actual proof that would hold up in court. What they did have, however—a potent weapon if wisely wielded—was detailed and intimate knowledge of the history of abuse in Clyde's family going back two generations and involving at least one male relative in each.

Doreen and her sister, Madge, related the whole story surrounding Tim's grandfather. His arrest, which they all called "the family secret," had been kept from the grandchildren, of course. When a young Tim asked, "What happened to Grandpa?" he was purposely ignored. And Grandpa's abuse, we discovered, had gone beyond that one daughter, Josephine. Way beyond. Doreen told Steele of one unpleasant encounter back when she was dating Clyde. "After I walked in the door of Clyde's house, my husband's father and his sister, Daphne, came out of the bedroom where they had been in bed together. Daphne told us later that she liked sleeping with her dad more than she did her own husband." Nor, Steele learned, was Grandpa the only family member who had been convicted of a sex crime.

Doreen went on to reveal that Tim's uncle Mel had been discharged from the army, arrested, and convicted of sexually abusing his daughter—Tim's first cousin. Mel knew a lot of family history, Doreen thought, but he probably wouldn't talk. She was right. But the trial was still ten weeks away, and Steele had a little time to pursue these leads and work his way back through Tim's life to find other evidence of his father's molestation.

Though friends and relatives could not shed much light on the case, a review of Tim's academic and medical records proved helpful in corroborating his story. His school records showed that, from kindergarten through the fifth grade, his performance was about average. His fifth-grade teachers noted that he was "a nice and cooperative boy, but he was disinterested and unmotivated."

After he entered the sixth grade, though, when the abuse began in earnest, Tim's academic performance took a marked turn for the worse—a trend that continued through his senior year in high school. From the seventh through the twelfth grade, he rarely received a mark higher than D, despite the fact that he tested average and remained a compliant, well-behaved student.

His teachers attributed his poor performance to the fact that he was often listless and frequently fell asleep in class. In fact, several had recommended that he seek medical advice. Indeed, he complained so often of health problems (starting at about age nine), that he made more visits to the doctor than someone ten times his age. Just during the fifth grade he made twenty-five visits to his pediatrician.

Tim constantly complained about lower-back and stomach pain, as well as constipation. His pediatrician, Dr. Andrews, originally diagnosed the young boy's ailments as related to the stress of his parents' divorce and the subsequent breakup of the family. However, after we had confronted him with Tim's admission of sexual abuse, Dr. Andrews made a startling admission: had he known then (in the 1970s) what he knew now about child abuse, he would surely have reported Tim as a sexually abused child. But society wasn't sensitive then to such issues, and doctors weren't trained to spot child abuse as they are today. Lower-back pain, frequent constipation, and an overly compliant personality coupled with the loss of the ability to concentrate in school—these are all warning signs associated with sexual abuse.

Latham, Steele, and I all agreed that it was likely Tim was telling the truth, but all we had were bits and pieces of circumstantial evidence. We needed a psychologist who specialized in sexual abuse, and preferably one who had experience with homicide, to help us put it all together. Finding this person was my responsibility.

I knew several good child abuse experts who would help, but they all lived out of state. Had Tim lived in a big city, any one of them would have been the right choice. However, because this was a small, conservative town, I was extremely reluctant to bring in an out-of-state expert. I started calling my contacts around the country and soon found the name of a psychologist who lived in the general area.

Dr. Kevin Drazune lived only about four hours away and specialized in evaluating and treating sexually abused children. Though he had a private therapy practice, he worked primarily as a prosecution expert in cases brought against parents who sexually abused their children. As with many of the psychologists and psychiatrists with whom I work, however, Drazune had not previously evaluated a victim who had killed one of his parents.

After I presented the basic facts of the case, Drazune expressed immediate interest, but also his concern about being seen by his colleagues and others as a "hired gun." Expert witnesses, especially psychologists and psychiatrists, are often criticized as being legal Silly Putty in the hands of whoever is paying them, molding their opinions and testimony to fit the side for whom they appear. Drazune felt strongly about his independence and told us that he wanted to evaluate Tim and arrive at his own conclusions without interference from me or Latham. He felt most comfortable, he said, as someone who would help the court arrive at a just result, rather than as merely an expert witness for the defense. Though a bit distressed by his attitude—given that it is necessary for your expert to at least identify with your side—I liked his honesty and integrity, rare commodities in the often duplicitous world of courtroom experts.

Dr. Drazune proved to be our ace in the hole. After more than twenty hours of interviewing and testing Tim, Drazune became a believer—and he did it all on his own. Any lingering doubts Steele, Latham, or I might have had about Tim vanished when we read Drazune's report. Though Tim had admitted to us that he was repeatedly abused over at least eight years, he'd been unable to be specific enough for us to nail down concrete events and incidents that would illustrate and strengthen our case. Embarrassment and excruciating psychological pain often engender a quasi-amnesia in abuse victims, and because Tim had suffered from this as well, we had needed someone with Drazune's expertise to get at Tim's memories, a delicate task.

While Tim will never remember everything his father did to him, Drazune was able to document meticulously more than twenty-five separate incidents of sexual abuse. Though my work routinely takes me into some of the most grotesque and dismal corners of the human landscape, the doctor's report was difficult even for me to read dispassionately. Drazune wrote:

> The fourth incident occurred roughly two months later, near the end of [the school year]. This was the first incident Tim could recall that he did not like. His father called him into his bedroom and asked that he rub his feet . . . then asked Tim to give him a "blowjob." Tim attempted to beg off because he was starting to become uneasy with the sexual contact, but his father said, "Do it anyway," and Tim complied. Tim then got a towel and wiped the semen from his father. Afterwards they watched TV together. . . .

> Tim had failed to do some chores his father had assigned. When he came home after drinking with his buddies, Clyde gave Tim the choice of extended grounding or [agreeing to] fellate him. His father had him perform fellatio on his knees while his father reclined on the couch in the living room. His father then administered fellatio to Tim, and Tim recalled that this was the first time that he himself had ejaculated while his father sexually stimulated him. . . .

> Starting in the seventh grade Tim began to become increasingly disturbed by the abuse. He was becoming interested in girls, beginning to realize that there was something wrong about what was happening between him and his father. He was beginning to feel socially awkward and felt that he was particularly inept at relating to girls . . . he attributed his difficulties to his developing fear that he might be a homosexual . . . and was afraid that

his friends would somehow be able to tell by the way he looked or acted that he was a homosexual. . . . Tim had returned home from a school dance . . . and his father requested that Tim fellate him. Tim refused. Clyde then stated something [like], "Then you're going to do something else." Tim again refused, but his father was becoming increasingly angry, and Tim felt convinced that he was going to be hit. . . . So he said, in effect, "OK, you win," and allowed his father to rape him anally. The penetration was painful despite his father's having lubricated his anus with Vaseline. . . . Clyde then wanted to perform fellatio on Tim, but Tim refused, whereupon his father angrily went to bed.

Though Drazune, like the rest of us, knew that, absent a confession from Clyde, there was no way to prove Tim's allegations 100 percent, he did have other methods to determine the truth. Drazune examined things such as the detail with which Tim was able to relate the events, his emotional state and demeanor during the recounting of the stories, and the consistency of his story over several interviews.

Drazune also looked for any external corroboration of the facts Tim could provide. Of critical importance to him was a foster child who lived with the Waylenses who verified that Tim had indeed slept with his dad almost every night after the divorce. Drazune was also persuaded that Clyde's long family history of incest and abuse, while not proof positive, made Tim's account of his father's depredations much more believable.

From the psychologist's efforts to develop a chronology of the abuse, our defense began to take shape. Drazune had identified a number of circumstances and events in the six months prior to the homicide that, while alone insufficient to drive Tim to kill his dad, had, taken together, pushed Tim over the edge.

After he turned seventeen, Tim had become more profoundly depressed by his father's escalating demands and the impossibility of escaping them. He attempted to "treat" himself by getting drunk and frequently smoking marijuana. It was this chronic depression, in fact, that led him to smoke all of the marijuana that a drug dealer had given him to sell. As the police later discovered, this forced Tim to go to his father for the money, a pivotal event since it led Clyde to press his son for sexual favors to escape the threat of the dealer. Even after his arrest, Tim could still hear his father saying, "I'm going to have you for a long time on this one."

It was also during this time that Tim lost his virginity, a source of great exhilaration, but one that dramatically increased his frustration and anxiety over what he perceived as an ever more hopeless situation. Tim's first experience of sex with a girl dramatically drove home the contradiction of his existence. "It was a real high having sex with a girl," Tim said, "but then on the other hand it made me feel shitty about what I was doing with my dad."

Though Drazune had confirmed our belief in Tim and provided us with valuable insight and acts, we were still not home free. We needed to translate Drazune's conclusions and everything else we had into a viable legal defense.

The state had charged Tim with murder in the first degree, for which he could receive a sentence of life in prison without parole. Murder is generally defined as the intentional taking of a human life. In first-degree murder, the slayer intends to kill and acts with premeditation, thinking about the idea of killing in advance of the act even if only for a minute. They also act with deliberation, reflecting on their actions and carrying out the crime in a cold, dispassionate manner. Murder in the second degree means that the person intended to kill, but did *not* do so with premeditation and deliberation. If the accused can show that she murdered because of a mental illness (not rising to the level of insanity) or because she was intoxicated with drugs or alcohol at the time of the homicide, then there is no deliberation or premeditation.

We had no doubt that the state could make a persuasive case for first-degree murder, something I find true in most of these cases. Parricide defendants typically present the police with a first-degree murder case on a silver platter. The police could prove that Tim shot Clyde when he was sleeping and that about two weeks before the killing, Tim stole the murder weapon from a next-door neighbor. He was not drunk or high on drugs at the time of the murder, nor was there any indication he heard voices emanating from his stereo commanding him to kill his dad.

We were not hopeful that the jury would convict Tim on a reduced charge of manslaughter. In voluntary manslaughter, the individual has the intention to kill, but there are "mitigating factors," extenuating circumstances, the most common of which is when killing took place during the "heat of passion." To prove the "heat of passion" circumstance, a defendant has to show that he acted only because he was provoked by the victim in a way that would enrage the reasonable or ordinary person, being severely beaten by the victim or watching the victim assault a family member, for example. Second, the law also requires that the killing take place during the interval when a reasonable person would not be able to reflect on the precipitating incident and therefore control his emotions. Since his father, by Tim's admission, had been sound asleep for at least four hours at the time of the shooting, we could hardly argue that Clyde provoked his son into a murderous rage.

To prove self-defense, we would have to show that Tim reasonably believed himself in imminent danger of being killed or having a dangerous felony like rape committed against him. To be found not guilty by reason of self-defense, the slayer must have *both* a reasonable fear of being harmed and a reasonable perception that the infliction of the harm is imminent. The problem with using self-defense in parricide cases, especially those such as Tim's where the parent is sleeping or otherwise unaware of the attack, is that the law has traditionally (and even to this day) defined "reasonable" in terms of the perception of an adult man.

The standard has changed little since feudal times—the fifteenth-century English farmer walking down a country path accosted by another man bearing a six-foot oak staff. To defend himself against the attack, the man could use his sword to slay the aggressor. "The person doing the perceiving in all this had long been thought to be a healthy adult man, like the gunfighter walking over to the O.K. Corral," said my friend New York criminal lawyer Michael Dowd.

The balancing principle inherent in self-defense is that a person can only react with that amount of force necessary to repel the attacker. So, in the traditional scenario, the slayer had to have been assaulted with a deadly instrument in a deadly fashion, i.e., not just randomly waving a knife, but lunging with it. If the aggressor merely hit the slayer with his fists (unless he was a karate expert or a professional boxer) or accosted him in a nonlethal way, then deadly force could not legitimately be used.

On the basis of these traditional scenarios, "imminence" meant that the attack was going to take place immediately or soon thereafter. If the aggressor merely threatened to kill at some time in the future, then the slayer could not legitimately claim self-defense on the grounds that it would not be reasonable to assume the danger was imminent. Similarly, the slayer could not legitimately be said to be acting in self-defense if he was hit with an oak staff on Wednesday and then jumped out of the bushes the next day or week and stabbed his unsuspecting assailant.

The assaults visited upon a child cannot be even remotely compared to any of the traditional self-defense fact patterns. The inequities of power and stature inherent in the parent-child relationship, along with the effect of abuse, fundamentally alter the parameters for defining and determining the presence of imminence. A child who kills the typically physically or sexually abusive parent is responding not to one or two incidents, but a series of hundreds, maybe thousands of assaults over that child's life. And while every assault may not be life threatening, it is the cumulative effect of the routinized attacks that is integral to understanding a child's perceptions.

The principal problem for Latham and me would be convincing the judge and jury that there was an imminent danger despite the fact that Clyde was sleeping. And it was going to be the expert's job to explain to the jury how the abuse fundamentally alters the perceptions of dangerousness and imminence.

While most of us instinctually know that child abuse is harmful, it is for the expert witness to explain how abuse fundamentally alters the child's perceptions of danger and imminence.

Tim, like most abused children who kill their parents, suffered from post-traumatic stress disorder (PTSD), a psychiatric disorder associated with being exposed to extraordinary events or traumas outside the range of normal human experience. In addition to child abuse victims, PTSD has also been found in Vietnam War veterans, concentration camp victims, and those who have been raped. While PTSD is technically classified as a mental disorder, it is one of the few kinds of psychiatric disorders that is considered a *normal response* to an *abnormal situation*.

The two most relevant aspects of PTSD in explaining the perceptions of an abused child who kills his parent are hypervigilance and the intrusive re-experiencing of the trauma. While obtuse clinical definitions of these concepts abound, perhaps the most succinct was stated by Dr. Lenore Walker, one of the nation's leading psychological experts on battered women who kill:

> Hypervigilance is the normal outcome of having been abused and traumatized. One of the most significant effects to somebody who has been traumatized is that they learn that the world is really not a safe place for them and that they may not be able to protect themselves all the time. This causes them to become hypervigilant to any potential cues of danger that will happen in their environment. It's almost like having a very finely tuned antenna for impending violence, and it picks up low-level cues that people who have not been traumatized would not see. These people are usually fairly accurate about [what will happen to them]; sometimes they're looking so carefully for these cues that they may be called paranoid. [Often] when a hypervigilant individual picks up on a danger cue, it will trigger an intrusive re-experiencing [of similar trauma]. In their mind they will be experiencing now not only the danger that they're sensing is present, but they will also be remembering previous incidents where there has been a similar kind of danger.

Even though Tim's perceptions of danger could be effectively explained to the jury, self-defense was going to be a hard sell because, according to Tim himself, the last incident of sexual abuse had occurred at least three months *before* the homicide. The evening of the killing, Clyde only threatened to have sex with him "sooner or later," not that he would rape Tim in the immediate future. Moreover, Tim never mentioned that his father had specifically threatened his life in any way.

Despite these problems, Latham and I believed we had a compelling defense. Our major concern, however, was keeping Tim out of state prison. Steele and Latham were not merely trying to scare Tim when they had told him he would get eaten up at the state pen. Tim was a slightly built teenager who, despite the violent nature of his crime, was by no means an experienced street fighter. Tim, as Latham often commented to me, would not survive even the time it would take to appeal his case.

Soon after Tim's arrest, prosecutor Rudy Clinton offered a deal: Tim would plead to first-degree murder with a recommendation of parole. The parole was not guaranteed, and we didn't believe Clinton could obtain the conviction anyway. To move the prosecutor toward a more conciliatory posture, I suggested an unorthodox tactic—permit Drazune to be questioned by DA Clinton in advance of the trial. I had never met Clinton, but understood that he was a conservative prosecutor who, once he knew that Tim was abused, would be uncomfortable publicly prosecuting a victim of sexual abuse for first-degree murder.

A guiding principle in criminal defense work is never let the prosecutor know anything about your case; as in times of war, surprise is the best tactic. Yet we didn't want to surprise the prosecutor, we wanted to educate and sensitize him. Our hope was that Drazune, a fifty-two-year-old, bespectacled, nonthreatening academic type who favored worn corduroy jackets with patched elbows, would be able to convince the DA that the homicide resulted from a set of very specific circumstances that would not repeat themselves. Clinton, too, would be impressed by Drazune's credentials as a prosecution witness.

Drazune was able to convince Clinton that Clyde Waylens sexually abused his son, but Clinton refused to drop the charges from first-degree murder. Sexual abuse, though tragic, was no excuse for murder, he said later. No deal. We were going to trial.

I flew into the small town four days before trial. Latham arranged first-class accommodations for me in the spare room of his small wood-frame house. Within two hours, his dining room had become our command post; by nightfall the entire room was covered with half-full bags of pretzels and chips, coffee cups, and empty beer cans amid piles of documents highlighted in bright yellow and blue.

The first thing I did the next morning was to visit Tim. Up to that point, Tim Waylens was a kid I had known only through newspaper stories, psychological evaluations, school records, and conversations with others. I knew the facts of his life, but I had no clear picture of who he was.

After being admitted by the captain of the jail, Latham and I walked down a drab-green concrete hallway lined with cells. Pairs of eyes followed us through the tiny viewing windows cut into the steel-plated doors. At the end of the hallway, we stopped in front of interview room six. The electronic lock banged, and we opened the door and sat down at a graffiti-marked table. A second later, the door on the other side of the room opened with another bang. A doe-eyed, baby-faced teenage boy came in staring intently at the gray concrete floor. Though not in handcuffs or leg irons, he shuffled in as if bound in chains, with his wrists pressed together at his waist.

When I shook his hand, he looked up for a second and gave a halfhearted smile, then stared down once again at the floor. Latham said, "Here's the guy I've been telling you about." Tim was silent.

"Come on," Latham pleaded with an air of fatigue. "You *know* who I'm talking about. This is the guy who specializes in helping kids like you—kids who kill their parents. He just wants to talk to you for a while."

Tim gave me a brief, searching glance, and I recognized a face I'd seen many times before—a face squeezed dry of joy. A child forced to walk an emotional tightrope his whole life, never knowing when he'd fall off. And who, in desperation, finally took the life of the one who gave him life, rather than crashing to a certain death.

I began to talk to Tim about what to expect when we went into court in three days. Mute, he just kept nodding his head. He was not being shy or obstructive; he was paralyzed with fear at the thought of soon telling a packed courtroom that he had been sexually abused. After about a half hour, however, Tim began to open up. He interrupted me in the middle of a question and said, "I know you've been helping Bill and Larry a lot, and I wanted you to know how much I appreciate it." I smiled in thanks, a first step closer for both of us.

Though I had read and reread his descriptions of his ordeal, I wanted to hear Tim say the words himself. I especially wanted to hear answers to the questions the jurors would have in mind as soon as they took their seats. This is what he told me:

P: Why didn't you run away from home?

T: Because it would have meant leaving my mom and brother. Mom wasn't living very good. She never finished high school—she was poor all the time. She needed me. I didn't want to be a burden on her or my brother. And I wasn't going to go live on the streets, I didn't need that shit. Besides, I also loved my dad. Even though he was an asshole, I had some pretty good times with him. We played pool. When he got a motorcycle, we'd go on rides. He taught me how to shoot when I was really young. My dad would take my brother and me for ice cream and rides in the country—things fathers and sons do together. I loved the sight of him and yet I hated him. I just didn't know what to do. . . .

P: Did you ever think about telling anybody about the abuse?

T: No, but once I thought about telling Mom. It was about a month before the homicide. I just had gotten so fed up with things. It was like six A.M. on a Saturday morning, and I rode over to her house and I went upstairs. I'm standing at the foot of her bed and she wakes up. I was going to tell her. Then she says, "Just a minute, we'll go downstairs." She got dressed and came downstairs, but by that time, I changed my mind. I told her it was a girl problem.

P: What was life like for you in the time immediately preceding the homicide?

T: In the last six months I was drinking and getting stoned all the time, trying to forget what was going on with my dad. I tried to stay out of the house as much as possible, because when I was home, I knew it was going to happen. . . . He was tying me up a lot then. He'd just

*come into my room and just do it. And I would be still
and let him do his thing and leave. He was doing it four
to five times a week. He was getting rougher. He'd have
anal intercourse with me more often. He'd stick things in
me. He'd poke me with pens and pencils. . . . I was getting
suicidal toward the end. Like a month before [the murder],
I had stolen a gun from my neighbors' house. That was
my way out. I remember thinking I was going to kill him
or myself. I also told friends that I wished he were dead.
I didn't sit down and write out a plan. I was just thinking
maybe I could kill him. It's going to be him or me. And
then a friend committed suicide about four days before
the murder, and I couldn't kill myself, I just knew I
couldn't put anyone through that.*

    *P: Why didn't you tell anyone about the sexual abuse
after you were arrested?*

    *T: I didn't want anyone to think I was gay. I didn't
trust anybody. You think people aren't going to believe
you. . . . People would think, "Oh, his dad's a great guy,
he couldn't do that to him. He's making this up, you
know."*

I was satisfied in my own mind that he was truthful, but I
wondered if we had the whole *truth.* Tim had never told us
exactly what he was doing between midnight when his father
made the threat and four hours later when he shot Clyde
except to say that he had been half asleep during this time.
We all, Drazune included, believed that something that Tim
wouldn't or perhaps couldn't tell us had happened. Two days
before jury selection was to begin, Latham and I were sitting
in his dining room, feverishly preparing questions, when the
phone rang. It was Steele, calling from the prison where he
went every day to visit Tim. As Steele got up to leave, pushing
one more time for Tim to be truthful about what had happened the night he killed his dad, tears welled in the boy's
eyes and he began to sob uncontrollably.

Clyde had not just threatened to have sex with his son—
he actually forced Tim to have oral sex. After the sex act,
Tim begged his father to stop molesting him. Clyde told Tim
things would never change, Tim was always going to be his.
Clyde then went back into his room, read for a little while,

and went to sleep. "I am always going to be his; it's never going to change," Tim said he thought to himself. "I couldn't handle it anymore. . . . I got up and shot him."

It was too easy, Latham and I thought. Worse, this new information threw a monkey wrench into our theory—namely that Tim killed because he feared an impending attack. On the other hand, I knew that after being removed from the abusive environment, victims, especially boys sexually abused by their fathers, never immediately reveal complete details. The information comes out in dribs and drabs for a long time. It is not unusual for the child to continue to divulge new information even after his trial and sentencing.

Though it is difficult for any person to reveal that they were sexually abused by their father or another adult male, boys are much more reluctant to discuss their experience than are girls. They are taught to quash their emotions and hide their fears. And because machismo and homophobia are pumped into them at an early age, the very last thing a boy is going to do is reveal that his dad has been having sex with him. New York University psychiatrist Dr. Dorothy Lewis, who works with death-row inmates, told me, "I've had individuals on death row [who said they'd] go to their death rather than reveal that they were sexually abused."

Unfortunately, it is not only the victims themselves who have a serious problem discussing their abuse; most of us do not even want to acknowledge the existence of such depraved sexual practices. A defense attorney, however, cannot afford to be squeamish about these matters. In court, the defense lawyer must walk a fine line, painting a real picture of the horror that pushed the child to kill without offending the average person's sensibilities. Luckily, Latham and Steele were up to it—in fact they were ready for anything. Unfortunately, some lawyers are not, such as the one who called me several months before Latham contacted me.

This attorney from a small Midwestern town was referred to me by a national children's rights organization. Though practicing law for about twenty years, he had never seen a case like this in his career. These were the facts: a fourteen-year-old boy, who had never even skipped class, had brutally killed his stepfather with a sixteen-gauge shotgun while the two were hunting. It had clearly not been an accident: the boy had told his friends that he was going to kill his dad, and he had shot his stepfather twice in the back from close range, reloading between shots.

The attorney was soft-spoken and deferential. So much so, in fact, that it took me an hour to get to the heart of the case. After pushing him for a possible motive, I suggested that something else might be going on.

There was a long pause. "Well, maybe. It's possible, from something the boy said, that the boy's stepfather was, ah, well, taking advantage of him in a certain way," he said.

" 'Taking advantage of'? You mean his father was sexually abusing him?" I asked. "Exactly what did your client tell you?"

"His father forced his head into his lap."

He fell silent, obviously sailing choppy seas, so I took it step by painful step. "And what else did the father do? I know it's difficult, but the jury's going to need details in order to decide in his favor. Did the father zip open his own fly and expose his penis?"

"Well, yes," said the lawyer uncomfortably.

"Did the stepfather force your client to give him a blowjob? I mean fellate him?"

"I think so, maybe."

And then came the political geography lesson. I get them all the time. It's probably because I still have traces of a New York accent, though I haven't lived there for over twenty years.

"I really have to pause here and tell you that this is a very conservative county," he said stiffly. "They're not big-city folk here; they're squeamish about this stuff. I've got to watch how I phrase things, if you know what I mean."

I knew exactly what he meant, but his attitude infuriated me. He was the kind of lawyer who played it safe, worrying more about what the jury would think about him than going the distance for his client.

I understood his problem, but he obviously did not. "How often did this 'taking advantage of' occur? Once a week?"

"About," he replied coldly.

"Did he try to masturbate the boy or orally copulate him?" I could just see him pulling the receiver away from his face, asking himself, "Why in the world did I call this guy?"

"I just don't see why it's so goddamn necessary to get that detailed," he said, disgusted. "It's enough that we can get out that he forced his son's head into his lap."

"Your client is being charged with first-degree murder, and the DA isn't playing 'Let's Make a Deal,' right?"

"Correct," he said with some resignation.

"Then you can't hold back. Let *me* get very detailed for you. The jury probably isn't going to believe your boy to begin with. So he's going to have to make it real for every juror, or he's going away forever. How real? While he's describing the oral sex, each one of those jurors should be able to see his father's semen rolling down his cheek."

A very long silence. "I think I get your point."

I have always understood the immense reluctance of abused children to talk about their ordeal, but during my first few years, it was a constant battle to remain tolerant of those defense lawyers who are either ignorant of the devastating effects of abuse or too timid to confront the matter head-on. Over time, I realized my impatience stemmed from my failure to realize that though it was the mid-1980s, child abuse was still a taboo subject, even among defense lawyers.

For the three days prior to trial, Steele, Latham, and I were working eighteen-hour days, shuttling between casebooks and last-minute interviews with witnesses. It was one-thirty in the morning on the eve of trial, and we were doing our final strategizing over some cold vodka in a local watering hole. We had worked our asses off, and despite the shortcomings in the case, we couldn't wait to blast into the courtroom in seven hours. As we waxed on about what a coup it would be if Tim walked on a not guilty, we caught ourselves.

A not-guilty verdict did not mean Tim's life would be peaches and cream. What could Tim do? He was traumatized, and he had no family support structure. His mother was burdened with her own problems; his dad's family hated him. He had absolutely no money to support himself, let alone to pay for the psychological counseling he so desperately needed. He was suicidal and had earlier sought refuge in alcohol and drugs when times were difficult. The streets would be a cruel alternative, but the system didn't care. We all would have done our job.

The case had more than its share of depressing facts; it was unnecessary for us to make the picture any darker. Sometimes, there are no answers. We finished our drinks in silence and left the bar.

Before we went to sleep, we had to deal with one last-minute problem. All trials are minidramas. Not only is it important what the actors say and how they say it, but how they look. Steele had already bought Tim a new three-piece, dark-blue suit, the right choice for the average defendant in the average murder case. But it was wrong for Tim, especially because it made him look older than his years. The jury had to see Tim as he was, a teenager, not an adult. We raided Latham's limited wardrobe and found two sweaters. After hastily removing an old spaghetti-sauce stain from a pastel-blue pullover, we put it in Latham's briefcase.

Steele, Latham, and I arrived at the nondescript courthouse the next morning at about eight-thirty. Though the courtroom would not open for another hour, a line of family, friends, and others was already forming. The jailers had taken Tim from his cell and brought him to an attorney interview room just off the courtroom.

When we walked in, he stood up and said hesitatingly, "Well, do I look okay?"

"Great, man, you look great," said Latham. "But the fashion king here wants you to look better." Latham took the blue sweater out of his briefcase and told Tim to take off his coat and tie. Tim looked a little dismayed. It was the first suit he had ever worn and he liked the way he looked. But when he put on the sweater, he shed five years.

Out of respect for Tim (a favorite of the deputies), and knowing that he was not going to bolt from the courthouse, the sheriffs allowed Tim to walk alone with us into the courtroom. With Steele behind, and Latham and I to his sides, Tim nervously walked the twenty steps to the courtroom door. As soon as the door opened, the television klieg lights came on and the packed spectator gallery became quiet, all eyes turning to see the boy who killed his father. We took our seats at the large wooden conference table in front of the judge's bench. Jury selection was about to begin.

Under the laws of our nation any person accused of a crime is guaranteed a trial by a jury of twelve "good and true" citizens selected from the community. The problem in parricide cases is that, though the jury is technically made up of "peers" of the child, realistically they are not his peers at all.

Adults often forget what life was like as an adolescent. Few have a realistic picture of this time: some romanticize their youth; others want to eradicate it from memory. My experience in such trials is that the jurors will react first as parents, second as the children they once were, and third as the impartial decision-makers they take an oath to be.

The jury selection process, voir dire, which occurs before opening arguments, provides the attorney the opportunity to investigate the jurors' attitudes, opinions, and prejudices about such topics as child rearing, family violence, and self-defense. It is a golden opportunity for the attorney to educate and sensitize potential jurors to the issues that will arise in the case itself.

I have developed a list of sixty-five questions that is designed to gauge a person's attitudes on matters from child rearing and child abuse to the use of self-defense in a family setting.

An added bonus of this selection process is that the judge, and sometimes the prosecutor, become educated about the issues. The legal profession prefers to think of itself as operating immune from personal and social prejudices, and that the "law" is grounded in a timeless objectivity. Nothing could be further from the truth as the raging debates over the appointment of all recent United States Supreme Court nominees since Sandra Day O'Connor have demonstrated.

I steadfastly believe that, when the average judge dons her black robe to preside over a parricide case, she is no different from the juror—reacting and thinking first as a parent, second as the child of her parents, and only lastly as a judge. From the moment the gavel goes down in a parricide case and the court is called into session, a judge's attitudes and biases are often as conspicuous as the diplomas that hang so proudly in their offices.

Ninety prospective jurors filed in. Some shuffled, others walked purposefully. Twelve of them would decide Tim's fate. I remembered what Steele said about the people in the county taking their duty seriously. One look at them told me he was right. They were split about evenly between men and women.

Most seemed to be over thirty-five; some were formally dressed for business, while others wore jeans or coveralls. Few talked with each other; even fewer smiled. They were indeed a solemn bunch, and they hadn't even heard the facts yet. It was as if they were preparing to hear a sermon. But as I stared at the group and tried to size them up, I could only think that these people didn't have any idea what they were in for.

In many jurisdictions it is the practice, especially in cases concerning sensitive subjects, to have each juror fill out a questionnaire. Before asking any questions, the judge and the attorneys then review each questionnaire to determine if there is anything in the juror's background that may prove to be a source of embarrassment should they have to discuss it in open court.

The questionnaire for Tim's case contained seven questions, the most critical of which was, "Have you or has anyone close to you been the victim or participant in incest, rape, sexual or physical abuse, or any kind of similar behavior? If so, kindly outline your experience."

About 90 percent answered with a big NO, or they left the answer line blank. That was to be expected. It happens in every parricide case, despite the fact that at least 25 percent of them, according to the statistics, should have answered yes.

The names of twelve prospective jurors were selected, and each took a seat behind the ornate wooden banister that surrounded the jury box. The defense and prosecution were each given twenty-six "peremptory strikes," with which they could discharge a potential juror without giving a specific reason. On the other hand, an attorney has an unlimited number of "strikes for cause." Strikes for cause are granted infrequently—only when the person is obviously incapable of being fair and impartial.

Juror number one was a silver-haired, sixty-three-year-old machine operator and a lifelong resident of the community. He wore a flannel work shirt and faded denim jeans. His scowl told me that he hated being in the courtroom.

Prosecutor Rudy Clinton rose to begin, asking general questions, trying to stay as far away from child abuse as he could. Clinton was determined to treat this homicide as if it were any other criminal case.

"Do you realize that serving on a jury is an important civic responsibility?"

"Yes."

"Based upon what you have been told about this case, that it involves a boy who killed his father, do you believe that you can be fair and impartial?"

"Yes."

"Can you follow the judge's instructions as he reads them to you?"

"Yes."

After about ten minutes of lethargic exchange, Clinton thanked the juror for his honesty and sat down. Now it was our turn.

Latham and I decided to alternate in our questioning. Because Latham had the home-court advantage, he went first. Under his breath he whispered to Tim, "Are you ready?" With a half-nervous smile, Tim nodded. "Then I am, too," Latham said, rising from his seat and lumbering across the floor until he was eight feet from the juror.

"Good morning, sir. My name, as you know, is William Latham, and I, along with Mr. Mones, represent Tim Waylens. I promise not to take much of your time, okay?"

The man gave a ho-hum nod.

"First, I would like you to give me your definition of incest."

The machine operator needed a minute to compose himself. Then he softly replied, "Well, ah, sex between family members, like between an uncle and his niece."

I glanced over at the remaining jurors, most of whom looked as if someone had thrown cold water in their faces. They sat up straight and fastened their safety belts. It was going to be a rough ride.

"Do you think it's possible to have incest between a father and a son?" Latham continued.

A long pause. "I guess it happens."

I looked at Tim, and it was obvious that he was trying to hold back the tears. One got away and rolled down his cheek, and I squeezed his hand to let him know it was okay to cry. Though he didn't realize it, Tim was in a giant group-therapy session.

In the next twenty minutes juror number one was asked dozens of questions about issues that he had probably never considered in his entire existence on the planet: Do you believe family violence is a private problem that should be handled entirely within the family? Some people believe that an abused teenager has only himself to blame if he doesn't run away from home; what do you believe? We thanked him, later using one of our peremptory strikes to get him off the panel because he had told us that the problem of child abuse was overblown.

Clinton then turned to juror number two. The process went on through the morning. Jurors talked about their philosophies of child rearing; how they were treated as children; what they thought of using a paddle; and whether a paddle had been used on them. Right before we adjourned for lunch, juror number six was called. She had answered the abuse question on the written form in the affirmative. We all went into the judge's chambers for the first time.

A small, heavyset woman in her midtwenties sat in the center of the small office. She was twisting a Kleenex around her index finger like a tourniquet, until the fingertip turned bright red, and tiny bits of white tissue fell on her powder-blue skirt. Her eyes darted everywhere around the room and all she saw were men: the judge, the prosecutor, two defense attorneys, a sheriff, and a court reporter. The room was silent, except for the humming of the heater. For all of our experience, none of us knew where to start. We were almost as uncomfortable as she was.

Judge Murdoch, a soft-spoken, experienced jurist, tenderly broke the ice by asking if she felt her ordeal, whatever it was, would prevent her from being impartial. That's all it took. Tears gushed down her rosy cheeks. The bailiff had to get more tissue because she had twisted hers to shreds. She couldn't even manage to answer the question. All she could say between sniffles and sobs was that her father had sexually abused her as a teenager, and her life had not been right since. She tearfully said she didn't want to serve on the jury. The judge asked if either the state or the defense had any objection in dismissing this juror. Both sides mumbled, "No objection."

The young lady got up quickly and walked out of the office ahead of us. She entered the packed courtroom with a flushed, tear-streaked face, and we followed, our heads hung low, embarrassed. After all, we were the ones who had made her cry. As terrible as it sounds, her crying helped our case, lending a human dimension to what had up until that point largely been abstract. Her distress helped establish, even for the most cynical juror, that abuse is real. Her tears were the first step in making the horror hit home.

When we came back for the afternoon session, Judge Murdoch called us into chambers. Rolling an unlit cigar around with his fingertips, he pointedly asked us if some settlement was on the horizon. Clearly disturbed by the morning's events, he was not looking forward to presiding over this case.

"If you fellows don't find a middle ground on this one," he began, "we *all* are going to find ourselves in a position that *nobody* wants to be in." Cryptic, but we got the message: No one would come off a clear-cut winner.

Clinton said that any deal would have to include some state prison time.

"Well, Judge," Latham said, quickly rising out of his chair, "if that's his attitude, we don't have anything to discuss. I've told him over and over that we won't accept a deal that involves state-pen time."

The judge glanced at Clinton, who just shrugged his shoulders and got to his feet. We all went back into the courtroom to continue the selection.

A twenty-five-year-old laborer who had an eight-month-old baby was next in line. He was a real macho guy who had worn a perpetual smirk throughout the morning proceedings. Macho men are dangerous jurors in parricide cases, especially those involving boys who kill their dads. Such men tend to believe that a son should be able to take whatever his dad dishes out. If the boy doesn't fight back or get the hell out, then it's his own damn fault.

This juror deflected every question I asked. He was determined to keep his feelings to himself, and he was doing a great job. After ten minutes of fruitless back-and-forth, I turned and walked back to my chair, resigned to striking him. Halfway back to the counsel table, a question popped into my mind.

"What's more important to you, your job or your kid?" I asked abruptly.

He leaned forward in his seat, pressing on the wooden

railing of the jury box to make his point, indignant that I could even ask such a stupid question. "My kid, of course. He's more important than anything in the world. All kids are!" That was all I needed. He had my vote.

On the afternoon of the second day of jury selection, Steele had arrived with the news that he had tracked down Mel, Tim's uncle. Unbelievably, Steele had convinced Mel to be a witness for the defense, no small task considering that everyone else on Clyde's side of the family refused even to speak with us. Mel had agreed to cooperate to do something positive to make up for the torture he had visited on his own children. He would testify, he said, in graphic detail to his father's abuse of his older sisters, his brothers, including Clyde, his mother, and amazingly, himself. At last, we had the key to corroborate the intergenerational abuse in Tim's family.

By the end of the second day of jury selection, we had thoroughly explored the feelings of dozens of potential jurors on a wide range of child rearing and family issues. Most importantly, we had heard some enlightening answers about the extremely deleterious effect of child abuse, especially sexual abuse. Juror after juror said they could understand why an abused child would not run away or report the abusing parent. They had their views on other subjects critical in the trial—the use of deadly force in defending oneself and the reliability of psychologists and psychiatrists in evaluating human behavior, for example. With our case resting in large part on the testimony of mental health experts, this latter area was one explored in depth. In fact, we had to use one of our peremptory strikes on a gentleman, a chemist, who said that he believed that psychology and psychiatry were "imprecise" sciences at best.

One of my cardinal rules in cases of boys who kill their fathers is to avoid selecting men over fifty-five; they are the least sympathetic, and therefore most likely to mete out the stiffest sentence. Raised when child abuse was unheard of, but children were still mistreated, these men tend to subscribe to macho philosophies such as: "My father beat the shit out of me and I turned out all right" and "If you can't take the heat, then get the hell out of the kitchen." As fathers, moreover, many tend to perceive the homicide as an attack against the authority of all fathers. Needless to say, then, on the morning of the third day of selection, when a distinguished-looking, white-haired juror I'll call Matthew was up for questioning, I was fairly sure how he'd answer my questions.

Matthew's questioning was conducted in chambers because he had written on his questionnaire that he had "strong feelings about child abuse." A tall, muscular man in his early sixties, Matthew worked as a school administrator. Unlike the others we had questioned in chambers, he projected self-assurance, sitting erect in his chair and answering our questions without the slightest hesitation.

Clinton began with the most general questions. When Matthew told Clinton that his job brought him into frequent contact with police officers, I could see my esteemed opponent relax into his seat. "This guy's on my side," Clinton's smile seemed to say. When Matthew said he was in charge of school discipline, Latham and I gave each other the thumbs-down look. This guy would kill us in the jury room. At that point, we didn't care why he had strong feelings about child abuse. No defense attorney in his right mind would leave on the jury someone who was, for all practical purposes, a cop himself.

With confidence, Clinton then moved on to ask Matthew about his child abuse answer. "I notice you've stated that you have strong feelings about child abuse. Could you tell us why?" Matthew took a deep breath, cleared his throat, and riveted his eyes on Clinton.

"When I was a little boy," he began, "I had a stepfather who liked to mete out discipline with the back end of a two-by-four." With each word his voice rose, measured but increasingly angry. "One day, just as he was about to beat me, I took that board away from him and grabbed him by the throat. I choked him within an inch of his miserable little life."

Hiding his sudden unease, Clinton remarked conversationally, "But *of course* you didn't kill him, right?"

"No, sir. I was lucky, very lucky." The truth of his answer struck so deeply that nobody dared speak. For a split second each of us was with Matthew as he choked his stepfather almost fifty years earlier.

The judge looked to Clinton and said, "Any more questions?" He knew the answer, but he asked it anyway. Clinton quietly responded, "No."

Believing we had heard all we needed to hear, Latham and I did not ask any questions. The judge, however, was concerned. Would Matthew's experience, the judge asked, affect his impartiality in this case? Matthew was adamant; he could separate his personal life from his public duty. Needless to say, when we went back into the courtroom, Clinton struck Matthew from the panel.

Matthew's examination was so fascinating that I wanted to find out more about him. Initially, he was reluctant to speak to me because he didn't want to relive his childhood pain. He mulled over my request for several weeks and finally agreed to be interviewed over the phone.

As he had in chambers, he began by speaking in a calm and deliberate tone:

> My stepfather was a hardworking man [whose] way of dealing with us kids and my mom was to yell, scream, and ridicule. My mom was a loving and caring person, but she was psychologically and physically unable to deal with him. Sis and I spent a lot of nights listening to him slap Mom around and belittle her. It probably happened ten times a month. She chose to stay, but kids don't have that choice. . . . On one occasion I remember we had a large garden full of spuds and corn. He said, "Come out here, you're working in the garden." And he put me in a pony harness with a cultivator. I was twelve. To this day I think back on it. I pulled for four hours with him behind the cultivator. I remember my mother and the neighbors coming out trying to tell him that it's not humane to treat your son this way. And the more people tried to tell him this, the more he said mind your own goddamn business."

Matthew would have been a great juror. And though I still am wary of silver-haired men, today I am much more willing to give them a chance.

A final jury was eventually selected on the third day. When we went back to the judge's chambers that afternoon, Murdoch reiterated his admonition. He did not want to see this case go to trial. Murdoch would not let us leave his office. He propped his feet up on his desk, lit a cigar, and said,

"Gentlemen, tell me how all of us are going to close *this* gap."

Since the first day of jury selection, both sides had been trying to find a compromise. At the end of the first day, Clinton wanted a guilty plea of second-degree murder and the minimum twenty years in the state prison; by the end of the second day, he offered a plea to second-degree murder with a minimum of ninety days of confinement in a state correctional facility and a suspension of remaining prison time. On this final afternoon, it was our turn to offer something to the district attorney.

"Judge," Latham said in a tired voice, "we can live with a plea to second-degree murder, but we simply can't take jail time." Clinton responded: he could not accept a plea that would place Tim on unsupervised probation. I saw his response as a major concession, because it was the first time he had not mentioned prison.

Would Clinton, I asked, agree to Tim's serving his "time" in a closely supervised therapeutic treatment program outside the state? The program, which I had used several times in the past, specialized in treating violent adolescent offenders. It was not a barred facility, but the residents were kept under twenty-four-hour surveillance. Tim would plead guilty to second-degree murder and be placed in the program for three years.

Because the case was so politically sticky, Murdoch and Clinton jumped at the proposition. Clinton was in an especially difficult position: he could not simply let Tim walk on a straight probationary sentence because it would appear that he was soft on crime. Yet, he could not risk what he now realized was the very real possibility of a not-guilty verdict.

Clinton did not agree out of any last-minute rush of sympathy for Tim. He had known the details of our defense at least four months before the trial—we had even put our chief expert in a room with him for three hours—but he had never been interested in dealing. What turned the tide was the voir dire, especially Matthew's examination. Clinton simply "underestimated the emotional impact of this type of scenario," Latham remarked. "He just wasn't prepared for how it was going to play with the individual jurors."

Throughout the months preceding the trial, Clyde's family and friends had repeatedly insisted that the prosecutor demand the maximum penalty to punish Tim. They maintained their position even after Clinton told them that he was convinced that Clyde had sexually abused his son. Yet their reaction was understandable, for they had lost a close relative by violence and wanted the killer, even if one of their own, to pay the price. When I asked Clinton how the family had responded to the plea bargain, he said, "All I can say is that they did not take it well."

A couple hours before the plea was going to be formally announced in court, Steele had to take care of one last detail. None of us could predict how those in the courtroom would react to the news that Tim wasn't going to prison, and Steele was leaving nothing to chance. When I walked into the courtroom two hours later, it was ringed with a formidable array of county sheriffs, all with their hands folded in front of them and large bulges in their jackets.

When Judge Murdoch emerged from his chambers, the jury was fully expecting the trial to begin. Instead, he told them that a settlement had been reached, thanked them for their participation, and sent them home. They gave a collective sigh of relief. Nobody had wanted to decide this boy's fate. But they also didn't want to leave the courtroom until they had heard Tim speak.

The courtroom was packed with all of Tim's family and friends, as well as his classmates and numerous townsfolk eager to hear his final statement. Murdoch asked if he had anything to say before sentence was imposed, and Tim rose, composed and serious, and walked to the wooden railing in front of the judge's bench. Neither Latham nor I had any idea what Tim was going to say. Clutching the railing, he spoke in a tearful but strangely calm and relieved tone.

"I've been abused for nine years. I loved my father, but there's nothing I can do to bring him back. I am seeking help, and I would like to thank the court for giving me that help." He could have continued, but there was really nothing more to say.

The location of the nonsecure treatment program is a secret, the only information released to the public being that it is in another state. Tim lives close by the program's offices in a simply decorated two-bedroom apartment with a male staff member. He spends his days doing odd jobs around the office, and he receives therapy five days a week.

The goal is to rebuild his personality. In the weeks preceding and following the homicide, Tim was suicidal. Before the homicide, he had thought about killing himself because he saw no other way out of his predicament; in the months following Clyde's death and even after he began the treatment program, Tim contemplated suicide because of the tremendous guilt he felt for killing his dad. As he said to me so often, "I hated my dad and I loved my dad." It was that love that drove him to consider ending his own life.

Like many sexually abused adolescents, Tim had a low opinion of himself. One of the primary objectives of his therapy is to make him relive in detail the reality of his childhood. For through confronting his victimization by his father, Tim will be able to shed the belief that he was to blame for that abuse.

I visited Tim after he had been in the treatment program for about a year. As we sat in the coffee shop of my hotel, it was obvious that he was a changed person. He looked me straight in the eye and spoke confidently and clearly. I knew he was still in great pain, but he was making a valiant effort at putting his life back together.

To me, the most interesting aspect of his treatment is his participation in a therapy group made up of adult male sex offenders. "The group is made up of Peeping Toms, guys who've exposed themselves, and a couple of child molesters," he said. "And most of them have had some kind of early childhood sexual experience." Though Tim was a victim, his therapist believes that those men would give him a unique insight into understanding his relationship with Clyde.

"Does it worry you that they were victims who became offenders?" I asked. "Yes," he responded quietly. "But because I'm seeking the help now, I will be able to recognize any of the symptoms that they have had because we've talked about it. So if anything happens, I'll know it."

"Do you have any fear you'll abuse any kids you might have?" I asked cautiously.

"I have a fear of having a family right now because I don't want to have happen to my kids what happened to me," he said. "But in five years, maybe longer down the road, I probably won't have that fear because I know it won't happen. I mean I doubt it will happen. Oh, I don't know about any of that. All I know is I have a lot of stuff to get out and I think it will take me a long time to do it."

Mike

On a Sunday afternoon in the spring of 1985, Michael Alborgeden and his father, Craig, went to have lunch at a relative's home. A little over five feet six inches tall, and weighing about 140 pounds, Michael looked like almost any other sixteen-year-old in the high school he attended in a suburban Southeastern town. The first thing one noticed about Mike was his large, watery-green eyes. Regardless of his mood, they conveyed melancholy. This day, however, they were hidden behind a pair of mirrored aviator sunglasses, and it wasn't because of the weather, which had been overcast and rainy. Nor did Mike wear the glasses to effect the cool and detached look so popular with boys his age.

"How'd you get that shiner?" his aunt Barbara asked as he walked through the door.

"I tripped and hit my eye on the coffee table," he said quickly, dismissing the seriousness of the injury.

"No, he didn't. I popped him," Craig derisively boasted. Michael looked down with embarrassment, but his father just cackled with delight.

Two days before Craig and Michael had had one of their typical arguments—whether Michael had folded and put away the dirty laundry without first washing it. Believing his son had lied to him, Craig had punched Michael in the eye.

That was Friday night, April 11.

Friday's black eye wasn't the exception; Mike had twelve years of practice in making excuses for bruised arms, cut lips, and bumps on his head. Though a strong, coordinated, and athletic kid, to others he always seemed to be slipping, tripping, bumping into something, or cutting himself on some sharp object. He was the king of prevarication.

Craig, a short, burly man in his early forties, with a full beard and closely cropped jet-black hair, was a fervent believer in the wisdom of physical punishment. It was the way he had been raised, and he was sure that the beatings would make his only son a better man.

Michael learned early that childhood was for sissies. Craig, a service station owner, instilled the work ethic in his son almost as soon as Michael could walk. Vacations were not spent tying lanyards at Boy Scout camp or playing Little League baseball. Instead, every summer from kindergarten through high school Michael passed sweeping the garage or pumping gas.

Most little boys occupy their time playing with miniature race cars, G.I. Joe dolls, and water guns, but not Craig's son—these toys were for children. When Michael was five, Craig gave him his first motorcycle; at seven, Michael got his first weapon, a shotgun.

Along with the adult toys came adult responsibilities for their care. At age five, Michael was allowed to gas up his motorbike, but after filling it, the boy had to put the can back in the garage. Returning home from work one afternoon, Craig noticed that his son had left the gas can in the driveway. He bolted angrily from his truck and raced toward Michael, who was sitting on his bike. Before Mike could say hello, Craig had thrown him off and began beating him with the gas can. As he slammed his son with the metal can, he screamed, "I never want you to forget to put this away." Michael never forgot again.

And so it was on that Sunday afternoon that, after hearing Craig brag about "popping" Michael, Aunt Barbara warned her brother, "One day he's gonna fight back and you'll regret it."

"Whenever he's ready!" Craig shot back contemptuously. "Whenever he's ready!"

* * *

About a week after that family gathering, Michael filed a missing person's report on his father. He hadn't seen or heard from his dad in three days, he told the two detectives. After conducting a search of the house, however, the two were dubious that Craig was merely missing. Both family cars were in the driveway, and Craig's wallet and watch lay on his bedroom dresser.

Craig's relatives also suspected that something was not right about Michael's story from his unusual behavior that weekend. He had had two all-night parties at the house, and he had skipped school for two days. Craig had such an iron-fisted grip over the household that when he was away on a business trip, Michael would not even dare dream of throwing a party, let alone of staying out all night in violation of his strictly enforced curfew.

Three days after Michael filed the missing person's report, a fisherman found Craig Alborgeden's bullet-riddled body under a boat dock. The police determined that he had been killed about four days earlier. Michael was arrested five hours later, and by that time, the police had much more than circumstantial evidence that fingered him as the killer. Many of Michael's friends who had played active roles in the cover-up had already confessed.

With the formal police identification of Craig's body, Billy Eckhart, one of Michael's closest friends, had turned himself in to the authorities. The freckle-faced seventeen-year-old nervously told police that he had been awakened at home by Mike late on the previous Friday evening.

"I did it," Mike had excitedly told his friend. At first Eckhart refused to believe Mike had killed his dad. Mike was too scared even to talk back to his father, so Mike's killing Craig seemed just too much to swallow. To prove his story, Mike cajoled Eckhart back to the Alborgeden home, where Eckhart saw the lifeless body. Mike then got extremely nervous; he pleaded with Eckhart to help him decide the next step.

Mike and Billy wrapped Craig's body in a blanket, put it in the trunk of Eckhart's car, and drove through the dark until they reached the marina. After hiding the body, they silently drove home, neither fully appreciating what they had just done.

On the Friday evening following Craig's disappearance,

armed with Eckhart's confession and mounds of circumstantial evidence, county homicide investigators Richard Caspar and Joe Angeli visited Craig's sister Barbara and brother, Dana, to tell them how their brother had died. The news didn't shock them, for they had already suspected the worst. Still, they would not completely accept that their nephew had taken his father's life unless he told them himself. With the detectives remaining in his house, Uncle Dana went to pick up Michael. Upon their return, in front of the detectives and other relatives, Uncle Dana said, "Please tell me, Michael, that you didn't do it." Michael was silent for a moment, then broke down, sobbing that he had killed Craig.

On that fateful Friday evening, Michael had gone skating with his friends. At first, Craig insisted that his son be home by nine-thirty, but after Mike pleaded, his father relented. Michael could skate until eleven. The boy didn't get home until one-thirty A.M. He was very late, and he knew his father would be livid.

As usual, his dad was lying on the couch, apparently asleep, the TV blaring away. As Michael tiptoed past to his room, his father bellowed, "You always gotta push it. Every time I give you a break, you always gotta push it! Come out here!"

Craig was propped up on one arm, with a .22-caliber rifle perched on the floor next to the headrest. "You got two choices," his father continued angrily. Michael thought that he was going to say thirty days in juvenile hall or forty days restriction, the option he'd been given when he had skipped school several weeks earlier.

His guess was far off the mark.

"You kill me, or I kill you," his father said. Since Craig routinely threatened to kill his son, Michael ignored him and began to walk back to his room. Then he heard two metallic clicks, the chambering of a round, then the cocking of the rifle.

"Come here, I'm serious," his father yelled after him. Michael wasn't sure if the gun was even loaded, but his father's tone made him turn. When he pivoted, he found himself looking down the barrel of the gun. Again Craig made his threat. Though he refused to believe his dad was serious, Michael did the only thing he could—he took the weapon, stock first.

The rifle was frozen in Michael's hand, the barrel no more than a foot from his father's head. Then the familiar taunting began.

"I hate you," Craig sneered. "You're not my son! I never intended to have you. I hate you!" Tears welled in the youth's eyes as Craig's attacks moved to his ex-wife. "I hate your mother. She's a cunt. If you don't kill me, I'm going to kill you, then kill her, and then kill myself!"

"I don't remember how many times I pulled the trigger," Michael would later recall sadly. "After I pulled the first time I kind of like blanked out. . . . I just kept pulling it till it stopped." When the gun was empty, Craig lay dead on the couch, six bullets in his head.

After his confession, Michael confessed, ashamed, that his father had frequently beat and verbally belittled him, but the homicide detectives did not want to listen. He was just one of those violent, rebellious, degenerate teenagers. After the arrest, the case was immediately assigned to Maurice Aton, the most experienced attorney in the prosecutor's office.

Aton agreed with the detectives: Michael was nothing but a coldhearted killer. Following a hearing in which the judge set bail at $250,000 and denied Michael permission to go to his father's funeral, Aton told the newspapers that "a turbulent relationship . . . is no excuse for homicide."

The brutality with which many patricides and matricides are committed tends to blind prosecutors to deeper motives, the real underlying causes of such crimes. As a result, DA's typically lump them together with stranger-perpetrated homicides—the teenager who stabs a stranger for a cigarette or the gang member who kills an innocent child in a drive-by shooting. Though a politically opportune comparison for many prosecutors to make, it is not an accurate one.

The majority of children who kill their parents do not have a history of violent lawlessness. If they have been arrested, it has usually been for a victimless, property-related crime such as shoplifting, vandalism, or theft. They are for the most part submissive and not aggressive personalities.

According to a 1987 University of Michigan study by psychiatrist Elissa Benedek and psychologist Dewey Cornell, which is the most recent comprehensive research on minors who kill, adolescents who kill strangers often have a long history of serious delinquency and dangerous, assaultive behavior. Teenagers who kill strangers, according to a 1976 study, had more impulse-control problems than children who killed their parents. In fact, most "stranger-perpetrated" homicides by minors occur in connection with the commission of another crime, such as robbery, and are devoid of the emotional elements common to parricides. Unlike children who kill their parents, these teens "tended to view the victim as an obstacle interfering with some immediate need for gratification."

Aton focused completely on events the night of the murder. Earlier incidents, from years to days before the homicide, were almost irrelevant—another common prosecutorial position in these cases. In fact, Aton even refused to accept that any argument took place. He believed that Craig was sound asleep when Michael walked in the door. Fearing the inevitable punishment because he had violated his curfew, and fed up with all the restrictions imposed on him, Aton's reconstruction went, Michael had snuck up from behind and simply executed his defenseless father.

In large part, Aton based his analysis on the autopsy report, which revealed that all six bullet wounds were clustered *behind* the left ear. This cluster pattern led the forensics experts to conclude that the wounds could only have been inflicted by someone standing behind, *not in front of,* Craig as Mike had stated.

Aton's theory was further bolstered by Michael's behavior after the crime. There was abundant proof of Michael's deliberate attempts to cover up the crime, and ample evidence that immediately after the homicide he neither felt nor showed any remorse—a fact that particularly perturbed Aton and the detectives. In the days following the killing, Michael was anything but in mourning: he had had two raucous, all-night parties at his house. His demeanor hadn't changed even after his arrest. While he cried during parts of his interrogation, for the most part he had come off as relaxed and unemotional.

Though Michael was not a hardened juvenile delinquent, neither was he a saint. The previous spring, while living with his mother in another part of the state, Michael had been arrested and put on probation for breaking into a neighbor's empty house. His family decided it was best for him to get out of the area, so he was sent to go live with his dad, who four months earlier had been divorced from his mom. The prosecutor reasoned that Craig had to be strict because the probation order legally obligated him to monitor his son's behavior, a position that Craig's relatives supported.

Craig's siblings emphasized to the homicide investigators that there was great love between Craig and his son. Michael was always in his father's company, worked with him on the weekends, and father and son spent all their vacations together.

Mike's aunt and uncle painted him as a headstrong teenager becoming steadily more difficult for his father to handle, especially over the previous two years. Skipping school, cutting class, ignoring chores, flaunting his curfew—his incorrigibility would have raised the ire of any parent. Though Craig had occasionally hit Michael, the punishments were no different from what they had received from their father and certainly never amounted to child abuse. Mike's problem was that he wanted too much to be his own man. He refused to obey his dad and finally killed him simply because he got tired of listening to him.

By the time Marty Griffin, Michael's privately retained attorney, called me for assistance some fifteen months later, plea negotiations had broken down and a trial in adult court was eight weeks away. Griffin, an intense, short, wiry man nearing fifty, is the quintessential general practitioner. His practice caters to moderate- and middle-income people; he handles everything from bankruptcy and incorporations to drunk-driving cases and real estate transactions. Michael's case was obviously a departure, both challenging and difficult.

Griffin was passionately devoted to Michael. In fact, in the year since Michael's mother's family had hired him, he had in effect become Michael's surrogate father. Such intense bonding between an attorney and the client he or she is defending is normally unusual, but occurs, I have found, with surprising frequency in parricides. The cement of the bond lies in the fact that these adolescents are eminently sympathetic characters, especially for a jaded defense attorney used to dealing with some very unsavory people. The teenager, for his part, attaches himself to the attorney with a passionate intensity. Not only is the defense attorney the first person to take a legitimate interest in the child's tale of woe, she is also often the first person to say, "I believe you, and I'm going to help you."

From our first, lengthy conversation, it was obvious that the year had taken its toll on Griffin. He appeared overwhelmed by the immensity of organizing the case for trial and taken aback at the aggressiveness with which Aton was prosecuting the case. The tone of the prosecution was set soon after the arrest, when Aton first offered a take-it-or-leave-it plea, which left Griffin no room to maneuver.

Michael had originally been charged in juvenile court with first-degree murder with the use of a gun. As a minor, if convicted, he would serve a maximum nine years. If he was transferred to adult court and convicted, he would serve twenty-seven years to life. Aton offered a plea whereby Michael would agree to be treated as an adult, then plead to second-degree murder with a gun, which carried a term of seventeen years to life.

Griffin countered with this offer: allow Michael to be tried as an adult, but he would plead guilty instead to voluntary manslaughter and serve a maximum sentence of thirteen years. Aton rejected it outright; he had, he said, offered his best deal. Griffin realized the DA wasn't bluffing when, several days following the offer, the same judge who had set Michael's high bail and had refused to allow him to go to his father's funeral had "informally" advised Griffin that it would be a big mistake to reject the plea. A jury could easily return a verdict of first-degree murder, the judge said, resulting in the significantly harsher sentence. In spite of this pressure, Griffin refused Aton's offer, which was really no offer at all, because, considering his age, even the minimum seventeen years would destroy Michael's life.

Griffin didn't have to tell me that Michael had been transferred to adult court. In theory, the transfer laws in all states specifically prohibit judges from transferring a child to adult court solely on the basis of the seriousness of the crime. Rather, the court should consider a whole range of additional factors such as a child's amenability to rehabilitation, his mental state, and prior criminal history. In all my experience, however, I have only seen a handful of parricide cases where the child remained in juvenile court. In the eyes of the average judge, positive character and all other evidence notwithstanding, the act of killing a parent is itself sufficient to require a child's transfer to adult court.

I agreed to help Griffin organize the case for trial and to assist him in the jury selection and the examination of the expert witnesses. Since time was of the essence, I flew to meet him three days later.

Griffin's office was the top floor of a converted Victorian mansion. I felt at home as soon as I walked in because his office looked just like mine—papers strewn all over his huge mahogany desk, books precariously stacked in the corners. Sitting on the mantelpiece were bronze busts of Mozart and Lincoln, alongside several Styrofoam coffee cups half full, I was sure, of ancient coffee.

In our initial conversation, Griffin had told me that he had some good corroborating evidence of the abuse. "Before we really get into it," he said that first day, "I want you to look at what we've been able to dig up about what this kid went through." He swiveled in his leather chair and hoisted three overflowing cardboard boxes onto a table next to his desk.

"There they are," he said proudly.

"There what are?" I said incredulously.

"The evidence, the statements, the whole thing," he declared.

The boxes bulged with file folders holding letters from friends and relatives, witness statements, sworn affidavits, interview summaries, and hospital and school records. Contrary to the usual conspiracy of silence that envelops these cases, here were people willing to testify on Mike's behalf. I was flabbergasted. From just a quick inspection of the files, I could see that Craig had not been a subtle man and had not been afraid to push, punch, burn, cut, kick, or vilify Michael in front of others. Though I was heartened to see this outpouring of support, organizing the data was going to be an immense chore.

Putting every person who witnessed Craig's wrath on the stand was out of the question. Though our primary goal would be to recreate the horror that was the child's life, previous trials had taught me that juries can only take so much. It is as if, especially in cases involving severe and prolonged physical mistreatment, the jury reaches an emotional saturation point, beyond which they become desensitized to the child's plight. Because of this, we would need to prioritize the incidents according to their severity, taking into consideration the age of child, the act itself, and incident that precipitated the abuse. For example, punching an eight-year-old in the back because he spilled milk on the living room carpet is perceived as much more reprehensible than a slap to the face at fourteen for violating curfew.

After thoroughly reviewing the documents, I realized with a sinking heart that we had another problem. Most of the potential witnesses—coworkers, friends, and neighbors—could only speak in generalities:

"Craig was too hard on Michael, always putting him down and calling him terrible names like asshole and fuckhead."

"Craig treated Michael like he could never do anything right. He would call him worthless and stupid."

"There was often terror in Michael's eyes when Craig spoke."

Luckily, Craig's wanton violence had made a more indelible impression on others. One friend of the family stated in an interview that, as early as kindergarten, Craig gave Michael household chores. On one occasion Craig told his son to have the yard cleaned before dinner. "When Craig came home that night, he saw that seven-year-old Michael had not done his job. When the little boy came running up to give his father a hug, Craig backhanded Mike on the head and then told him to pick up a piece of paper lying on the ground. And when he bent down, Craig kicked him in his ass."

A person who lived behind the family wrote about an incident when Michael was about twelve. "I saw Craig hit Michael with a two-by-four in the back of the neck. Michael was supposed to fix the fence in their backyard so that the puppy would not get out. He had fixed the fence, but not good enough for Craig. Craig pulled one of those boards out of the fence and hit Mike with it. The blow knocked him to the ground." Another neighbor recounted the following: "Mike was always bruised. I saw Craig beat him several times on the back with a garden hose because the boy did not roll up the hose as Craig had wished."

Craig was an imposing and intimidating figure. Few adults ever dared argue with him about *anything,* least of all how he treated his son. When people did try to intervene on Michael's behalf, Craig put a stop to such meddling quickly and forcefully.

Kenny Stuggans, a friend and coworker, stated that, in the ten years he had known Craig, he had witnessed his friend punch Michael at least a thousand times. This did not include the countless times he'd seen Craig kick or hit Michael with an object such as a shovel, nor did it include the time that Craig pinned his eleven-year-old son to a wall, picked up a knife, and growled, "Why don't I just cut your goddamn throat out."

Only once did Stuggans try to stick up for the boy, but that was once too often for Craig. "I went back to Craig's house with him after work. Michael [about ten at the time] didn't finish all of the yard work. Craig punched Michael in the chest with a closed fist, knocking him to the ground. He then got on top of him, hitting and punching him with closed fists.

" 'Stop,' I screamed, 'you're going to kill him.' Craig got up, gave his son a very hard kick in the side with his boot, and then doubled me over with a punch in the stomach. He said to me, 'Keep your fuckin' mouth shut or you're not going to walk away.' " Kenny never opened his mouth again.

Joan Daniels, a neighbor, was another Good Samaritan. One day after school, she caught her son Justin and eight-year-old Michael playing with matches. As any parent would, she reported the incident to Michael's father. There is absolutely no disputing the fact that children must learn not to play with matches. I still remember the whack on the seat of the pants my father gave me when, as a six-year-old, I tried to start a little campfire on the living room carpet of our tiny Bronx apartment.

As soon as Craig heard what his son had done, he bolted out the door. When he found little Michael in the backyard, he grabbed his wrist and held the boy's palm over the flame of a butane lighter.

"Michael was screaming, his palm was burning and blistering, but Craig told him to shut up and act like a man," Joan said. "I grabbed Craig to make him stop, and he told me that if I touched him again, he would deck me." Joan witnessed further incidents of Craig's mistreatment of Michael, but erring on the side of safety, she kept her mouth shut.

Though Craig was remarkably brazen in his treatment of Michael, he meted out even more debilitating punishments when no one else was around. And it was only after the homicide that anyone discovered what happened when the front door was closed.

Over the years, Michael grew accustomed to a bizarre and agonizing pattern of treatment. In what he described as the "good weeks" he would get kicked, hit, or slapped perhaps twice, and in the "bad weeks" he would get assaulted every day. These were not soft kicks but rather were, as Michael described them, "like a full field-goal kick square on my buttocks that sent me flying across the room." During both good and bad weeks, Craig threw things at Michael for just about any reason or no reason at all.

Craig even had a special name for his punishments. There were the GPs, "general purpose" punishments, that Michael received every day regardless of his father's mood. When Michael was later asked to distinguish between GPs and other forms of punishment, he said:

"The other hits would be if he was mad at me for something. A GP hit would be for no reason. If I was sitting there and he happened to walk by, he would close his fist and hit me . . . [on the] chest, arms, or legs."

Michael never told a soul, lying over and over again about the origin of his many injuries. As a little boy, Michael cried when Craig hit or screamed at him, but he stopped around the age of ten because Craig wanted his son to "take the punishment like a man." Tears after a pounding just brought on more blows. To survive, he became highly proficient at blocking his feelings, denying the pain. In the beginning Michael clenched his teeth and fists at the same time. After several years of repeated punishment he simply acted like a mannequin, stone cold and limp.

Eventually he buried his emotions so far in the corners of his soul that even he couldn't find them. Complaining, let alone discussing his feelings with others, was out of the question. Not only did the truth shame and embarrass him, but his father often reminded him that it would be bad for his health to go to the authorities. Michael was smart enough to take his father at his word.

Many people, especially prosecutor Maurice Aton, could not understand why, if Michael was being treated so terribly, he didn't tell others about it. I was not at all surprised. Unfortunately, this type of uninformed criticism rears its head in almost every patricide and matricide case. People believe it is completely abnormal for the child to remain absolutely silent about his or her dreadful predicament, because it runs contrary to the basic instinct to survive.

Michael's explanation for his behavior was, however, eminently logical: he was scared and embarrassed. There is also a much deeper reason, one that most of us are unaware of, that shows his response as, in fact, normal under the circumstances. Implicitly, we all take a loyalty oath when we are children. We are taught and continually reminded that "family business" is sacred, inviolable, and above all private. You may even remember your own parents, at one time, saying something to you like: "Whatever goes on within these four walls stays here" or "Anything, and I mean anything, your father or I say to you or to each other does not leave this house." Such loyalty is crucial to human development itself because it fosters an individual's identity with his family and fortifies the boundary between the family and the larger society. In fact, while many of us profess that our first loyalty is to our country, in reality "family patriotism" is often greater than what we feel for our national government. Michael didn't tell, in short, because *nobody tells*.

Pathetically, the one person with whom Michael was especially evasive was his mother, Peggy. But it was easier to understand his deception with her than with others, because it was from his mother that he first learned to conceal the truth about Craig.

From almost the moment they met in junior high school, Peggy began covering up the truth about her relationship with Craig. To the average teenage girl, wearing makeup to school is a rite of passage. As a ninth-grader, Peggy was no exception. She didn't wear her "eye makeup" to make herself look more beautiful or grown-up, though. She used it to hide the fact that, the night before, Craig had given her a shiner. And because Revlon didn't manufacture a makeup cream heavy enough to cover black eyes, she used one made by Colgate. It served a dual purpose because she could also brush her teeth with it. Her ruse also included avoiding physical education class at all cost (a common ploy of physically abused boys and girls) because that would mean taking a shower and revealing those bruises that she could never cover with toothpaste.

Very young and starry-eyed with love, she thought the beatings would stop. Of course they didn't. The cuts and bruises just got worse and worse. After each beating, Craig warned he would kill her if she told anybody. Then he apologized and told her he would never hit her again.

Peggy was pregnant with Michael before she entered the tenth grade, but even this did not stop the beatings. When she was in her ninth month, Craig punched her so hard in the belly that he broke her water, complicating Michael's delivery. Soon after she turned twenty, Peggy told a friend that she wanted to leave Craig, but was too afraid. Craig had threatened to track her down and kill her if she left him, and she was smart enough to believe him. When she was twenty-one, Craig almost made good on the second part of his promise. It was Mother's Day.

"Michael was about four years old then. I had just gotten off the phone to tell Mother that I was coming home. I'd had enough of Craig's beatings. But as soon as I turned around, Craig punched me in the face twice," Peggy said. With blood flowing out of the corner of her mouth, he made his wife call her mother back to recant, especially the part about coming home. She complied. Craig did not allow her to go to the doctor until three days later. He had broken her jaw so severely that she was immediately hospitalized for several days and her jaw wired shut for over two months. Sadly, before Peggy gathered the strength to divorce Craig twelve years later, she would make several more trips to the hospital for concussions, broken bones, and cuts.

While they were married, Craig had avoided hitting Michael in front of his wife, though he had no problem beating Peggy when Michael was around. Peggy described the awful bind that she knew her son was in: "Craig would never hit Michael in my presence because he knew that I would take action against him. But Michael never spoke of Craig's violence against him because he knew that I would take some action, and then Craig would retaliate against me, which Michael was seeking to avoid."

Even after the divorce, when Peggy was supposedly out of harm's way, Michael kept his mother in the dark. He believed that the truth would impel Craig to retaliate against both of them. Michael's concern for his mother's safety even made him lie to her about one of his worst ordeals at Craig's hands, an incident that occurred shortly before his sixteenth birthday:

> I told my father that I wanted to go to seminary class . . . in the morning at school. I was sitting across the way from him, and he told me to come over to the couch. "So you want to go to seminary class," he said. And I said, "Yes." "Well, only faggots go to those," my dad said. "Do you still want to go?"
>
> I told him that I did. He had his buck knife and he was sharpening it. He told me to put my hand on the table, and he held my wrist. He held the knife over my finger and he asked me if I still wanted to go to church. And I told him that I did. He pressed the tip of the blade down—he like slammed it—and my finger started to bleed real bad.
>
> And then he said, "Oh, God, I don't believe that I cut you." He put peroxide on it and bandaged it. . . . I later told my mom that I cut it doing dishes.

Fortunately, as the voluminous files of eyewitness evidence demonstrated, Mike's efforts to shield his father had not been completely successful. Yet, as much as I welcomed this crucial support to Michael's defense, there was something about it that angered me deeply. Though countless adults had either directly or indirectly witnessed Craig's wrath, few ever attempted to protect Mike. Sadly, this is not a unique situation.

Every day relatives, friends, neighbors, and strangers look on as a parent abuses his child, and almost no one intervenes. In circumstances like Mike's, intimidation by the abusive parent is certainly partly responsible, but here again we run up against deeply ingrained social restraints. There is no tradition in our nation for becoming involved in the family affairs of others even when a situation warrants it. On the contrary, most of us are so completely obsessed with protecting our own right to privacy that we feel compelled *not* to interfere in the family circumstances of others. As angry as I was at those who had stood by and let Mike suffer, I could at least understand their motivation. Amazingly, there were those who broke the mold, making valiant attempts to protect Michael. How and why their efforts failed to help the boy is more tragic still.

When Michael came to live with his dad after the divorce, he fervently hoped there would be a change for the better. This was not a vain hope, for, as in most abusive relationships, good times, even great times, punctuate the periods of darkness.

For all the abuse he visited upon his son, Craig was a generous father. He gave Michael motorbikes, cars, and several hunting rifles between the ages of five and sixteen. The motorbikes and rifles were used on the numerous camping trips that father and son often took. Though working for his dad meant that Michael had to give up weekends and summer vacations with friends, it was not a poor bargain. By the time Mike reached sixteen, he had not only learned how to fix cars, but had become so skilled that he was often put in charge of operating the service station. In addition to what he learned, Mike also received a respectable salary.

Briefly, very briefly, Mike's new living situation seemed to be happy and fulfilling, the problems with his dad gone as if they'd never existed. It didn't last. One of Peggy's relatives described the first few weeks after his arrival:

"When Michael first came [here], he was a happy-go-lucky teenager who was very pleasant. After two or three days of living with Craig again, his attitude changed markedly. He became quiet, somber, and slouched around the house. . . . Craig constantly put Michael down and asserted his authority over him for no apparent reason."

Michael did not release his tensions and anxieties with drugs or alcohol, nor like many severely abused children, did he show any overt signs of depression or other emotional disturbance. He was not lethargic or perpetually glum, nor did he isolate himself, disappearing into his own world for inordinately long periods of time. Instead, he found his peace, as ephemeral as it was, in steadfastly denying the reality of his existence. He made up for his home life by hungrily seeking friends and pursuing an active social life.

Immediately following his move to his dad's home, he started going steady with Jennifer, an articulate, vivacious girl fourteen going on eighteen. As she told me in her bouncy voice, her initial impression of Michael was that he "was a very fun and outgoing guy." Her mother, Anne, a housewife with two older children, agreed: "He was a very sweet young man. And you could really sense in him the desire to please. . . . He found out my favorite flavor of ice cream and would bring it by."

Despite his jovial personality, both mother and daughter observed that Mike was curiously quiet when it came to discussing his family. As soon as Michael introduced her to his dad, she completely understood this silence.

One day after school Jennifer and another friend were watching television with Michael in his living room. Craig came in the door and immediately lit into Michael for leaving the wash unfolded on the living room couch. Michael froze, the lightness rushing out of him; the pleasant chatter of teenage conversation turned to an awkward silence. Not wanting to embarrass Michael, his two friends discreetly stepped outside. Several minutes later, Craig called out to them, "You can come in now. I'm done thumping on him."

As Jennifer later recounted, "When I came back in the house, Michael wasn't there, so I went into his room. He had red marks all over his face and neck. I asked him what was that on his neck, and he goes, 'I don't really want to talk about it right now.' He was very embarrassed. I didn't pursue it because I didn't want him to feel like he had to be embarrassed in front of me."

This was not the last time that Jennifer saw marks on her boyfriend's body. "He always said that they were from working or from this or that. But you can't do that many things to yourself working. I mean, every single day there would be some mark." The signs of abuse also did not escape Anne's scrutiny.

"Very often when he would come over to our house," Anne told me, "it seemed like he would have a different mark on him. You know, a bruise on his arm, a fat lip, or something on his cheek. I would ask him about it and he would always have a reason like 'I fell off my bike.' I was just getting to know him and had no reason to disbelieve him. But then it began to happen with such frequency that I told my daughter he has something wrong with him. It's beginning to concern me."

One day Jennifer stopped pretending that she believed his excuses. Mike had come by to pick her up for a date, and she couldn't help but notice the split lip.

"What happened?" she demanded.

"You don't want to know," Mike sheepishly replied.

"Yes, I *do* want to know, I do want to know," she pleaded.

"No, you don't," Mike shot back, but soon relented. He told her what she had already known, but hadn't wanted to admit. "My dad punched me in the mouth last night," he said, ashamed.

When Jennifer told her mom, they decided to help, but they didn't know what to do. Anne ruled out going to the authorities, since Michael had told her that he could handle living with his dad, despite the beatings. So they tried to work around Craig by getting Michael out of the house as often as possible.

Several evenings a week Anne, Jennifer, and several of her high-school friends went to a local track for exercise walks. Michael told Jennifer that if she called his dad and asked his permission for Michael, Craig would more likely agree. Each time she called, Craig said, "He can go with you if you bring a leash with you." Everyone just thought it was bad joke, another example of Craig's humiliating his son.

"So this one time," Jennifer said, her voice laden with embarrassment at the memory, "his dad says, 'Yeah, [he can go,] but you have to bring a rope.'

" 'A rope?' I said.

" 'Yeah, a rope!'

"There was something different about the way he said it, [and] I thought to myself, he means it. So I said, 'Okay.' "

"When my daughter got off the phone," Anne later told me, "I said, 'Surely he's kidding, right?'

" 'I don't think so,' my daughter said. 'We have to play his sick little game to get Michael out of the house.'

"Jennifer went to the garage and found a yellow piece of rope that we tie our tents down with."

Michael and his father were in the living room when Jennifer knocked on the door, holding the yellow rope in her right hand. Craig told her to tie the rope like a lasso. "I was afraid. . . . He wasn't yelling at me, but it was like you'd better do it . . ."

Several minutes later, Michael came down the driveway—on all fours, like a dog, one end of the yellow rope tied around his neck, and a mortified and horrified Jennifer nervously holding the other end in her right hand. When Mike got into the car, it was eerily quiet. "All of us were hoping it to be funny and silly," Anne told me softly, "but it wasn't. It was something sick and we were the last ones to know it."

When they got to the track, everybody was still speechless. Everyone except Michael. Ever the pleaser, he joked around, trying to keep it light and happy as if nothing had ever happened.

Though Michael appeared to have an endless tolerance for his father's behavior, his friends didn't. Seeing Michael continually degraded and mistreated by his father profoundly disturbed them, especially watching the frightening transformation that Michael underwent around his father. In Craig's presence, Mike was always quiet and eerily removed from everything, even himself. Mike's friends were particularly incensed that Craig treated his son "like a slave," making the boy responsible for every household chore from food shopping to cooking, cleaning, and doing the laundry. Jennifer often heard the directives Craig left for his son on their telephone answering machine—"If you don't clean house and fold clothes, you're dead" or "If you don't do these chores, I'll put my foot so far up your ass that you won't be able to see daylight."

After several months of trying and failing to cajole Michael into doing something on his own, such as reporting his dad or running away from home, his friends decided to intervene.

One crisp fall morning before classes, Jennifer, her older brother Dale, and the two friends, Rob and Kirk, who had witnessed the dog-leash incident went to see the vice-principal, Mr. Hastings. They told him that they wanted to help a friend who was being abused by his dad. Hastings, known as an intimidating administrator, heard them out impassively, gazing back without a word. After learning the identity of the student, the administrator hastily told the group to have Michael in his office after lunch.

Lunch hour in a high-school cafeteria is a time to chat about weekend dates, discuss movies, and complain about the boring, tasteless food. On this day, the agenda at one table was clearly more serious.

"I'm not going to see him," Michael protested. "If my dad finds out, he'll kill me."

Jennifer leaned across the table. "You've gotta do it," she said emphatically. "It's your only chance." Rob, another friend, chimed in, "We went in there and told him you were abused. You're gonna have to tell him."

Michael continued to resist their pleas for the remainder of lunch, but relented right before the bell. As a show of support, his four friends accompanied him into the office for the interview.

This was not the first time Michael had been in Hastings's office. In the past year he had been sent down there for cutting up in class, and it was Hastings who had meted out the discipline. Now Michael sat in his office, not as a disciplinary problem, but as an "alleged" victim of child abuse.

A short, balding man in his early fifties, Hastings sat behind a large, shiny wooden desk. Michael sat in the center of the room, directly in front of the desk, his four friends several feet behind him. As soon as they had all taken their seats, Hastings leaned back in his imposing leather chair and brusquely asked, "Are you being abused?"

Michael didn't respond. The silence made his friends cringe.

His brow furrowed in apparent doubt, Hastings looked at Jennifer and said disgustedly, "Do you think Michael is abused?"

"Yes," she passionately declared. "Michael *is* abused."

Michael gave Jennifer a look that said, I can't believe you told him! Then to their surprise, Hastings abruptly confronted the boy. "I don't like you," he said, his tone hard. "And if you're not going to say anything, you can just leave."

Knowing he had to get Michael to press on, Rob asked Hastings if he could have a moment outside the office with his friend. It took Rob thirty seconds to convince Michael to go back in and tell the truth.

When the two returned, Hastings asked again, "Are you

being abused at home?" Michael bowed his head and quietly said, "Yes."

"Why are you changing your story now?" Hastings demanded.

"I didn't want to tell because I didn't want there to be an issue over it," Michael said sheepishly.

"Can you tell the day you were abused?" asked Hastings.

"Pick any day of the week and that's the day," Michael flatly replied.

Hastings pressed Michael for specifics. His father had hit him in the jaw about two weeks before, Michael said.

The vice-principal's skepticism was obvious. "I have to fill out all of this paperwork just because of you," he concluded, "and I don't even know if you're telling the truth. I hope you don't think you could just bullcrap me around just for nothing."

Michael and his friends were shaken by the encounter, which they had imagined quite differently. "It was like Michael did something wrong," one of them later said. Michael and the others had done what they were supposed to do and yet in return had only received a callous rebuff. Now escape for Michael seemed almost impossible. It was not, however, until about a month later that Michael literally gave up all hope.

Michael was talking to his mother on the phone, and his dad was at work. "In the middle of the conversation, the operator broke in and told me to get off the phone so I could take an emergency phone call," Michael said. "It was my dad."

"He demanded to know who I was speaking to, and I said my mother. He screamed at me, 'I told you to stay off the phone. When I get home you're dead meat.'

"I said, 'I was just talking to my mom.'

" 'I don't care,' my dad said. 'You just stay right there; when I get home, you're dead.' "

It wasn't the first death threat his father had made. In fact Michael had long ago accepted death threats as part of his life. But this time something in Craig's voice told Michael he meant it.

"Fuck this," Michael said to himself. He had to get out. He called Rob, and his friend's mom, Sue Ellen, told Mike that he should come stay at their house that night. It was only a temporary reprieve, but Mike was desperate.

Michael and Rob went to Jennifer's house for dinner that evening. As soon as he walked in, Anne went over to Mike and said sternly but compassionately, "We have to do something about this, don't we?" Michael looked down, quiet.

Anne pleaded with him, as her daughter had months earlier. "Please, please tell me what we're going to do. Who can we tell? What can we do to help you?"

"I can't tell anyone, he would kill me," Michael said. Even as the words left his mouth, they all heard an ominous pounding at the front door. Blood rushed from Michael's face, his eyes opened wide in fear. Jennifer went to look through the peephole. Before she could say it was Craig, Michael was out the back door and over a six-foot-high brick wall.

Craig was very polite. Jennifer steadfastly denied that she knew Michael's whereabouts, and Craig left after several minutes. Michael returned later that evening, feeling good that for the first time he had successfully evaded his father. Maybe with the help of people such as Anne and Rob's parents, he thought, things would be okay.

At six A.M. the next morning Sue Ellen drove her son and Michael to morning Bible classes. As they turned into the school parking lot, Michael let out a bloodcurdling scream: "Oh, no. That's my father!"

When she discusses the incident today, Sue Ellen still speaks with all the fear she must have felt those few minutes that day.

"His father barreled out at us in this big truck. I turned around in the middle of the street and started driving fast. His father was yelling out his window. Then he drove his truck in front and stopped my car. I was hysterical. He got out and jumped on the hood of my car spread-eagle and started pounding the windshield. He was cussing my son and myself. . . . He got off and I drove around him. Finally we got to another street where he stopped my car again. There wasn't really anywhere to go.

"I could have got around him," Sue Ellen continued breathlessly, "but Michael said, 'I'm getting out.' . . . His father dragged him by the arm and put him into the truck and drove away."

Most people would have been too frightened to stay involved, but not Sue Ellen. "I went home and called the police. . . . They told me that Michael was a kid in trouble and his father was just trying to get him to mind him. And if I believed the things Mike told me, I was stupid. . . . They said if I continued with this, all I would do is cause myself problems. His father had every right to press charges against me for aiding and abetting on Mike's running away from home, so I just better stay out."

When Craig and Michael arrived home after the car chase, there was a message from Mr. Hastings, who wanted to see both father and son at his office that morning. "You know what this is about?" Craig demanded. Michael shook his head no, praying that action was finally going to be taken on the abuse complaint he had made several weeks earlier.

On the way to the school Craig was crying. He told Michael that he had been very worried about him the night before. The threat to kill him had only been a joke. Michael wasn't moved. "He was trying to make me feel bad, but I didn't," Michael said later.

The meeting in the vice-principal's office was conducted with all the sensitivity and fairness of the Spanish Inquisition. On one side of the room sat Hastings and Michael's probation officer, Ms. Haller; on the other side, Michael and Craig. Michael was so close to his dad that he could actually hear him breathing.

"Are you being abused in the home?" Hastings said to Michael, as if accusing rather than supporting him.

Michael looked at his father, then back at Hastings. He lowered his head. "No," he said quietly.

From that point on, the meeting degenerated into what Mike described as a "what's wrong with Michael show." After Hastings lit into Michael, Haller let loose with the final crusher: "We think the problem is with you."

This meeting represented the sum total of the child abuse investigation supposedly instigated by Mr. Hastings. No social service worker separately interviewed Michael or his father, nor did any investigator seek out any of Michael's friends or other family members, any one of whom would have instantly corroborated the boy's charges.

Michael later told me how he felt after the meeting with

Hastings and Haller. "Wacko . . . mad. I hated them all. I was gonna try to do something to get arrested, to get put back into juvenile hall. 'Cause I didn't want to go home." As bad as juvenile hall was, Michael was probably right that he would have been better off going there, for, once at home, his father seemed almost drunk with his new sense of power. "He thought he was king. He said, 'You're gonna live under my rules. You *can't* get away.' "

Craig used the incident as a lever to tighten his stranglehold on Michael. He had to come home directly after school, and Craig prohibited him from going out on weekends at all.

In the following weeks, Michael became noticeably withdrawn and angry toward his friends. His diminished self-interest was starkly illustrated in his answers to a school health evaluation:

Can you recall the last time you felt highly motivated to do something or were excited by some activity? *No.*

Can you name an event or possibly an individual who is causing you to feel unable to achieve your highest level of ability? *My dad. He puts me in a I don't care mood.*

It was not just Craig's tighter grip that made Michael's life increasingly unbearable, for he also had to contend with his father's deteriorating mental state. After the final divorce papers had come through five months earlier, Craig had begun to sink into a depression that appeared to worsen daily. He vacillated between hating his wife for leaving him and hating himself for pushing her out. Michael naturally bore the brunt of these drastic mood swings, a handy, ever-present target for his father's anger and frustration.

"I have Michael sitting here," Craig bellowed into the phone to his ex-wife one night. "And I have a gun in my hand. . . . I'm going to kill him and take away the only thing you love. Then I'm going to kill myself."

Peggy had heard Craig threaten to kill himself before—in a phone call several months earlier he even fired a weapon into a pillow, but she had never heard him threaten to kill her son. She begged him not to kill Michael, then told him she was calling the police.

Craig did have a .357 magnum in his hand, but Michael

was not sitting next to him, he was asleep in his bedroom. Waving the gun in his hand, Craig woke his son, confessing nervously, "Your mother called the police because I told her I was going to kill you, then kill myself, but you know I couldn't hurt you. So when the police come, just make sure you don't say anything."

Michael told the police that he was sleeping and didn't hear his dad make any threats. Craig watched him from across the room. After speaking with Craig for several minutes, the officers left without incident. They never asked Michael if his father had threatened him at any other time, nor did they even ask if Craig owned a gun.

As soon as the front door closed, Craig began ranting and raving against his ex-wife. "Well, what do you think about her calling the cops?" his father demanded.

"I don't want to get involved," Michael wearily said as he walked to his bedroom.

Kenny Stuggans also witnessed this mental deterioration. "One evening Craig called and said, 'I need to talk.' [He came over and] went on for about an hour talking about how depressed he was. Then he looked to me and said, 'I'm too chicken to commit suicide. How about it, Kenny? Will you take me out and shoot me?' " Stuggans took it as a bad joke and tried to settle his friend down.

Several weeks later, while Stuggans was working at the gas station with Craig and Michael, Craig smacked Michael in the head with a hammer handle because the boy broke a pane of glass. As he usually did, Michael walked quietly away with his head bowed.

When Michael was out of earshot, Craig again turned to his friend and said plaintively, "I wish I could go out and kill myself, but I don't have the guts. How about it, Kenny?" Kenny had no response.

Michael's suffering at the hands of his father was also aggravated by his increasing isolation from those who tried so hard to help him. Not only had Craig forbidden Michael to have anything to do with Rob and his family, but Jennifer's parents, fearing their daughter was becoming too involved with Michael, had made her break off their relationship.

"You are my whole world," Michael wrote her, "and they took you away like it wouldn't hurt and it didn't, no, you see it was more than hurt. Because you are my love, and without you I feel like an unread book placed on a shelf alone all by myself."

Eight weeks later, Michael killed his dad.

Psychologist Dr. Marci Flanigan, an expert in adolescent abuse, evaluated Michael shortly after his arrest. While parricides are not, of course, predictable, she was not at all surprised that Michael had killed his father. The most significant determinant of this outcome to her mind was Craig's severe long-term physical abuse and domination. Based on Michael's own statements and declarations from some forty witnesses, there was no question in Dr. Flanigan's mind that Michael had been physically and verbally brutalized by his father almost since birth.

"In light of the continuous history of threats and injuries," Flanigan wrote, "there appears to be data suggesting an honest and reasonable belief in the necessity [for Michael] to defend against imminent peril to his own life."

While noteworthy, Dr. Flanigan's conclusions with respect to the violence were rather obvious. In fact, one of Craig's siblings had earlier predicted that her brother's assaults would one day provoke Michael to retaliate. However, what I found most profound and compelling was Flanigan's analysis of the greater family's role in the ultimate tragedy.

Flanigan believed that the patricide would probably *not* have occurred had some family member decisively intervened on Michael's behalf. By turning a blind eye to what they had to have known was a critical situation, and thus remaining passive, these relatives forced Michael into the untenable position of resolving the situation himself.

Dr. Flanigan's analysis also helped us understand what Craig's threat to kill Peggy meant to Michael and how this might have later influenced his own actions. Over the years, Michael watched as his family, friends, and neighbors all ignored Craig's blatant abuse of Peggy. Even Peggy's parents, Michael knew, had never intervened to help their daughter even before she married Craig. And the boy was acutely aware that the divorce papers were just that—paper, and not a solid shield protecting his mother. Given his father's previous brutality, earlier threats made real, and Michael's hopelessness that anyone would ever intervene, it was logical for him to assume the night of the homicide that his father would kill him then his mother.

The failure of the school and the social service system to protect him (they, in fact, made the situation even worse), and his isolation from Jennifer and his other school friends, Dr. Flanigan pointed out, only exacerbated his feelings of abandonment.

After reviewing all the evidence and spending many late evenings strategizing with Marty Griffin, I felt we had a good chance of getting a verdict of not guilty by reason of self-defense, or in the absolute worst case, voluntary manslaughter. First- or second-degree murder seemed out of the question. There were, however, two serious problems.

First, the number of bullets and configuration of the wounds *behind* the left ear suggested, as Aton contended, that Michael had ambushed his sleeping father from behind, later inventing the whole you-kill-me-or-die scene. Second, Michael's behavior after the crime also seemed to indicate planning and premeditation.

As to the wounds, the first hurdle was convincing the jury that an argument had occurred. Not only did we have evidence of verbal abuse and threats extending back at least ten years, we had mountains of airtight evidence that Craig's behavior had changed radically in the two months before the final confrontation, evidence I felt would convince the jury beyond a doubt that he had threatened to kill Michael. That the wounds were behind and below the left ear presented a more complicated problem—one for which I had no explanation.

Fortunately, Griffin was more skilled in ballistics than me. His theory, which we tried out on his office couch with me playing Craig and he Michael, was that, when the first shot was fired, Craig had been propped up against the arm of the couch, his head turned slightly to the left. The impact of the first shot, which was fired from only about a foot, was so powerful it propelled Craig's head up and back to the left. The other five bullets, fired in rapid succession over the next two to four seconds, entered his head in the area of the first shot.

Griffin's theory was persuasive, but it did not address why Michael emptied the entire clip of bullets into his father's head. Wouldn't one shot have sufficed, if he was actually acting in self-defense?

Prosecutors commonly perceive "overkill" as evidence of premeditation, as well as depravity. In the moral hierarchy of homicide, a person who shoots his victim once in the heart is somehow less wicked than one who shoots his victim twenty-five times. As we saw with Tim and as is true in most parricide cases, overkill seems to be common and has much more to do with the child's fear of the parent than it does with the child's intent to inflict injury. Here, Flanigan's report helped us immeasurably.

She wrote, citing a recent research study on adolescents who kill, "Overkilling is believed . . . to reflect the fear and panic that the victim, perceived as an omnipotent figure by the adolescent, will get up and retaliate [rather than] to be the result of explosive rage." Substantiating her argument, she pointed out that Michael did not want to touch his father after the shooting because he was afraid he would wake up, something Billy Eckhart had witnessed.

Providing the jury with a convincing explanation of why Mike dumped Craig's body would be more difficult to explain. If Michael legitimately believed he had killed in self-defense, the average juror might think, why did he then engineer an elaborate cover-up? If you are innocent, you should have nothing to hide, right?

Other than what Michael said himself—that he was scared and confused—we had no explanation. To the outside observer, this might sound like a lame excuse, but it is one that is uniformly given by kids in these circumstances. We would have to hope that the jury would accept Michael at his word.

There still remained one perplexing problem that Griffin and I struggled with up until the night before jury selection, a problem we could do virtually nothing about: the prosecutor was out to hang Michael.

Aton was intelligent, one of the smartest prosecutors I had ever come up against; he was certainly sufficiently experienced to predict how a jury would react to the facts. Despite the strength of his case, I simply could not believe that he did not see Michael as at least a partially sympathetic defendant. His confidence was so boundless that we thought he must know something we didn't or have some star witness waiting in the wings to skewer Michael or solid evidence of something Michael had done or said that would blow our case out of the water.

Beneath his apparent cordiality, Aton seemed poised to pounce from our first encounter in court the day before jury selection. Aton wore his medium-length hair slicked straight back. He was dressed impeccably, a dark suit over a heavily starched white shirt with a knife-point collar that said, "I mean business."

If the number of law books and file folders piled beside him was any indication of preparedness, we were in trouble. Sure enough, Aton fought us tooth and nail from the beginning, challenging everything from the admission of most of the evidence pertaining to Mike's and Craig's behavior before the night of the homicide to the use of psychological testimony.

Since the case dealt primarily with physical abuse, our goal in jury selection as defenders was to pin prospective jurors down on what I call their "domestic discipline policy." The impaneled jury would be exposed daily to firsthand accounts of some disturbing forms of physical abuse, and therefore it was important to determine during selection not only how they felt about various kinds of discipline, but how they themselves had been treated as children.

Without asking any questions, I knew that almost every prospective juror had been physically disciplined as a child or had used some sort of physical punishment with his own children. As family-violence expert Dr. Murray Straus relates, "there is almost an obligation to hit if the child misbehaves. . . . Physical punishment begins in infancy for about one out of four children, [and] reaches a peak of 97 percent at age three and declines steadily after that."

Considering the prevalence of physical punishment, our goal was to choose a jury of people who observed strict limits in disciplining their kids. In my experience, women make the best jurors in this kind of case because they are generally more sensitive than men to family violence. Also, because most family violence is by men against women, it is much more likely that the women have themselves been victims of abuse or had a friend or relative who was.

After a three-day give-and-take with Aton, we ended up

with a jury of six men and six women, most around forty years old, who in general believed in using some form of physical punishment. Eight thought that such discipline should be limited to spanking on the backside with an open hand, while three believed a parent was within his or her rights to use a switch or belt, but only on the buttocks. The head and face were off-limits, all agreed, and hitting a child with a closed fist was abuse. Interestingly, while several admitted that they had been hit with razor strops and switches, they did not believe these were appropriate. Finally, we had a single juror who considered any form of physical punishment abhorrent.

When the trial began on a crisp, clear spring day, would-be spectators lined the halls of the ultramodern courthouse. Most of those who waited patiently were Mike's friends and relatives, some of whom were to be defense witnesses. Though murders were a rare occurrence in this quiet suburb, the trial did not draw the intense community attention, or anything close to it, that I'd seen in other cases. No one was crying for blood, and in fact, everybody in line looked uncomfortable, no doubt anticipating the heartache and ugliness that the trial would inevitably bring out.

Aton presented the case as I predicted. In his opening argument to the packed courtroom, he portrayed Michael as a dissolute teenager who, tired of following the reasonable commands of his father, had summarily executed him.

Griffin's opening argument began with a phrase that I often recommend attorneys use in these cases. "*Abuse* is a mild word to describe what Michael Alborgeden was forced to endure during his years with his father." The jury immediately sat up, attentive.

Aton's case was over in two and a half days. His primary witnesses were cops, cops, and more cops, plus a smattering of the confederates who'd assisted Michael in covering up the crime. Throughout, he pounded home the themes of his opening argument.

There was really no need to do any serious cross-examination of most state's witnesses because they had nothing really damaging to say. There was no question that Michael had killed his father, then attempted to cover up his actions. Our only goal was to show why he took his father's life.

Aton repeated a single theme throughout his direct and cross examinations: Michael was exaggerating and lying about his treatment at the hands of his dad. Regardless of how Craig treated Michael, Michael did not have to do what he did. That night he had a choice. He could have run out of the house and sought assistance from relatives or friends.

Using Griffin's voluminous files, from which we had culled the clearest, most unquestionable witnesses, we set out to show that the physical abuse had been severe and long-term. Though two dozen people testified, Michael himself was by far his own best witness. He remained fairly stoic as he discussed the grisly details of his ordeal—long years of enduring abuse had trained him not to cry, not to break down in public.

He related in stark detail the sordid history of beatings; on the witness stand he shed his clothes, except for a bathing suit, to show the physical legacy of prolonged battering. From the top of his head to his fingertips and the back of his legs, he graphically pointed out fourteen irregularly shaped lumps and scars. While Michael spoke without emotion, the jurors weren't so sanguine; many winced and a few turned completely away, unable to look at the scars.

Ironically, Aton's boundless passion to convict Michael, the thing that had so worried Griffin and me, in the end helped us. In hammering home his theory during cross-examination, Aton actually elicited more graphic, excruciating detail from Michael. The harder he tried to "break the witness," the more he fleshed out the horrible, inescapable reality. Witnesses answered questions more passionately because they were so rigorously challenged. Michael's predicament came alive; jurors could almost see the beatings and hear Michael's silent screams.

In cross-examining Michael, Aton adopted a predictable "take no prisoners" posture. The following is a small excerpt from Michael's second day of cross-examination:

> *Aton:* . . . *So the fact that your dad had talked about killing himself had nothing to do with why you shot him that night?*
> *Michael: He had talked about killing me and my mother and then himself.*

> *A: But that just made you angry, is that correct?*
>
> *M: It made me fearful. And it made me angry that I was going to die.*
>
> *A: Now wait a second. You said before that the reason you had killed him is that you were very angry at him because of the words that he used?*
>
> *M: I was also very fearful for my own life.*
>
> *A: You were afraid?*
>
> *M: Yes, I was.*
>
> *A: When did you become afraid of dying?*
>
> *M: I've always been afraid of dying.*

At this point in the examination Michael lost his composure. Tears welled in his eyes, his voice cracked as he continued.

> *A: I see. But you weren't afraid of killing?*
>
> *M: Yes, I was. I've never thought about killing. I think that anybody would be afraid of killing.*
>
> *A: I see. Well, which were you, Michael? When you shot your father, were you angry with him and mad at him, or were you afraid of him?*
>
> *M: I had a lot of emotion. I was both. I was fearful and I was also very upset and very mad.*
>
> *A: Other than that, before that night he had threatened to kill you; is that correct?*
>
> *M: That's correct.*
>
> *A: On how many occasions?*
>
> *M: That he was going to kill me? On three.*
>
> *A: On three occasions?*
>
> *M: Yes.*
>
> *A: And on each of those three occasions he'd not killed you, is that correct?*
>
> *M: That's correct.*
>
> *A: On each of those three prior occasions at the same time he was saying he was going to kill you, he was also beating on you or kicking on you?*
>
> *M: At the three occasions that he said he was going to kill me, he was using it as a threat that if I did something, like if I turned him in for child abuse, that he would kill me. . . .*

123

>   A: And he didn't hit you on those three occasions
> either . . . he just said he would kill you?
>   M: Yes, he did.

While succeeding in getting Michael to admit that his father had previously threatened to kill him but had never followed through, the prosecutor actually starkly dramatized Michael's desperate situation. Michael did not step off the witness stand a cold-hearted, evil killer, but a confused, tormented young man.

After four agonizing days of deliberation, the jury reached its verdict. They trudged back into the courtroom visibly drained and upset. Several men and women had cried during Michael's testimony, and now they looked as if they had been in tears all through their deliberations. Judge Grassly, a portly man in his sixties, who from the beginning of the trial showed little sympathy for Michael, ordered Michael to rise and then turned to the jurors and said, "Madame Foreperson, have you reached a verdict?"

The foreperson, a petite grandmotherly type rose and softly said, "Yes, we have." Her voice unsteady, holding back tears, she said, "We, the jury, find the defendant Michael Alborgeden guilty of involuntary manslaughter." Michael's mother, who had been sitting in the back row, raced forward and threw her arms around her son. While relatives and friends crowded around weeping in joy that he was not found guilty of murder, Michael did not permit himself to cry.

In literal, legalistic terms this verdict, the lowest degree of homicide, meant that the jury had concluded that Michael did not even *intend* to kill his father. Instead, the death was the result of negligent disregard for the consequences of his actions.

In actuality the verdict, as is common in these cases, was the result of a compromise, what attorneys call jury nullification. As one juror later told Griffin, the jury was evenly split: six for murder one; six for acquittal. The former were disturbed by the disposal of the body and Michael's efforts to cover his tracks. The other six were equally firmly convinced that Mike had acted purely in self-defense.

The jury, of course, did not have the last word in this case.

Judge Grassly rejected Griffin's suggestion of probation outright. Instead he followed Aton's recommendation: Michael received the maximum prison time allowable under the law—four years for involuntary manslaughter and another two years for using a gun in the commission of the crime. Explaining his sentence, the judge said firmly that he couldn't "think of a more aggravated manslaughter case than this. . . . I hope we don't see you again."

Sixteen at the time of the crime, Michael would serve his sentence in a facility for youthful offenders. I went to visit him about a year after he was sent away to the State Reformatory for Young Adults. Except for the double Cyclone fence topped with razor-edged barbed wire and the presence of an armed, uniformed guard at the entrance, the reformatory looks like a small college campus. In addition to the seven two-story, yellow-brick buildings, each holding about eighty males between the ages of sixteen and twenty-three, there is a school, a mechanics shop, and a large recreation facility.

Michael was one of the few inmates in here for homicide; most had been convicted of drug and property-related offenses. And of those that had killed, most were gang members; only one other resident, a twenty-year-old who killed his mother, was in the facility for parricide.

I spoke with Michael in a sunny, green-tiled room, normally reserved for therapy sessions. He was dressed in a loose-fitting, light-blue uniform and wore brown work boots. In the year since the trial, he had changed enormously. He had gained about thirty pounds, all muscle. He was now almost as massive as his dad, but his soft eyes hinted at a gentler character.

The other change was in his demeanor. He smiled and seemed more relaxed. He did not enjoy prison, he told me, but it was, not surprisingly, less stressful than his previous life with his father. But to my surprise, he also told me that the controversy concerning his verdict had followed him to the institution.

Soon after his arrival at prison, Michael had appeared before the parole board, five corrections staff persons who would determine exactly how much time he would have to serve and when he would be eligible to apply for parole. For Michael, the experience was a mocking replay of the visit he and his father had made to vice-principal Hastings's office, and Aton's cross-examination.

Michael sat in a straight-backed wooden chair across from the five men. He was livid as he recounted the story to me.

"This one guy said, 'You show no remorse. There's more to this case than is being told. . . . I don't buy this one bit that you shot him like you told the court. . . . This isn't involuntary manslaughter, this is murder one. You just got away with it.' "

"I felt mad," Michael continued, "but they just wanted me to get mad [so that they could give me more time]. I just sat there. I just answered them, 'Yes, sir. No, sir.' "

What really incensed Michael, however, was the final comment one of the esteemed board members made after telling Michael he would be eligible for parole in three years.

"I think your father was hard on you," the man said patronizingly. "My dad was hard on me, too . . . but I'm glad I didn't kill him. He turned out to be a hell of a nice guy." Michael just bit his lip and said nothing.

As with some jurors, there were those in the community who felt real compassion for Michael. Their feelings, I believe, were summed up by Anne, Jennifer's mother, who wrote the following letter to the editor of the local paper:

> I am sorry that Craig Alborgeden is dead . . . but I believe with every fiber of my being that the responsibility for what happened that night lies fully with him. For as Michael and Craig stood together in that room for what would be their last time, they learned together, possibly at the same moment, just how effective Craig had been. He [Craig] had in fact, with all the threats, abuses, and emotional blackmail, finally made a believer of Michael.

All the debate about motives and what Michael should or should not have done loses sight of one heart-wrenching fact: Michael really loved his dad and expended every ounce of his strength trying to get his dad to love him.

About a year before he shot Craig, Michael wrote his dad a poem.

FATHER AND A SON

A father and me is closer than
the wind blowing against a tree
closer than the fish and the sea.
For with no father there would be no me. And I hope my
Father can see that my love
is stronger than if we were
three. Father I am telling you
this because I want you to love me
So just remember Father these words
are coming from me, "I love you so
much I just hope you can see."

love always,
Michael

When Craig received the poem, he tearfully confided to a friend, "I wish I could show affection to Michael instead of hitting him. . . . I don't know how to show love to him. I regret it. But that's the way my dad brought me up. Never in my whole life did my father ever tell me, 'I love you.'"

George

The eight highway patrol officers were flabbergasted, expecting a raging gun battle from the youth they had just cornered after a high-speed chase. With their revolvers and semiautomatic shotguns aimed at the driver's door of the late-model, two-door Ford, they ordered the dark-haired teenage boy to exit the vehicle slowly. Before they could even tell him to put his hands up, George McHenry had collapsed onto the roadway like a rag doll and tearfully blurted out, "I did it. I killed my father."

If they had known George, they wouldn't have been surprised at this outburst of honesty—George hated liars. He didn't even wait for them to tell him he had the right to remain silent and instead launched into his confession as soon as he was cuffed. Homicide detectives pray for suspects such as George who have a compulsion to talk, because confessors take the detecting out of detective work. George's desire to bare his soul, however, had exactly the opposite effect on his appointed attorney, David Blount.

Blount was not appointed to the case because he was a homicide specialist. His area of expertise, in fact, was not even criminal law, but rather medical malpractice. There was a slight irony to his appointment, for the forty-three-year-old attorney's specific area of expertise was obstetrical malpractice: he sued doctors and hospitals on behalf of children critically injured during childbirth.

Blount was appointed to represent George because the judge in charge of assigning cases considered him a hard-working attorney used to uphill battles, someone who could give this boy a fair defense in what was sure to be a hostile community. Ken McHenry's death had indeed sent shock waves through the large Midwestern city where the family lived. Though Ken was by no means well-known, his killing drew great attention, symbolizing, for many, all that was wrong with modern youth. Mirroring the anger of the community, George's bail was set at $250,000.

Blount sounded fairly relaxed as he introduced himself to me over the phone. He had read an interview I'd done with a national newsmagazine and wanted to get my advice on George's case. He prefaced his words by admitting that he had no money at that time to pay me, but would try to get the court to approve funds for my involvement.

Because teenagers rarely have sufficient finances to retain a lawyer privately, parricides are usually publicly funded cases, and thus payment for my services is usually a problem. Even if the family is wealthy, the child is typically unable to get access to any money either because the estate's assets are frozen until the case is resolved, or because the surviving parent simply refuses to pay for the defense out of deep anger and resentment toward the child.

I always give the attorney initial advice without a written guarantee of payment, knowing that something will inevitably work out. I also know that good intentions are often not enough; as a result, I provide free assistance in about a quarter of my cases.

I accepted Blount's assurances, and he proceeded to fill me in. Ruefully, he told me the first thought that had come into his head after interviewing George was, "The old 'I didn't do it' or 'I didn't mean to do it' defense is not going to work this time. The guy was sleeping, and George had talked about it for weeks."

"Welcome to the world of parricide," I said.

But Blount had a more immediate problem than his trial strategy—George's mea culpa behavior. "I advised him *not* to talk to the police under any circumstances," Blount told me, exasperated. "Yet, even after his confession, I got a call from one of the deputies who said George was talking to them. He spoke to them on no less than fifteen occasions. The deputies advised him that he had an attorney and shouldn't be talking to them. But George didn't care. I went to talk to him about not talking to the police and he nodded his head in agreement, and the next thing I know is that he's down there again."

Teens such as George are eager to please authority figures. His confessing zeal reminded me of another parricide case where the teenager, an electronics whiz, volunteered to fix a video camera that had broken down during the taping of his confession. The detectives sat dumbfounded as the fifteen-year-old boy—who had just killed his whole family—repaired the machine.

What these children never grasp, of course, is that the detective wants to use the information to put them in prison for as long as possible. These kids open up to their interrogators because the detective is usually the first person to express genuine interest in their saga. Talking to the officer also has a cathartic effect, helping to release the tremendous pressure of the guilt many feel following the homicide.

Typically, lawyers worry that any talk by their client could lead to an admission that the child killed the parent, but that is not a concern here. The defense is not based on whether the kid did it, but why. Moreover, the child rarely makes an admission that hurts him, and sometimes, his candor even benefits his defense, demonstrating a legitimate motive.

I advised Blount to strike a compromise with George: he could talk to the cops as much as he wanted, providing he stayed mute about his conversations with his lawyer.

In all his confessions, George made no attempt to whitewash his role in the homicide; in fact, he provided the most specific details to the investigators. Though hysterical immediately after the arrest, with the police he was calm and rational, admitting that he had thought about killing his father for several weeks. He even revealed the various plans he considered to carry out the homicide. Though George was precise on the "how," he did a dismal job in explaining the "why" of the homicide.

Veteran detective Harry Anders was George's confessor.

In his formal confession to Anders, George could only say, "It was over homework, and . . . about me in general, basically." Anders asked George to elaborate, but the boy couldn't.

At the end of the interrogation, Detective Anders asked, "Is there *anything* you'd like to add to your statement at this time?" George thought a moment. "Yeah," he answered dejectedly. "Pretty stupid and childish of me to do this. If I could go back in time, I would have changed everything."

Anders was uneasy, bothered by the fact that all of his experience screamed that a seventeen-year-old boy doesn't kill his father over homework. It disturbed him so much that he did something uncharacteristic for a cop; he tried to give the kid an out.

"Does your dad ever hit you?"

"Not while I lived there, no," George said.

"Has he ever hit you before?"

"When I was younger, but that's about it," George said.

After forcefully insisting to an anxiously awaiting press that the slaying was one of the most cold-blooded crimes ever committed in the city's history, a police department spokesman added that the "boy and his father argued over the boy's conduct, but evidently it was nothing to the point where anyone would expect something like this." The town was up in arms, and George's neighbors were equally baffled.

"George was friendly to just about everybody, a perfect gentleman," one neighbor told an inquisitive reporter. "And he treated his father with respect."

With Blount, George was no more forthcoming about his motivations than with the police. Initially, he would only say that Ken was a strict parent and that he despised living under his father's roof. But for all his animosity, he adamantly denied that he had been physically mistreated (let alone sexually abused) at, or even remotely near, the time of the homicide. At the time I was not concerned about his denials since so many find it difficult to speak openly about their abuse immediately following the killing. However, what was bewildering was that George had only lived with his father for eight months before he killed him.

Before this case, everything that I knew about parricide told me that it only occurred in situations where the child had lived with his parent for his whole life. Yet here was a seventeen-year-old who had not lived with his dad for nine years. It was simply beyond my comprehension how the enormous intensity of emotion that invariably accompanies these killings could have built up in such a short time.

It was obvious to Blount and me that we were not getting the whole story. And it was not that George was consciously holding anything back; he was simply unable to help us with the facts of his early life. Not only did he have a spotty memory of his childhood, but he knew little about his family history. We would not find the answers in the events of the preceding eight months or eight years; it was necessary to go back much further.

When I finally met Barbara Moran, George's mother, she was working as a manicurist at a beauty parlor. Though I had seen no picture of her, I could immediately pick her out of the group of women, not because she looked like her son, but from the sadness in her face. When we sat down in the back of the shop, I saw that her son's arrest had taken a heavy toll. A slight woman with thin lips and wispy brown hair, she seemed much older than her forty-seven years because of the dark rings around her tired blue eyes. Though she had been divorced and remarried for more than ten years, her voice was heavy with remembered pain when she discussed her years with Ken.

"I met him at a dance, I was nineteen. . . . He was a big man, over six foot tall, and he seemed pretty sure of himself, you know, pretty together," she began.

"I found out that his mother was divorced, and he was more or less helping raise his brothers and sister. I admired him for that, you know, to have a person that young take on the responsibility of being a father. . . . He was nurturing towards his brothers and sister," she said.

However, as Barbara spent more time with Ken, she quickly saw that there was little to admire about his life. As opposed to the stable, supportive environment in which she was raised, Ken's childhood was volatile and violent.

"His father was divorced and married quite a few times, and so Ken had a lot of stepmothers. When there were arguments, his father would always stick up for their stepmother—always. The kids were always wrong, especially Ken. Ken and his dad would get into yelling and screaming matches, and his dad had punched him a few times that Ken has told me. . . . And on the other side, I know when his mother remarried, his stepdad was also quite abusive to Ken and the other children. There was total rejection in his life."

When Tommy, their first child, was born in 1966, there was nothing that the nineteen-year-old father wouldn't do for his son. "I gave birth to him," Barbara told me, "but he was *Ken's* child. . . . He wouldn't trust anyone to even baby-sit for little Tommy." When Tommy was a year old, Barbara became pregnant with their second child, but during her first month, Ken was shipped off to Vietnam.

After Ken came home from the war, Tommy was still his special little man. Inexplicably, however, Ken absolutely rejected George. Barbara shook her head in tearful disbelief as she spoke. "He would have nothing to do with George from the time I brought him home from the hospital. . . . When Ken introduced his two young sons, he would say, 'This is my son Tommy and this is George.'"

Tragically, when Tommy was seven years old, he was killed in a car accident. Barbara responded by holding little George closer; Ken reacted by pushing George even further away. "At first Ken would tolerate George, but after Tommy got killed there was nothing," Barbara lamented. "George was lost, his father just shut him out. . . . He would try to get attention from his dad and Ken would say, 'Get out of here, I don't have time for you.' George would look at me and ask, 'Mom, what's the matter?' This went on until George just shut his father out. . . . George always caught hell for everything, it didn't matter what it was . . . [like] if there was a chip out of a dish or something."

If Tommy had not been so tragically ripped from his family, might things have been different? Would Tommy have been able to protect his younger brother from his father's wrath, or at least to cushion the blows by providing moral support to George? My inclination is to say, yes, things might have turned out better for George, but how much better, I simply do not know. What I did discover, however, is that Barbara and Ken eventually had four more children, and Ken proved to be a good father to them. But his attitude toward George remained cold and distant. "George remained the low man on the totem pole," Barbara said, "even though he was the oldest."

Ken physically punished George about two or three times a week, smacking the boy on the rear with an open hand, "for doing what a little boy would normally do, like playing with his trucks in the front yard." Though these beatings often left handprints on George's buttocks, Barbara did not believe that Ken was a physically abusive parent.

Ken's switch was his tongue. Starting when his son was in grade school, Ken routinely called George a "bastard" or "stupid." But the most stinging criticism—which George heard throughout his life—was: "You're a wimp and you will never amount to *anything!*"

Several weeks after his appointment to the case, Blount got a call from Stan Lertner, who lived next door to Ken and who felt compelled to recount a troubling incident that had been gnawing at him for over twelve years.

"I was outside in my yard one day," he told Blount, "and saw Ken working on his car. He had the hood up and George was standing right next to him. George was about five years old. Ken yelled over, 'Hey, hey, Stan. Come over here, I want to show you something.' I thought that Ken wanted to show me something under the hood. When I got there, Ken looked at George and said, 'Have you ever seen a dumber kid in your whole life? Look at his eyes . . . damn, you're so dumb!' George just sat there quietly with a hurt and pained expression on his face. Ken treated his other kids differently. He wasn't hard on them like he was on George."

Some of those who witnessed Ken's tongue-lashings tried to intervene, but it was to no avail. Barbara eerily recalled one incident—remarkably similar to one Mike Alborgeden experienced—that foreshadowed the future. George was only five years old. He and his family went to a relative's house for a holiday visit.

"George's uncle Harry was trying to help him ride a little bike," Barbara began, "and Ken goes, 'No, I'll do it!' Well, Ken went over, and every time George would make a mistake, he'd say, 'You're stupid!' or 'What's the matter with you!' And then he'd just jerk him off the bike. When Ken walked back across the yard, Uncle Harry told him, 'You know, that

kid tries so hard, [but you don't seem to] know he is alive.
. . . [He's] going to get you one of these days for the way you
treat him.' Ken just laughed."

Ken's treatment of George was far from the only problem
in the McHenry household. Ken had occasionally struck his
wife before he went to Vietnam; after his return, however,
the physical and verbal violence drastically escalated. Though
the war and Ken's use of drugs and alcohol cannot themselves
be blamed for all of the problems Ken had when he came
home, they certainly took their toll.

"When he got home from Vietnam," Barbara said, "I'd
have to roll out of bed in the middle of the night and go
underneath it because he'd start in with his dreams and his
yelling. . . . And that's when he started in real heavy with
the drugs. . . . He used to hit me quite a bit, and . . . I took
the wrong approach. I decided that if . . . well, he's putting
me in the place of a man, and at least a man fights back, so
I started fighting back. . . . If he was going to punch me, I
was going to punch him, even though when I got punched
back, it was twice as hard."

Ken left Barbara with cuts and bruises on numerous occasions. With great anger, she related her fruitless attempts
to get help from the police. "They stood in my front yard and
said that there was nothing that they could do, because they
didn't see him hit me, and I was standing there with a swollen,
black eye." As debilitating as those times were, it is not her
own agony that she remembers most vividly.

"When Ken hit me," Barbara sobbed, "George would go
and hide under his bed or in a closet. Sometimes he'd just
stand there with this nobody-home look."

Though continually ignored or belittled, George never ex-
ploded in anger or resentment at Ken. On the contrary, he
ceaselessly tried to please him. He could not keep the smile
on his face forever, and sadly, around the third grade, George
began to shut down emotionally, shunning all affection, refusing to let even his mother hug him. And with this withdrawal came anger, an anger that eventually consumed him.
To Barbara, his behavior seemed to say, "I can't get attention
for doing something right, so I'll do everything wrong."

George's problems at home soon spilled over to school.
Though he tested above average, he usually did poorly. Even

when he did well, his academic performance was eclipsed by his behavioral problems. He had a poor attention span and was frequently disciplined by teachers for disrupting the class. Especially sensitive to being teased, he frequently scuffled in the playground as a result.

Ken and Barbara divorced when George was in fourth grade. Though Ken had little contact with his son—his visits were erratic, often not even one a month—George's behavior did not improve. His report cards for the next few years repeat the same phrases over and over: "needs to learn self-control"; "erratic in his performance"; "I would like to meet with you at your convenience." As he got older, his problems at school grew more serious, too.

As a result of truancy and his poor academic performance, George was forced to repeat the seventh grade twice. Throughout this time and into the eighth grade, he continued to get into fights at school.

He just could not walk away from the slightest cut or joke at his expense without blowing up or raising his fists. Hand in hand with this, by the time he entered ninth grade, he had become obsessed with what one friend described as "getting stronger and stronger," pumping iron and keeping himself in superb physical shape. One friend recounted that George wanted to be just like the character he developed for Dungeons & Dragons (a board game particularly popular among boys where the players take on the identities of various warring characters): "incredibly powerful, totally immortal—you could never hurt the guy." Barbara noticed this power obsession, too, and thought that it was "because his dad always told him that he was weak, a sissy."

Despite his volatile disposition, George was a bit of an anomaly. He was not the classic school-yard bully who was in and out of reform school on assault and sundry charges by his fourteenth birthday. He never once hit a teacher or hurt another child seriously, much less with cruel intent, in a fight, nor was he ever arrested for any act of violence.

By the time George entered high school, he was smart enough to realize that he had to control his explosive temper. Avoiding fights that would inevitably result in discipline, he opted for taking out his frustration with others on himself by punching walls and throwing things. After an argument with his high-school girlfriend, for example, he punched a plate-glass window. Because he could predict when he was about to "go off," George had an agreement with the high-school principal (surely an enlightened man) that allowed him to go to the gym to work off his fury. After sprinting ten laps or lifting a few hundred pounds of weights, he would return to class.

Despite Barbara's tireless efforts, including individual and family counseling, she was unable to help her child. The family strife was unfortunately exacerbated by the fact that George could not get along with Elton, Barbara's second husband, either. "George knew Elton loved him," Barbara said, "but he had been so conditioned by his dad to get a bad response from men that he was confused. He knew my love, but not a man's love. My husband tried, but he got frustrated."

Elton and George's always acrimonious relationship fell apart completely shortly after George's seventeenth birthday. The daily fights and yelling matches were consuming the whole family, and so, for the sake of her marriage and her other children, Barbara told George that he had to leave.

For several weeks, George lived with two older friends until Ken, who had spent only a total of two months in the past nine years with the boy, invited his son to come live with him. Why Ken made the offer, and why George accepted, no one really understood.

Several of Ken's friends and relatives said he wanted to repair his relationship with George as he had put his own life back together after divorcing Barbara. His drinking was under control, he had found work as a foreman at a local auto parts factory, and he had remarried and had a baby girl, Felicia, with his second wife. Ken acknowledged that he had made mistakes with his son, but he was, he thought, better prepared now to help him. What worried him most was that his son was going in the wrong direction—failing in school and with no skills or plans for after graduation. Perhaps in his son Ken saw somebody he had known twenty years earlier who really needed help.

A few of George's friends remarked that he had accepted the offer to move in with his dad for a good reason: he had no money and no place to live. Barbara and others thought his motivations were more complicated, deeper. Incredibly, despite years of mistreatment at his father's hands, George still had immense respect for him, longing for his love and approval, hoping this would be the chance to prove himself. The truth of his motivation probably lies somewhere in between, but one thing is certain: the minute George walked through his father's door the fuse was lit.

In the first few weeks things went smoothly between father and son, with both trying as hard as they could to put their best foot forward. But the honeymoon didn't last too long; they soon realized that little had changed since the early days.

Sadly, Ken's image of his son was frozen in time. "He didn't know how to deal with an adult son," one of his relatives said after his death. "He treated him like a three-year-old." George was still a loser who couldn't do anything right. And behind all his good intentions, George hadn't forgotten how his dad had treated him as a youngster. Though he was now almost as big as Ken, his dad still made him feel as if he were five years old.

Describing to me the first few weeks living with his father, George said, "I was baby-sitting [Felicia] from like nine in the morning until five in the afternoon. [When my dad came home,] he jumped my shit because the house would be a disaster. After trying to pick up things for so long, I just let the kid tear the house apart . . . then I would reorganize it." And it was not just housekeeping that caused arguments between father and son.

"We'd have arguments about nearly everything two people could have arguments about, stupid arguments about stupid things. Like 'who left the toilet seat up' kind of arguments. Or how much noise I made in the shower; or my time limit on the phone. He timed me with a little bell." There were even rifts over bowling: "If I beat him, he would say, 'You didn't beat me! I lost.'" Regardless of the subject of the argument, Ken usually ended them by calling George a liar, an accusation that cut George to the quick each time.

As in the past, George never confronted his dad or challenged him in any way. He was scared. Though Ken never once slapped or punched his son during this period, George lived in constant fear that his father would physically retaliate if George made his true feelings known. He continually told his friends that he was terrified that his dad would hit him, as he had some five years earlier when he learned that George had gotten his first D. Ken had turned on his son and punched him in the face so hard that it "splattered me against the wall."

But now George was older, with more opportunities open to him to escape his intolerable living situation. Though he knew he would have to live with his dad during his senior year, he didn't have to be home the whole summer. Attending National Guard training camp promised relief from the pressure, as well as a chance to show his dad he was a man. George figured that the grueling training program would be worth it; it would make his dad proud of him. He was wrong. Joining the Guard was like throwing gasoline on a fire.

Before his son even left for the program, Ken had begun referring to it as "doing wimp service in a wussy outfit." The training his son would receive in the Guard, he insisted, could not compare with the training *he* had gone through in the army. George's friends reported that Ken, on numerous occasions, told him, "You're stupid for joining, and you'll never get anything out of it. You may be my son, but you ain't gonna make it. You're not tough enough. You're a wimp!"

When George returned after the two-month exercise, Ken maintained that the only change he saw in his son was a new haircut. He did not see that George's sense of self-worth had been greatly boosted. George had successfully completed eight grueling weeks of basic training, something his father had insisted he could never do, and that in itself made him proud and self-confident.

After boot camp, his relationship with his father deteriorated further. Neal, one of George's closest friends, had heard him complain about his dad, but he never realized how difficult things were for George until several weeks after George got back.

"George came over to my house one evening," sixteen-year-old Neal began. "He said he had to be home by eleven P.M., so I walked back with him. We were goofing off, so George was a few minutes late. George walks in the door, and his dad pushes him into the wall and says, 'You're five minutes late.' It was a *heavy* push. I tried to explain to his dad why we were late, but he wouldn't let me. I was stunned. I didn't know what to do. My dad would *never* do that."

That he was under a great strain the eight months he lived with his dad was obvious to others as well. The mother of one of George's girlfriends at the time immediately noticed something was amiss in his life.

Leona Hampton, a cheerful middle-aged homemaker with three teenage daughters, described the polite young man who visited her home as "someone who was lacking in love; he was looking for someone to notice him." George was so starved for affection that he'd call Mrs. Hampton "Mom." "George would come in and say, 'Okay, where's the food, Mom?' or 'Mom, can I help you rake up these leaves?' It always tickled me because he was like the son I never had."

Ever silent, George did not vent his deep frustrations about his home life around Mrs. Hampton. He did, however, tell Mary, her teenage daughter, as well as other friends, that his dad and stepmom were driving him crazy. Several times he even went so far as to say he would "end up shooting these two" someday. Nobody took him seriously because that was George: it was typical for him to rant and rave, and past experience had taught them that, though he had a temper, he would never really hurt anybody.

Yet, George was growing more and more desperate and even went, on two separate occasions, to his National Guard recruiter, Captain Emil Jervis, to tell him that he wanted to kill his dad. Before he formally entered the summer training program, George spoke to Jervis for several hours about his problems at home. Jervis later said, "[George stated] he wanted to kill his father, [who] didn't approve of him, and [that] he'd be better off without one . . . that he might as well kill him." Assuming that George was just a typical teenager mouthing off about frustrations at home, Jervis did nothing, told no one.

Shortly after the homicide, Captain Jervis stated in an interview that George had done fairly well in training, "but after his return I could tell he was under stress. It was like he was being overwhelmed. . . . George was proud that he finished [the training], but his father was not proud of him."

Just three weeks before the killing, George went to see Jervis, his baby sister in tow. It was the first time in Jervis's experience that a male teenage recruit had brought a baby into his office. It was also the first time such a recruit asked to be temporarily excused from a meeting so he could change a dirty diaper. Before he left that day, George again told Jervis that he wanted to kill his dad. But Jervis simply regarded the threat as the mere musings of a frustrated teenager.

The care and devotion George showed for his little sister perfectly illustrated the complexity of his personality. He had such a short fuse he'd blow up at the slightest criticism and was so angry and irritated with his father that he freely voiced his murderous intentions. And yet on the other hand, compared to most teens his age, especially males, he was exceptionally warm and sensitive. There was nothing he would not do for his little sister. "I like little babies," he said. "They're really neat. It's hard to believe they're so helpless." Perhaps because he was a boy of such extremes, he was never truly understood by anyone, even himself.

Hoping to help his son improve his grades, Ken required George to finish homework as soon as he came home from school. As with every other rule, it soon became a constant source of battle between father and son, indirectly touching off the confrontation that led to Ken's death.

"I didn't do my homework Friday night," George later said. "I waited until Sunday night [because] I only had five problems to do." But Ken didn't care if George only had five problems, he was furious that the boy had waited until the end of the weekend, disobeying him yet again.

"I waited till now because I only have five problems to do," George said.

"You should be doing it now!" Ken bellowed just inches from George's face.

"Let me just unwind a little more, drink a cup of coffee, smoke a cigarette, and then I'll do it," George responded angrily.

That was it for Ken. "This is typical of you. You were a screwup as a little kid, you're a screwup now, and you'll be a fuckup for the rest of your life." George could not respond, nor could he even hear everything his father was saying, choked and blinded as he was by his own anger. "I wanted to jump up and grab ahold of him and squeeze the shit out of his neck. . . . It was really no different than any other night, it's just that this night it got too much," George later said. The screaming lasted ten minutes, and then, just before leaving to go to a friend's house with his wife and child, Ken warned George to finish his homework before their return.

"I ended up finishing my homework, but then I don't really know what got into me." It was at this point that George took a rifle that a friend had given him and stashed it in some bushes outside the house.

Ken, Madge, and little Felicia returned about an hour later. George went to bed, and Ken and his wife stayed up watching TV. At about three A.M., George got dressed and went outside to smoke a cigarette. Then, quietly, he came back in with the rifle. First, George unplugged the two house phones, then he crept into Ken's bedroom and walked to the foot of the bed. George raised the weapon and aimed it at his sleeping father's head.

Madge later said she heard a loud pop and then felt something warm flowing onto her body—it was her husband's blood. She immediately woke up and saw the barrel of a rifle no more than two feet from her head.

"What is going on? What's happening here!" she shrieked. She looked at her husband, realized what had just happened, and screamed, "Please don't, please . . ."

Shaking from head to foot, George curled his index finger around the trigger but couldn't pull it. His finger froze in its crooked position.

"I couldn't . . . I couldn't. I was just terrified," George later said. A detective surmised that George was literally paralyzed by what he had just done. "He had not planned what the hunting rifle, fired at close range, would do to a human skull."

After the killing, George did not immediately flee. First, he warmed a bottle of milk for his baby sister to calm her down. Then, after bringing the baby to Madge, George took the car keys from her purse. Before leaving, he even reconnected the phones, allowing Madge to call the police immediately, thus hastening his capture no more than a half hour later.

It didn't make any difference to the prosecution that the victim and the assailant were related. George's confession gave them an airtight case for first-degree murder. All the elements were there to establish intent and premeditation. George had spoken about his desire to kill his father during the two months before the homicide to many people—his mother, stepfather, several friends, and Captain Jervis. One of George's friends told the police that the night before the homicide, he had overheard George tell another friend words to the effect that "if my dad messes around with me, I know where his gun is and I'm not afraid to use it." The police also had George's own statement that he had earlier planned how to carry out the homicide.

Parricide cases such as George's are undoubtedly the most difficult to defend, because it was primarily George's mind and soul that his father pummeled. In our society, we consider psychological and verbal abuse less serious than either physical or sexual abuse, perhaps because they leave no outer scar. The old taunt "Sticks and stones may break my bones, but names will never hurt me" still captures the prevailing wisdom. Such thinking, however, merely betrays our ignorance, for psychological abuse can be as crippling as physical violence and have as lasting, debilitating effects.

Of all forms of abuse, we know the least about emotional abuse, complicating our efforts even to define and identify it. For example, most of us generally accept that parents can yell or curse if a child does something dangerous or acts foolishly. No law, moreover, requires a parent to tell her son, "I love you, you are the most precious part of my life." Nor does it say anywhere that a parent cannot scream, "I hate you, I wish you were never born," to his daughter. Despite these problems in defining verbal and emotional abuse, certain behaviors are clearly more harmful than others. Constantly berating and criticizing a child regardless of the child's actions, coupled with statements like "I wish you were never born" or "I hate you, you are not my child," for example, clearly constitute psychological abuse.

Just as children are physically fragile and undeveloped, they are emotionally and psychologically immature and unformed as well. But while a broken arm may heal and bruises fade, severe, prolonged psychological abuse can attack a nascent psyche, twisting it, disrupting its normal growth forever. Specific effects on the child's personality are harder to quantify, but can include poor self-image, lack of self-confidence, depression, and self-destructive behavior.

Straus and Gelles characterize emotional abuse as:

the most hidden, insidious, least researched, and perhaps in the long run most damaging form of intimate victimization. . . . Defining physical or sexual abuse is relatively easy compared to the formidable task of setting forth what constitutes emotional abuse. . . . There is little doubt that direct or indirect attacks on one's self-concept leave deep, long-lasting scars . . . emotional wounds [that] fester beneath the surface forever. . . . We suspect that one reason so little research on emotional abuse has been conducted is that so many of us are guilty of occasional or even frequent emotional attacks on loved ones that the behavior is too close and too common to allow for objective research."

A further problem is that the determination of whether a particular parental behavior amounts to emotional abuse not only depends on what the parent says and does, but also on the child's inherent emotional and mental health. For reasons that are still largely unknown, certain children are able to cope with the verbal violence better than others. Some have girded their personalities by forging strong bonds with other family members or friends. These outside relationships enable these kids to withstand their parents' attacks, because they are validated by other people and therefore understand the abuse is not their fault. Still others cope through inner strength gained from some outside activity such as school or sports.

The import of all these problems for parricides is that they severely limit the defense options. Without an underlying history of severe and prolonged physical and/or sexual assaults, it is virtually impossible to use self-defense, a bitter irony since what we are literally arguing is "defense of the self." The same logic applies to a manslaughter defense, which requires the killer to have been "adequately provoked" by the victim and then to have killed in the heat of passion. Where a jury would understand a fractured skull and broken leg, or anal rape, as sufficient provocation, pleading ten years of petty insults and belittlement just doesn't have the same force.

Complicating George's case, Ken was sleeping when he was shot. Further, the scolding over unfinished homework could hardly be considered a life-threatening, provocative act. Despite his constant fear that his father would severely beat him, by George's own admission he had been neither touched nor had his life threatened during the entire eight months he lived with his dad. In fact, as George told Detective Anders, the last beating had occurred almost five years earlier.

With self-defense and manslaughter out of the picture, we began to focus the defense on simply getting a second-degree murder conviction. Though legal arguments about the degrees of murder seem irrelevant to outsiders—murder is murder, right?—to the defendant and his lawyer, they are critical. The degrees of murder exist because they concretely distinguish between greater or lesser guilt in the same crime, the level of guilt being the touchstone for later sentencing.

If convicted of first-degree murder, George might face life in prison without parole; a second-degree murder conviction, however, could mean a life sentence but with the possibility of parole in twenty years. Second-degree murder meant that George killed his father intentionally, but did not premeditate the act. Legally, we would have to prove that George committed the crime under diminished capacity, that he could not have premeditated "due to a mental disorder, and not amounting to insanity and not due to emotions like jealousy, fear, or anger," as the statute read.

Obviously, we needed the services of a topflight psychologist or psychiatrist to help us prove that George was indeed suffering from some identifiable mental disorder. Initially, however, the judge disagreed, refusing Blount's informal request for funds to pay for this because he did not believe that they were necessary to the defense. I should have expected this obstructive response since the judge also denied my necessity for the funds for my services, which Blount had picked up out of his pocket.

Because of the denial, Blount then had to conduct a full-blown pretrial hearing on the necessity of psychological testimony. In an affidavit I prepared for the hearing, I was forced to state what I thought was the obvious: "The defense of a parricide case hinges in large part upon explaining to the jury how the dynamics and functioning of the parent-child relationship affected the defendant's act of homicide. . . . The explanation of the cause of the homicide can only be accomplished through the construction of a comprehensive profile of the family system. The development of this profile requires the testimony of both psychologist and psychiatrist."

In all his wisdom, the good judge eventually granted funds for hiring two experts. As it usually happens, choosing and preparing the experts was my responsibility. George was evaluated by two doctors with whom I had worked in the past—Dr. Bill Hazeler, a psychologist, and Dr. Martin Loftus, a psychiatrist.

After evaluating him separately, both concluded that George did indeed suffer from a mental disorder. Neither found George to be insane; he didn't hallucinate and was in sufficient touch with reality.

George, however, "lived his life expecting, without reason, to be harmed or taken advantage of," Dr. Hazeler wrote. The boy perceived others as "being deliberately threatening or demeaning," and as a result he was angry nearly all the time. "[Similar] individuals frequently have histories of poor relationships with their parents, including in particular a lack of perceived support and nurturance from parental figures. Underlying their aggressive demeanor are intense and unmet needs for attention, security, and dependence. . . . The behavior of this young man is characterized by a pervasive apprehensiveness, intense and variable moods, prolonged periods of dejection and self-deprecation, and also episodes of withdrawn isolation and unpredictable anger."

While Ken, both doctors acknowledged, was perhaps too strict with George and at times even verbally abusive, they did not believe he had done anything in the time his son lived with him that warranted George's ultimate response. They, moreover, largely discounted the effect of the entire father-son history, and the effect on George of witnessing Ken's earlier abuse of Barbara. Instead, they saw the homicide as primarily being the product of a dysfunction in George's own mental process. At the time of the homicide George, Dr. Hazeler theorized, was suffering from a "paranoid personality disorder, with features of a borderline personality disorder."

Dr. Loftus for the most part agreed with Hazeler's findings that George was probably paranoid and had been demonstrating serious coping problems for at least six years. George's acting-out problems were so obvious, Loftus told me, that he was "appalled" that there had been no intervention by the school.

It was George's inherent personality disorder, Hazeler concluded, and not Ken's treatment of him, that was responsible for the "ongoing conflict" that ultimately resulted in the shooting. "As a consequence of this disorder," Dr. Hazeler wrote, "George felt more threatened physically by his father than was probably justified objectively. The point here is not whether or not Mr. McHenry was a menacing individual, but that, as a result of his disorder, George's subjective experience of threat was likely greater than warranted by circumstances."

Similarly, George's paranoia impaired "his ability to cope with his father's harshness and rejection. . . . Because George felt his personal autonomy threatened by his father, his attention was focused selectively and narrowly on his own anger at this perceived maltreatment and on his need to end it by whatever means [necessary]. . . . The long-standing nature of this disorder diminished George's ability to respond to the conflict with his father except through violence. George had, in effect, spent much of his life angrily preparing for combat and was therefore severely limited in his ability to evaluate . . . other options for coping with the conflict."

In sum, George, in the experts' opinion, did not have the ability to premeditate the crime because the paranoia diminished his capacity to understand the consequences of his actions and even to think about other solutions or actions short of violence to cope with his deteriorating relationship with his father.

Though their opinions provided the evidence needed to refute the premeditation element of first-degree murder, I was not completely satisfied with their findings. I am not a psychologist and could not say whether George suffered from paranoia, but experience told me Ken's treatment had to have played a critical role in influencing George's overall behavior. To persuade the jury to accept the mental disorder that ruled out premeditation, I knew that it was crucial for us to tie the genesis of the disorder to the father's treatment, to show that

Ken was at least partly responsible for his son's problems. This was not so farfetched, because some recent research does show that long-term child abuse can produce in certain individuals identifiable psychiatric disorders. For reasons that are still largely unknown, certain abused children emerge mentally intact while others develop a wide range of serious mental disorders including posttraumatic-stress disorder (the most common), multiple personality disorder, and borderline personality disorder. Research has also shown that certain preexisting mental illnesses such as paranoia or schizophrenia are exacerbated by abuse.

Though our experts were of a different opinion, it was clear to anyone who knew George that his poor self-esteem and tremendous anger were in no small part due to his father's treatment.

Joey Danforth, George's twenty-year-old friend, did not have any advanced degrees in psychiatry or psychology, but he did have a keen insight into George's behavior. In the aftermath of the killing, Joey said, "His dad never really gave him the time . . . never accepted him . . . he wanted his dad to accept him. He didn't really mean to actually kill his dad. He was trying to get a point across so his dad would see that he was there."

Despite my disagreement with Hazeler, I knew he was a perceptive clinician. Hazeler noted that the homicide could throw George into a major depression, and that he was "at risk to decompensate under increased stress," i.e., become more disturbed and suicidal. Hazeler was definitely correct. Though George stayed relatively calm his first month in jail, toward the end of the second month he lost his appetite, could not sleep, and thought of suicide. Six weeks before the trial, Blount got a note in the mail:

Dear Mr. Blount:

The thought of death leaves me at perfect peace for I have a firm conviction that our mortal spirit is a being of indestructible nature. . . . This place and the pressure are eating me and I'm losing a war against myself. I don't like this. . . . Please tell my mom I love her a lot and I shall miss her.

Mr. Blount, I have chosen the appropriate punishment

for my crime, and the method I am using is crude, but
effective and slow. I would like to have my body used as
shark bait since it will be of no use. . . . My thoughts are
at the present blank. . . . I didn't choose to be here so
I am going to leave this world. . . . For the wages of sin
is death. Romans 6:23.

P.S. Goodbye. —

Blount immediately rushed over to the jail to see George,
whom he found listless and unresponsive. When Blount asked
him about the letter, George was silent for a long time. "I
didn't mean it," he said finally, his voice distant. Blount had
the sheriff put his client on a twenty-four-hour suicide watch,
which continued up until the day of trial.

Because Blount was paying me out of his own pocket, our
agreement was that I would provide assistance up to the day
of trial. As a result, I was not there for what Blount later
described as "one of the saddest cases I ever worked on"—
this from a man who routinely represents deformed babies.

Typically, the child is the principal defense witness in parricides. However, in the case of *State* v. *George McHenry,*
the jury never heard from the defendant. Blount and I had
discussed putting George on the stand many times. Because
George had not rebounded from his depression, Blount was
worried that he would be too unpredictable. Finally, he decided that it might be more prudent to let others tell the story.

George's primary witness was his mother. For three gut-
wrenching hours, she tearfully told George's tragic history to
the packed courtroom. Natalie, George's fourteen-year-old
sister, followed her mother to the stand.

"How did your dad treat George?" Blount asked the young
girl in a simple blue print dress.

". . . Differently than the rest of us. . . . He called him
stupid."

In addition to the family members, the defense witnesses
were Stan Lertner, Captain Jervis, and George's two friends
Neal and Joey.

After five days of testimony and only five hours of deliberation, the jury reached a verdict. George stood expression-
less before the jurors as their foreman read the verdict—guilty
of murder in the second degree.

Despite the voluminous evidence that the prosecution had presented about George's plans to kill Ken, the jury rejected the premeditation altogether. And it was the expert testimony that made the difference. After leaving the courtroom, several jurors told reporters that, based upon the testimony of the defense experts, they were persuaded that George could not have premeditated the murder.

Four weeks later George was sentenced to a minimum term of not less than twenty-six years in the state prison. He made no statement, but sat, staring impassively at the judge, his wrists crossed in front of him.

With a touch of pride, George rolled up the sleeve of his neatly pressed, forest-green county-jail uniform and made a muscle, saying, "I'm up to fifteen-hundred push-ups a day now. I do them Mondays, Wednesdays, and Fridays." For years, George had worked out and lifted weights preparing for the *final* fight, the fight with his father that never came. Now he really needed to pump up for protection. He was going to the state pen, where the chance of assault was very real.

We were speaking at the local county jail in a garishly lit room with freshly painted white walls about six months after the verdict. George's coal-black eyes were clear and calm, but he was definitely on edge. In four weeks he was going to be transferred to a maximum-security prison, where he would be thrown in with seasoned adult criminals. Though he was in top shape and had learned self-defense training in the National Guard, he still faced tremendous risks of attack, primarily because of his age and inexperience.

Despite the obvious perils of a new type of abuse that awaited him, George was adamant that he was not afraid. He was determined to make it through on his own without help from *anybody*. "I believe in God and stuff like that, but I don't ask him for anything. I keep a low profile."

After a while, I turned the conversation to the subject I was most interested in—how he distinguished the earlier fantasies he had about killing his father from the actual murder.

"When you told your friends and others that you wanted to kill your dad, did you think you had the ability to kill him?"

"No," he answered quickly, his amazed reaction telling me

I had asked a ridiculous question. "It was childhood fantasy. *"You* wanted to kill your parents when you were younger, right? You felt frustrated, mad, even angry at them at times, right?"

"I . . . I was angry, yes," I stammered, uncomfortable at the sudden role switch. In my work, I am routinely called upon to discuss the tension and acrimony that exists between adolescents and their parents, but to tell a client about the problems I had with my parents proved, for several reasons, to be extremely difficult.

While I did admit to getting angry and frustrated, I didn't tell him that killing my parents never crossed my mind, even during the worst times, because I was afraid he would interpret it wrongly, that he would feel I was one more person condemning him. Society had already meted out a severe punishment; I didn't want to make it worse. On another level, I remained silent because I knew he was right.

During those turbulent teenage years, when our emotions are on a seemingly endless roller-coaster ride, many of us at one time or another have thought, or even said out loud: "I wish Mom was dead"; "I could kill Dad for doing that to me"; or "I wish I was an orphan or that they would both just go away and leave me alone forever." For practically everyone, these ruminations remain just what they are—fantasies that are usually forgotten the next day. Mental health professionals say these volcanic feelings are normal and even have a therapeutic effect on the child. It is no more than a way to release the feelings of anger and resentment that are a healthy outgrowth of family living. Tragically, for a few such as George, the fantasy becomes reality.

While I was still groping for a response to his question, George interjected, "Well, that's how I felt, angry. My only difference was I carried it out, I got too angry for my own good. I think I'm a nice guy, you know. I'm blunt, okay, but just your average guy. When I shot him, I wasn't thinking about the outcome at all. If I was, I wouldn't have done it. . . . What I should have done, and what I really wanted to do, was scare the hell out of him. Wake him up with the barrel that far away from his head," he said, holding thumb and index finger so they were almost touching, "and say, 'If you move, I'll kill you.' And then I would've backed away and told him to go in the living room and just sit down and not interrupt me at all."

We talked for seven hours that day, and with each passing moment the tragedy of his life and Ken's death loomed ever larger in my mind. As I walked out of the jail that afternoon, I thought of a film I had seen many years before, a film about tidal waves.

Tidal waves are not simply big waves that roll in from a few miles offshore. They are triggered by powerful earthquakes and volcanos that erupt hundreds, sometimes thousands, of miles away on the deep ocean floor. The wave lumbers across the ocean, getting bigger, picking up more momentum with each passing hour. It may travel for days, often weeks, before it finally strikes land and unleashes its catastrophic force.

We may never be sure why young George McHenry took his father's life. Strangers will probably say that he hated his father, but he didn't. Underneath the rage, he was like most boys—he looked up to his father and spent his life desperately trying to gain his father's approval. When most boys would have given up on their fathers, George went back to see if he could get what he always wanted—the admiration and love that his father showed for George's older brother, Tommy. And Ken was not a bad father who hated his son. He knew he made mistakes in the early years; asking George to come back and live with him was an attempt to repair the damage. Sadly, however, both men's visions were obscured by the tragedies of their pasts. Ken's vision was obscured by the pains of his own childhood, the terrible loss of his young Tommy, and the war he brought home with him. George's vision was clouded by the anger, confusion, and pain of being rejected by the man who brought him into this world. George spent his life directing his sadness and bitterness to everyone but his father, and all the while the pressure was building in him.

PART II

GIRLS WHO KILL THEIR FATHERS

Introduction

"In our culture, women are not supposed to use violence," says Dr. Lenore Walker, one of the nation's leading experts on battered women who kill, "even to defend themselves against a potentially fatal attack."

According to the FBI's Uniform Crime Report, women only commit about 10 percent of the approximately twenty thousand homicides each year in the United States. When it comes to homicide within their own families, the same holds—daughters are perpetrators of only 10 percent of all parricides.

Imagine that on her way home from school a teenage girl is forced into a car by a stranger. He rips her clothes off, forces her to orally copulate him, and then brutally rapes her. She sees the stranger the next week near the school and shoots him. The collective community reaction would probably be that shooting was too good for the rapist. Many people might go so far as to say that it was lucky for the community that she got him before the cops did, because *they* would only throw him in jail; people like that should be hung or at least castrated. A woman who killed her rapist would become something of a hero, particularly in the eyes of the average man, because men become especially enraged at *other* men who rape and assault "their" women, whether children, wives, or girlfriends.

The irony is, however, that regardless of her age, it is six times more likely that a female will be sexually or physically assaulted by a male family member or friend than by a stranger. And despite the fact that fathers and other male relatives pose a far greater risk to young girls than do strangers, society has historically reserved its most severe retribution for strangers. Revenge rises quickly to the surface of our collective consciousness when it comes to dealing with strangers, but when the perpetrator is the father, our reaction is of a different sort. "We're downright almost polite to these guys," a detective friend of mine once said.

This double standard is immediately apparent just in the terminology. Aside from the blood relationship, "incest" (as well as sexual abuse) is principally distinguished from "rape" in legal terms by the fact that it is allegedly not accomplished with force, and therefore penalties are not as stiff. Until 1977, when the Supreme Court declared the practice unconstitutional, rape carried the death penalty in many states. Not surprisingly, however, in those same states, incest was *never* punishable by death or anything even close to that severe a penalty.

As utterly heinous and injurious as sexual abuse is, few daughters ever resist; most never report the incest to their mothers, siblings, teachers, or others who could help. And the number who take the dramatic step of killing their fathers is so minuscule as to be almost insignificant. The overwhelming majority of sexually victimized girls react with the utmost passivity. They suffer quietly, then go forth into their lives crippled by emotional problems. Some pull themselves together, but many never heal and may even permit the cycle of sexual abuse to continue into the next generation by marrying men who are carbon copies of their abusive fathers. Very, very few ever even confront their fathers in any way, much less kill them. Almost all of these women die taking their secrets to the grave.

Cindy

Cindy Baker had a storybook life. She wore a million-dollar smile and had a lifestyle to match, living in a sprawling house in the nicest neighborhood of a large Southwestern city, owning a walletful of credit cards from fancy department stores, and attending an elite private school. Her father, Henry, was a wealthy businessman with movie-star looks; her mother, Elaine, was a successful interior designer. Cindy also had two intelligent and beautiful older sisters, Nancy and Kerri.

Though Henry's many professional and community responsibilities kept him constantly busy, his family was his number-one priority—and he never let anyone forget it. Most fathers keep a photo of their children in their wallet or on their desks. Not Henry—he dedicated a whole wall to them in his huge mahogany-paneled office: the girls standing in front of the Eiffel Tower; Nancy and Kerri skiing in Aspen; Henry and Cindy at the family's Texas beach home.

His children didn't look up to him; they worshiped him. He loved his three daughters very much, but Cindy was his favorite. "My little princess," he called her. Both tall and slim, with angular noses that tipped up ever so slightly, and Caribbean-green eyes set off by their light sandy-blond hair, father and daughter were alike as two peas in a pod.

In reality Cindy's life was anything but a fairy tale; it was a bizarre, X-rated horror movie in which she played the dual roles of favorite daughter and sex slave. For most of her life, she lived, like every other incest victim, a nightmarish existence filled with contradiction and insanity at the hands of one who supposedly devoutly loved her. Then, at age sixteen, the little princess tore the cover from her storybook fantasy, killing her knight in shining armor with two blasts from a sixteen-gauge Remington shotgun loaded with double-aught buckshot.

Five weeks after the homicide, I received a call from John Halpern, an attorney for the Baker family, who had gotten my name through the legal grapevine. From his stern, gravelly voice and ultraformal manner, I imagined, correctly, that he was one of those elder-statesmanlike lawyers from a blue-chip firm. Halpern dispassionately sketched out the bare bones of the case, only briefly mentioning that his client maintained she was sexually abused, and I gave him my initial impressions. He and his client were interested in retaining me, he said, but he first wanted to review my credentials. In about a week he called back and asked me to come to town at the end of the month for a formal review of the case, and "of course to meet Miss Baker."

Halpern picked me up at the airport on a bright Sunday afternoon. Though younger than I thought, only about fifty, he affected the look of an elder Brahmin lawyer from his dark-blue, pinstripe, three-piece suit to the shiny-black wing-tip shoes. His red bow tie was tightly knotted, and not one of his prematurely silver-gray hairs was out of place. Though I thought he would be put off by my less than formal attire of faded blue jeans, T-shirt, and sneakers, he welcomed me warmly.

Curiously, however, he did not mention the case once on the drive to my hotel, discussing instead the great weather and baseball, his great passion. Not having watched a whole game since my dad took me to see the New York Mets in 1966, I had little to contribute. Though I tried during the half-hour trip to steer the discussion to the case, he would only say, "Yep, this is going to be a son of a gun to try, a real son of a gun."

I spent the next morning at Halpern's office reviewing police reports, the medical findings, and the various witness statements. During lunch, Halpern and one of the firm's junior associates briefed me on the case.

Halpern was bothered by two things. Despite Cindy's allegations of abuse, they could find no physical evidence of it. Worse, the case was assigned to the county's most uncompromising prosecutor, Arlene La Platta. In a strained voice, he recounted to me his first conversation with her after the arraignment. "John," La Platta told him coldly, "let me tell you right off the bat I don't give a good goddamn if you can even prove your kid was sexually abused. She blew her father's head off. He wasn't a sleazy molester; he was a bright, caring fellow. I don't care what he did to her, she didn't have to kill him. There are going to be no bargains."

I told him not to worry about finding corroborating evidence—because with the trial ten months away, there were still numerous areas to explore. As to Ms. La Platta, however, I could of course offer no words of encouragement. "I guess we're going to have to tie our dancing shoes tight," I joked, trying to relax him, "because it's going to be rock 'n' roll in front of that jury." He responded with a half-smile.

After the meeting, I drove to the regional juvenile detention center, a large, modern, one-story concrete structure, squat and ugly, set five miles out in the desert. The boys are housed in the east wing and the girls in the west. The residents are mostly kids from poor families, about 60 percent of whom are Hispanic, 25 percent Native American, and the remainder African American and white. Most of the inmates had been arrested for selling and using drugs, or minor property offenses such as car theft; several were in for assault and battery. When I visited, four teens were being held for homicide, three boys and Cindy.

She was sitting in the tiny, poorly lit interview room, her eyes fixed on the blank wall in front of her, and her hands neatly folded on the table. In her simple state-issue blue jeans and white blouse, she looked like what she was—a schoolgirl. I shook my head.

Cindy rose as I entered the room, extending her hand to give me a firm handshake. She asked if there was anything I needed before we started. Despite her dire situation, I was impressed that she had the presence of mind to treat me as if I were a guest in her home.

"I'm fine," I said appreciatively.

"I know why you're here," she said in a businesslike tone, after taking her seat. "You're supposed to help my lawyer defend me. Just ask me what you want." Then she looked away.

I immediately realized that the detailed list of questions I had painstakingly prepared was useless. There is no one right way to begin to interview a sexually abused adolescent, but as I have often found, there are innumerable wrong ones. Even for the most caring parents discussing sex with their normal, healthy teenage children is not an easy thing; imagine, then, the immense difficulties I have, as a male attorney, persuading someone such as Cindy to relate the intimate details of her relationship with her father.

"I know how difficult it is to talk about what happened," I began. "I've represented many girls and even boys who've had similar experiences. I'll try to make this as painless as possible," I said reassuringly.

She swiveled around in her chair and glared at me contemptuously. "Bullshit," she spat. "You don't understand. You could *never* understand what I'm going through." She was right.

Cindy was bubbling with rage at everyone around her. Halpern had earlier told me that though she had not told her mother and sisters about the abuse, she was furious that they had never helped her. In her gut she believed they knew her father was sexually molesting her. At least, she thought, they should have realized something was wrong about her relationship with him.

Cindy was also incredulous and angry that the police wouldn't believe her story. More insulting still, soon after her arrival, one of the counselors—guards by any other name— taunted her by saying, "Everybody's saying they were abused these days, and you're just jumping on the bandwagon." As just another part of the whole disgusting process, she was also angry at me.

We sat without a word between us for five long minutes.

"How about this," I said finally. "I don't want to hear anything about the problems with your father now. Why don't you just tell me about your family in general. Maybe you could even mention the good things about him."

She paused for a second, then stood and stretched. Reaching a hand into the pocket of her skirt, she took out a photo. "This is a picture of him," she said, her voice empty of emotion. "It was taken in Paris. I was fourteen." The worn photo, which she obviously carried everywhere, was of just the two of them, father and daughter sitting at a small outdoor café. She had a glass of red wine in one hand, and he had his arm draped over her shoulder. He looked engagingly at the camera; her smile was wide, creasing her face from ear to ear. They looked like a commercial for the "good life."

"I'll give you an example of what kind of person my dad was," she said in the same flat voice as I gazed at the photo. "When I was in middle school, my friends used to tell me that they wished they had him for a father. . . . My dad was actually more than a dad. He was our mom, too. Whenever my sisters or I had problems, about anything, and I mean anything, we'd go to my dad—never Mom. My mom is an okay lady, but she was kind of . . . invisible when I was growing up. . . . She was off in her own world—and still is. When you meet her, you'll see what I mean. She's ditsy, but nice. But it's not like she's stupid or anything. . . . My sister Nancy once said Mom went to college to meet Dad. She was probably right."

Cindy walked back toward me, then assertively took her seat as if to say, "Let's get down to business."

"My father was a very moral person," she said with a touch of pride. "That sounds kind of weird to say, I guess, considering everything. . . . He used to tell us it was our responsibility to help others. He was always appearing at community functions and getting his picture in the paper for helping some organization out. And he would always get us to do the same thing. I remember him saying when I was little, 'You children have everything. A big house, nice clothes . . . you can get anything you want. But lots of children aren't as lucky as you are. I want you to remember that.' All three of us worked as hospital volunteers, and every Christmas we would go door-to-door in the neighborhood collecting cans of food for poor children."

Cindy talked about her father's good side far longer than I expected. The longer she rambled on about him, the more relaxed she became, sometimes crying softly at her memories, and just as often smiling as she spoke. Clearly, on a very conscious level, Henry Baker was still her hero.

"From the time I was in grade school, he always made me feel important, like I could accomplish anything. He did the same for my sisters," she said, wiping tears from her eyes. "He never spared any expense when it came to things we wanted to learn. When Nancy wanted to take piano lessons, he bought a piano. She got tired of it after only a few months, but he didn't care. And when I wanted to take ballet lessons, he hired a private teacher. I was only seven. That's the way he did things."

The interview that day ended without a single question about the incest or the killing. I would be back the next day, and we would get to the hard parts sooner or later. It was a good start, and I felt once again that fundamental contradiction that these cases threw in my face—as much as the parent had violated them, the child still loved, would always love, only wanted love from, the parent.

After dinner that night, I met the rest of the family at Halpern's office. As I approached the conference room, I could see them through the drapes, the two sisters pacing the room while an older woman, their mother, sat, silent at the long, highly polished oak table. And all wore very uncomfortable looks. Nancy and Kerri definitely resembled their mother—tall, reddish light-brown hair, hazel eyes, and high cheekbones.

After brief introductions, I discovered for myself what Halpern had told me earlier—neither Cindy's mother, Elaine, nor her sisters had any clue that the sexual abuse was happening. All three claimed that, as far as they knew, Cindy had a wonderful relationship with her father.

"All any of us had known," Elaine said carefully, "was that Hank and Cindy had gotten closer since Nancy and Kerri went away to school. Cindy was Hank's favorite. He treated her royally. If there was a problem, it was that he indulged her too much. He gave her anything she wanted." Her two daughters nodded in agreement.

Kerri and Nancy were both living in other parts of the country, Nancy in college and Kerri working. Both had little to say to me, and I understood why. Not only were they devastated by the incident, but it was obvious they harbored great malice toward Cindy. Kerri, the oldest, seemed to be speaking for Nancy when she tearfully confessed, "We don't know what happened, but it can't be anything that Dad did to her. . . . Maybe she had it too good, maybe she was crazy, who knows. But whatever, Dad would *never, never* do what she's saying he did to her. Never."

Though the family was paying for my time, it was obvious to me that these three women resented me, especially the sisters. They realized my job was to prove that their father was a lecherous man who brought about his own demise, and they didn't want any part of it. Though they didn't say it, it was clear that no one cared very much if the youngest member of their family went to prison for the rest of her life.

The meeting lasted only about forty-five minutes, and I knew just a little bit more when it was over than I did before it started.

Every year tens of thousands of girls are sexually abused by fathers or adult relatives, yet it is impossible to know the exact numbers. Sigmund Freud originally regarded his female patients' descriptions of childhood sexual abuse as mere fantasies, or wish fulfillment. However, as he heard more and more women relate the same tales of sexual abuse at the hands of their fathers and other male relatives, he began to accept that these abusive incidents were not figments of their imaginations. Addressing the Viennese Society for Psychoanalysis in 1895, he offered the theory to his colleagues that childhood sexual abuse was at the heart of adult female neurosis. The medical community was so outraged at this suggestion of rampant incest that Freud feared he would be ostracized by his colleagues. Several years later, he recanted his theory, according to some critics, because his professional credibility was threatened.

Times have changed, but only reluctantly have we begun to acknowledge the extent of this problem. "When I started in 1971, it was supposed to be one case of incest in every million people," says Henry Giaretto, a California psychologist who founded one of the nation's first treatment programs for incest victims and their families. "That year I had twenty-six cases. Now we're running more than a thousand new cases a year, in a metropolitan area of a million people. That's of epidemic proportions, isn't it?"

In statistical terms, the phrase *female sexual abuse* is used to mean all behaviors, ranging from the penetration or touching, however slight, of the vagina or anus with penis or mouth, to any intentional touching of the breasts, genital area, groin, or buttocks for the purpose of sexual gratification. Neither the duration or frequency of the assaults is relevant in determining whether sexual abuse has occurred. According to the National Committee for the Prevention of Child Abuse and Neglect, of the 2 million reported cases of child abuse and neglect in 1988, about 270,000 were sexually abused girls. Leading family-violence researcher David Finklehor of the University of New Hampshire says that one out of three females has been or will be sexually abused before the age of eighteen by a family member or relative; and in a 1985 national poll conducted by the *Los Angeles Times,* 27 percent of women admitted that they were sexually abused as children.

Incest is not an accident, is rarely spontaneous, and almost never occurs only once. Though the abusive parent or relative frequently suffers from serious psychological problems, specifically his lack of control over sexual and emotional impulses, the sexual exploitation of children does not occur impulsively or haphazardly. To the contrary, such sexual victimization of children takes place over the long term, in deliberate, escalating stages. And the key to understanding it is grasping the parent's abuse of his fundamental role as supreme authority figure in the child's life.

Most sexually abusive fathers are consciously aware that their security lies in their children's silence. In the early stages (grade school or younger), silence is guaranteed through the child's pure trust and respect for the parent. Children of tender age (up to ten years) rely on their parents for their very survival. It is not until the child is twelve or thirteen that she begins to think for herself and question her parents' behavior, and the authority that they listened to in the first place.

In the later stages, passivity is ensured by the child's embarrassment and self-blame as well as direct threats. Though Cindy ultimately chose a radically different solution to her appalling dilemma—only a handful of cases like hers are reported each year—in all other respects her father's incestuous behavior and the twisted relationship he forced on her followed a classic pattern of sexual abuse.

I arrived at the detention center the next morning at eight. "Have a good breakfast?" I asked Cindy.

"I guess you've never been locked up," she said. "The food here tastes like shit." She was right—it was a stupid question. Still, her good-humored response at least assured me that today she felt more relaxed.

After talking generally about her father's behavior, I asked her if she could remember the first time he touched her in a way she now knew was inappropriate. "The very first time?" she asked incredulously. "I can't do that because it probably started before I remember it starting. . . . Anyway, I was about nine I guess. I didn't have any idea that he was doing anything bad to me, because he was always physical with us. . . . He'd always be coming up behind me or Nancy or Kerri and tickle us—those sorts of things."

"So I was in the living room watching TV and my mom and my sisters were out shopping someplace. He came in and said he had a headache or stiff neck or something like that, and 'would you be a good girl and rub Daddy's neck?'

"I did it, and then he asked me if I wanted a back rub and I said yes. He started rubbing all over my body and not just my neck."

Cindy stopped talking for a moment and stared into the corner of the room. Was she angry? Sad? Maybe just emotionally drained? I couldn't tell. "Do you want to stop for a while? Get a soda or something?"

"No," she said. "It's okay, I was just thinking about something else."

"What?" I said.

"Oh, nothing. It was really nothing."

I didn't push her.

"Anyway," she continued, "he put his hand in my underwear and rubbed around between my legs. I just thought it was part of the back rub. I don't remember it as hurting or anything. . . . The back rubs became a normal thing between us. I never knew if he was giving back rubs to my sisters. . . . We would only do it when nobody was around. . . . And sometimes he would give me rubs when he came in to say good-night to me.

"One day he asked me if I ever told anybody about our back rubs. I told him no. Then he said that I shouldn't tell anybody, and it would be a secret just between me and him. I remember that very well, because I was always jealous of my older sisters. Nancy was fourteen and Kerri was sixteen and so they of course got to do things teenagers do. I was always feeling left out when they wouldn't take me places. So when Dad told me that we were going to have this secret from everybody else in the family, it made me feel very special."

These "back rub" sessions remained pretty much the same until one late-summer evening, right before Cindy was to start the seventh grade. "I was rubbing his shoulders, and he turned over and said he wanted to show me another way to relax him. He unzipped his pants, and I remember being scared by his penis," Cindy said. "He just told me to hold it and rub it. I didn't know about climaxing, so when this white stuff came out after I rubbed him, I thought I hurt him or something. After he wiped it up, he took me in his arms and said how much he loved me for making him feel so good." Much to her relief, after this incident Cindy got a reprieve from her father's touching and poking. Though she hated masturbating him, it was much less unpleasant than having him squeezing her nipples or sticking his fingers in her vagina. The reprieve was, however, short-lived.

"When I was fourteen and a half, he did *it*," Cindy said angrily. Father and daughter had gone by themselves late that summer to the family beach house; he had come into her bedroom to say good-night. "He told me that we were going to try something different from the usual thing now that I was getting older. I knew what he was going to say, and I was just hoping I wasn't right. I was right. After he told me to move over in the bed and lie on my back, I told him I was scared. He said, 'You know I wouldn't hurt you, princess, don't you?' I can still hear him saying it—'You know I wouldn't hurt you.' I didn't know what to do. He opened my nightgown, and he just lay on top of me and did it."

As frequently happens in cases of incest, the next day Henry paid a bribe—he went to a jewelry store and bought his daughter a $300 pair of gold earrings. Not only was he celebrating his "new" relationship with Cindy, but he was hoping as well to assuage any of her resentment and buy her silence. Cindy was as dazzled by the jewelry as she was by the candlelight dinner later that evening. Feeling he had won her over, he came into her room later that night and forced her to have intercourse again. "On the drive home the next day, I told him that I felt bad about what we did," Cindy said. "He told me that I shouldn't feel bad because it was just a way of showing love for each other. Then he told me how great I made him feel and that I should feel good about it. He asked me if he made me feel good, and I said yes because I knew that's what he wanted to hear. But I didn't feel anything but terrible the whole time."

That evening Cindy went out to dinner with her parents and of course said nothing about the weekend, except how great it had been. Cindy went to sleep that night very confused. "You see, he was always right about everything," she said emphatically. "And he never would do anything to hurt me. He never hit me once when I was a little girl, and I can almost count the times he even yelled at me."

Following the trip to the shore, Henry Baker did not touch her for what she said seemed like forever. Cindy thought her father had seen the light and would never again make those late-night visits to her room. No one will ever know what happened: perhaps he had second thoughts, maybe he was even scared. Whatever the reason, it was not enough to make him permanently stop. The nightly forays into his daughter's bedroom started again shortly after Thanksgiving of that year. "My mom was always working or having meetings in the evening, so it was just me and him. It got so that I was afraid to come home after school. . . . So I decided after thinking about it to try to reason with Dad."

Cindy figured if she broached the subject when he was working, she would have more success convincing him to leave her alone than if she did it when he was on top of her. "After dinner one night I walked into his upstairs office. I just stood at the door for a few minutes watching him work. And then I said something like, 'Dad, this isn't right. We shouldn't be doing what we're doing.' I couldn't even say the word. He looked at me like I hurt him. Then he said that he thought I liked the time we spent together. I told him that it wasn't the being with him that upset me, it was the stuff we did at night. That made him angry, but he didn't yell at me. He was trying to control himself. He asked me if I trusted him, and I said I did. . . . I didn't know what [else] to say back to him. . . . I left his office and that was my talk with my dad.

"When he came in to say good-night that evening, he asked me if I was thinking about telling anybody about what *we* were doing with each other. I told him that I wasn't. Then he said that talking to anyone about it will cause terrible problems for everybody in the family. And if the police got involved, he said he could go to jail and I could be taken out of the house. Then he started to cry and told me how much he loved and needed me. I never saw him cry before and so I started to cry. I felt like I hurt him or something. I felt sorry for him." Predictably, however, the forced sex started again several days later.

Though perhaps he hadn't consciously planned that reaction to her complaint, he could not have given a more perfect answer. Exploiting his daughter's ignorance and inexperience would no longer work, so he turned up the flame. By invoking prison and family in the same breath, he was tying her very survival and the survival of her mother and sisters to her continued silence. More insidious still, he had deftly shifted the psychological burden of the relationship to his daughter in that the incest was now her problem—one, in her eyes, that she had helped to create. A pattern often seen in such cases, the tandem processes of physical rape and psychological intimidation bind the child's emotions in a Gordian knot, thus leaving the young girl so debilitated she does exactly as her father wants.

"I couldn't tell Mom. She just wouldn't be able to handle it. She likes things very neat and ordered. It would have blown her mind. Besides, she probably would have said it was all my fault. And I guess it was kinda. [So] I tried to learn how to put up with it by thinking about other things when he was doing it to me . . . putting my mind outside my body. From the moment he'd lie on top of me till he was off me, I tried drifting away. It was something like playing the game 'make-believe.' You make yourself think you're someone else living in a different place. . . . I was doing *it* for my family."

Her eyes glazed over and her voice drifted off with these last few words. It was obvious that she was reexperiencing a particularly horrible incident. It was time for a break.

When we returned to the interview room about twenty minutes later, my first question was one I knew she would be asked on the stand. "You're a very intelligent, well-spoken person," I said. "Did you ever tell anybody what your dad was doing to you?"

She physically recoiled at the question. "It would have been *terrible* to tell," she said dismissively. "Besides, who is going to believe me? . . . I heard about child abuse authorities, but I didn't know who they were or what they would do if I called them. My dad is a smart man and has very good lawyers. Nothing would have worked. . . . I knew if I told anybody that nothing would really happen."

Amazed that she had revealed as much as she had that morning, I didn't want to push Cindy any further. Before leaving, she said to me, "You're coming back, right? I mean, you're not mad at me, are you?"

"Why should I be mad?" I said.

"Because I yelled at you."

"You're allowed to get mad at me. And don't worry, of course, I'm coming back."

She smiled slightly and waved good-bye.

The remainder of the day was spent back at my hotel room reviewing all the material Halpern had given me on Henry Baker. While many perpetrators of incest share certain traits, such as narcissistic personalities for example, they are indistinguishable in their public appearance or behavior. As John Crewdson noted in the *Sexual Abuse of Children in America,* "it was not very many years ago that incest was thought to be principally confined to what Tennyson called 'the crowded couch in the warrens of the poor,' to urban ghettos or isolated rural families in the hills of southern Kentucky." The meteoric rise in the reports of child abuse in communities throughout the nation through the 1980s shattered these preconceptions.

Perpetrators of incest attend church, play on the company softball team, and hold legislative office. They can be dirt-poor or filthy rich. They pay their taxes, vote, and have rarely violated any law other than the speed limit. They look just like everyone else. There could be one on your block.

Henry Baker, however, was more than an "anybody." At fifty, he was a successful entrepreneur who built shopping malls and apartment complexes. Despite his wealth, Baker had never forgotten his humble beginnings, giving generously to charitable causes and actively participating in a variety of community affairs. Most notably, Baker's pet project was an organization that provided toys, tickets to the circus, and other surprises to critically ill children. "Nobody is going to say squat against my dad," Cindy had said to Halpern during their first interview; she was right.

As I might have expected, not a single person came forward to report the slightest suspicion of the sexual abuse. Not one relative, friend, neighbor, or business associate said anything in their interviews with the police that could be construed as the least bit negative about him. There was, if anything, uniform praise.

The case interview summaries prepared by the homicide investigators read like flowery eulogies to a fallen hero.

"I knew Henry, Elaine, and the girls for at least fifteen years, and you couldn't find a more devoted husband and father. Elaine not only lost her husband, our community lost an important man."

"I was friends with her oldest sister, Kerri. They just seemed to have the perfect family. I knew him since I was a little girl. He was the ideal dad."

Unfortunately, Cindy's classmates and friends were equally in the dark about her plight. It was not surprising that none of her peers knew about her problem, because Cindy was a loner. There was, however, a time when Cindy had such a busy social life that Henry put a phone in her room.

Throughout grade school, Cindy had been outgoing and vivacious, especially close friends with four girls who lived within blocks of her home. They ate lunch at the same table every day and spent their afternoons at each other's homes playing in the yard or getting in trouble in mom's closet.

Dierdre, now sixteen and a half years old, with closely cropped, jet-black dyed hair, an earring in her nose, and ambitions to be a rock star, was one of the girls in this group. We spoke the morning after my second interview with Cindy. Dierdre hadn't wanted to meet in the law office, so I conducted the interview at a taco stand that was a local high school hangout.

"The thing that blows my mind about this is that we all admired Cindy," she said, puffing a nonfilter cigarette. "I mean, she had the coolest dad. The rest of our dads were . . . well, you know, pretty typical as dads go. . . . Mr. Baker took us to the mall, bowling, anything we wanted. My dad would never even allow five twelve-year-old girls to sit in his parked car!"

"If you were such good friends in grade school, why did you drift apart in junior high?" I said.

"We didn't drift apart," Dierdre said. *"She* drifted away from *us*. It wasn't like we changed schools or moved away or anything. But starting in the end of the seventh grade, Cindy stopped hanging out with us."

"Did you have any idea why?" I said.

"No, not really. We just thought she wanted to spend more time studying. But some of us thought that Cindy started acting snotty. Like she was too good for us."

The day before, Cindy had revealed something that at least partially explained her "drifting" away from her tight-knit group of friends. "In seventh grade, my friends started talking about sex," Cindy had said, as if annoyed. "It wasn't like any of them were doing it. They would just talk about how good-looking this boy or that boy was. Typical stuff that would make us all giggle. . . . I guess I started thinking that what I was doing with Dad was probably like sex. . . . I usually tried to be quiet when my friends were talking about it, because I was afraid I'd let something slip. My friends thought I was just embarrassed. . . . If they only knew."

"Cindy could have had a million friends in school if she wanted, but she just wanted to be by herself. . . . Of all the girls in our group, I stayed in contact with her the longest," Dierdre said. "I pretty much stopped right after she tried to run away from home. It wasn't like I thought what she did was so bad, but she just seemed to completely close down."

As soon as the interview was over, I walked over to the phone in the corner of the taco shop and called Halpern. "What the hell is wrong with you? How come you didn't tell me that she tried to run away from home?"

"What are you talking about?" he said defensively.

"I just spoke with one of her old friends, and she told me Cindy tried to run away," I said, irritated.

"Oh, yeah, I heard something about that. Cindy didn't make a big deal about it. But she really didn't get anywhere," he said. "From what she told me, it really wasn't a serious attempt."

Whether she got one mile or one hundred miles, the fact that Cindy tried to run was critical, especially since there was such a paucity of corroborative evidence. Running away from home, while not in and of itself positive proof that Cindy was sexually abused, was evidence that there was *something* wrong in Cindy's relationship with her parents.

Later that afternoon I arrived at the detention center. "It's going to be a long interview. You don't have any pressing plans for tonight, do you?" I asked.

"Is that supposed to be funny?"

"Yes," I said, "but you don't have to laugh." She shook her head as if I were a little crazy.

"Your old friend Dierdre told me that you tried running away. Can you tell me what happened?"

"Oh, you spoke with Didi," she said, suddenly curious. "What did she say about me?"

"Nothing bad, if that's what you mean. She just said you once tried running away."

"Well, she's right . . . but it wasn't a big thing," Cindy said. "I was about fifteen. Mom had just left on another buying trip. I was sitting in my room doing my homework and thinking about what was going to happen that night. It was going to be me and him, just me and him for three and a half weeks. All I knew was that he was coming home that evening, and I didn't want to be there. I mean, no matter how I looked at it, my dad was having sex with me."

Cindy briefly considered going to stay with Kerri, but decided against it because it would have meant telling her sister why she left. Instead, she went down to the Greyhound station and bought a bus ticket for California. After two hours on the bus her fear of being on her own took over; she got off and called her father, begging him to pick her up. "I waited over five hours . . . and guys were coming up and trying to pick me up. When he came through the door, I could tell he was upset. He told me that I worried him and that I owed him an apology for what I did. I apologized, but it didn't seem to do anything. He was quiet the whole trip back. When I went to bed that night, I couldn't remember feeling more horrible. . . . The next morning he came into my room like nothing happened. He said that he wasn't angry anymore. Then he got into bed with me."

But this was not the last time Cindy tried to get away, I knew. "Was the bus incident the only time you tried to signal that you were in trouble?" I asked softly. She looked away immediately, guessing that I had found out, too, about her most serious escape attempt.

"I don't want to talk about it," she said quickly, putting her head in her hands. At last she looked up. "Okay. So it happened early last year. I was mad at myself that I couldn't stop what was going on. And I was mad and hurt that nobody was helping me. . . . It seemed every day I was feeling worse. It didn't seem to matter if he was doing it to me or not. I just hated myself for letting it happen."

Tearfully, but with rage growing steadily in her voice, she continued, "On the outside I had to be this intelligent, happy teenager, but I wasn't that at all. It took lots of energy to even get out of bed. I also started getting sick a lot. I was always really healthy, and then all of a sudden I started getting diarrhea all the time. [And] I was so nauseated that I couldn't keep anything down. I would have to go vomit between classes. . . . Anyway, I first thought, 'This is it, I'm pregnant.' I didn't tell Dad. I went down to this clinic and got a test. Well, I wasn't. So the doctor told me all my pains and throwing up were probably from being under too much tension. He was right about that one, wasn't he?" she said, half-smiling.

"Anyway, he tried to be nice and help me," she continued. "He asked me if I was nervous or was worried about something. I just couldn't tell the truth. . . . It was a Friday night and I was in my bathroom vomiting. I couldn't stop, and I started crying. I just felt awful. . . . I went into my sister's bathroom across the hall and got a bottle of old pain medication, and I took whatever was in the bottle. Anyway, the next thing I remember was in an ambulance with my dad."

As result of the suicide attempt, Henry and Elaine placed Cindy in an exclusive private psychiatric hospital. The psychiatrists diagnosed her as being depressed, but they were unable to identify a specific cause beyond anxiety about leaving home for college the next year. In all the hours of evaluation and therapy, the subject of abuse in any form never came up.

Though Cindy did not volunteer the information, that the doctors' failure to uncover the truth is, I am convinced, indicative of the medical community's wider failure to recognize and become more sophisticated in dealing with abuse in the way they have come to understand and treat other sociomedical problems such as drug addiction and venereal disease. Despite the strides made since the early 1970s in the identification of sexual abuse, research is still in a relatively nascent stage. As a consequence, numerous mental health professionals lack a sophisticated understanding of the problem.

"Mainstream psychiatry," Van der Kolk writes in *Psychological Trauma*, "has usually studied individuals as self-contained entities, relatively divorced from the social contexts within which they mature and thrive. Despite the abundance of family studies and the prominence of social psychiatry in the 1960s, clinicians have not consistently recognized the virtual inseparability between individuals and their social frameworks." This, in a nutshell, is a basic problem thwarting greater understanding of abuse in this community. Further, he notes, diagnosing sexual abuse is more difficult because it "is often obscured by chronic depression, self-destructive behavior, and drug and alcohol abuse."

Cindy remained in the psychiatric program for forty-five days, living on a locked ward. Though she received no help for her problem, she did like one aspect of the facility. "That place was full of some very strange people, but it was better than being with him at home. At least when I went to sleep, I didn't have to worry about him coming into my room."

Cindy described the period immediately after her release from the hospital as being some of the best times she had had since she was a young child. "It was the way things should have been all along. Like things are supposed to be," she said longingly. Henry became a regular father, and there was no touching of any kind. I can only assume that he felt remorseful, judging himself responsible for her suicide attempt. His fear of exposure might have motivated the change, but I doubt it. Hadn't she just proved conclusively that she would rather take her own life than reveal the truth?

Unfortunately, this idyllic time was too good to last, ending abruptly after several months when Cindy's mom went away on another extended business trip.

"Nothing had happened with Dad in a few months, so I wasn't worried that she was going away for a while," Cindy began.

"Things were really great for a few days. . . . Sunday started out as a normal evening. Even a good one. We went out to eat and talked about college, which was on my mind since I was graduating a year early. I was really nervous about where I was going to get accepted. When we were driving home, he told me he had a special graduation present—a car. I was so happy I cried. . . . When we got home, I went to watch TV in the sitting room. He came in and sat down very close to me on the couch. He told me how much he was going to miss me when I left for school. Then he put his arms around me and started to kiss my neck. I tried to wriggle out, but he just held me tighter. Then he put his hand up my skirt.

" 'Please do it tonight,' he said. It was like he was begging me. He was saying this would be the last time and that sort of thing. . . . I kept saying no and trying to pull his hand away from between my legs. . . . He was trying to go under my panties. I started to cry, and then I shoved him hard and was able to push myself away. I don't remember exactly what I said, but it was something like, 'Can't you leave me alone? I just want to watch TV.' As I ran up the steps, he was yelling at me and saying things he never said before. He called me a 'bitch' and a 'cunt' and a lot of other names. He said I didn't show him any respect . . . didn't give him anything in return for how he treated me."

Cindy had maintained her composure to this point. But now she started to cry, and her sobs echoed through the small room. A guard knocked on the door to ask if everything was all right. I nodded and looked at my watch, shocked to see that we had been talking for over four and a half hours.

"Let's take a break," I said, pushing a glass of water across the table.

"No!" she said defiantly. "I'm okay."

She wiped her tears with her left sleeve. "I'll admit it," she resumed, "I was mad when I ran upstairs. Really mad. I knew I couldn't do this anymore. I walked past the closet where we kept the shotgun, pulled it out, and went into my room. If he came in, I was going to tell him that he was going to have to stop it. I thought I could scare him into leaving me alone. It must have been about ten or fifteen minutes later, maybe even a little longer, that I heard him coming up the steps. When I saw the doorknob turn, I raised the gun up. I *only wanted* to be listened to.

"He took a step into the room and turned to me. I fired before he said anything. I don't remember firing the second time, but I guess I did.

"I stood over him and couldn't believe that was him lying there. I started screaming, 'Get up! Please get up!' Then I started shaking him, telling him I was sorry. He didn't move. . . . I went back to the closet to find more shells, but there weren't any. I was going to shoot myself. . . . I went back to him and held him in my arms for a long time. Then I called the operator and told them to send an ambulance. 'I think my dad is dead. I killed him.' "

"I killed my daddy, I killed my daddy," was what Cindy had, in fact, wailed to the police officers as they tried to pick her up from the floor. Though she was far from strong, it took two hefty men to wrest her away from her father's body. Cindy was handcuffed and rushed to an emergency room because she was so covered in blood that the police thought she was wounded, too.

Back at the station for questioning, Cindy waived her right to remain silent, but then said little to the two detectives. "It was an accident. I really didn't mean to do it," she told them.

"But why did you have the gun in the first place?" the detective asked. "Was there an argument about something?"

"No, not really. I don't know what happened. I just took it out to look at it," she told them. "He came in my room to speak to me, and it went off."

Al Trubo, a soft-spoken, burly detective, was patient with Cindy. "It was obvious she wasn't telling us everything," he said later, "but I just had this feeling she really wanted to do the right thing."

Two and a half hours after her arrest, Cindy, by this time hysterical with grief and rage, told the investigators that she killed her father because he was going to rape her, and that he had been forcing her to have intercourse with him since she was about thirteen.

Trubo immediately called the child abuse and sex crimes unit, and Cindy was rushed back to the hospital.

A thorough gynecological examination revealed no indication of a recent rape or for that matter, any other kind of sexual assault. There was no semen in her vagina or anal cavity or anywhere on her body, underwear, or clothes, and a combing of her pubic hairs did not turn up foreign hair as would have been expected if she'd been recently raped. Similarly, the coroner later found no indication that Henry had recently ejaculated.

Cindy had no scratches or bruises on the inside of her thighs, or anywhere in the pubic region. There was only one bruise on her whole body; her left shoulder was swollen and discolored from the kick of the shotgun.

Following the routine procedure for sexual assault cases, a police officer took detailed thirty-five-millimeter photos of Cindy's naked body to document any injuries. Next Cindy's panties, skirt, and other clothing were carefully examined for rips or tears; nothing was found.

Throughout her recounting of her arrest, Cindy's voice was dreamlike, as if from a distance. Her last words to me that evening were, "It was like it was all happening to someone else. . . . Only when they brought me here, and I lay down in the bed, did I realize it was all happening to me."

On my last morning in town, Halpern took me to the courthouse to meet Judge Denton and the prosecutor, Ms. La Platta. The meeting was held in the judge's chambers.

When I walked in, the judge walked around his desk and welcomed me cordially. Denton was about forty-five and had been on the bench for just two years. He was a refreshing change from the stodgy judges I often encounter, judges who have a need to be worshiped. Denton made a point of telling me that he had never had an out-of-state practitioner in his courtroom, and he kindly offered to answer any questions I might have about local court rules.

La Platta didn't even get out of her chair when Halpern

and I came in the room, nor did she extend her hand to greet me. When we shook hands, she looked away.

"You are going to make a formal motion to participate in the case, aren't you?" she asked coldly. That was her only comment during the entire meeting.

"Of course," I said with a smile, trying not to escalate the tension.

As we walked out of the courtroom, I said to my gracious adversary, "I understand from John that you've already ruled out a plea bargain. Is that still your position?"

"Yes."

"Would you mind telling me the reasoning?"

"Listen," she said, suddenly tough, "the grand jury indicted her on second-degree murder. Personally I think they should've hit her with first. We're not going below second, and I seriously doubt that you or Mr. Halpern are going to let your client plead to second. . . . I don't see the sexual abuse playing a part in it, because she wasn't abused. Look at her. She had smarts, lots of money—the works. If it was so bad for her, why didn't she get some help, tell somebody, or just leave? Thousands of kids are sexually abused every year, and they find other ways of dealing with the problem. We see them every day in our office."

Halpern tugged at my sleeve to insure I didn't get into an argument with her. Now I saw why he was worried about La Platta. But it was not her intransigence that bothered me: I regularly encounter prosecutors equally pugnacious and uncompromising. What irked me was her insinuation that Cindy's wealth and intelligence somehow made it more likely that she would have found help.

I was infuriated at this patronizing assumption, so common among prosecutors. I can understand how a person unfamiliar with the detrimental effects of child abuse could believe that bright, rich teenagers are somehow in a vastly superior position to help themselves as compared to poor kids. But district attorneys, most of whom have, at some point in their careers, prosecuted child abusers and defended abused children, should know better.

Anyone who has spent ten minutes interviewing an abused child knows intelligence and logic have little to do with a child's ability to report abuse. Cindy was a solid-B student, but had she been the valedictorian it would have made no damned difference in her ability to deal with the confusion, embarrassment, and intimidation engendered by the abuse. Just because an adolescent can master advanced calculus or read *The Iliad* in Greek does not mean she is in a superior position to understand, let alone report her father to the authorities. The reasoning abilities that allow a child to perform well on the S.A.T.'s are useless for helping her cope with an abusive parent. Above all, the decision to remain, run, or report is one based on emotion, not logic.

Second, there is no correlation between a child's economic status and her ability to deal positively with any form of abuse. Child abuse cuts across all class boundaries, and it is ridiculous to believe that wealth can shield children from its ravages. In fact, a particularly cruel paradox of our times is that middle-class and affluent youth are, I strongly believe, the *least* able to protect themselves from parental abuse.

The more money a family has, the more they are able to maintain control over their lives, particularly their privacy, and thus to protect themselves from the scrutiny of others. Middle-class and affluent families tend to live in more isolated surroundings than other members of society. Their apartment walls are thicker, their fences higher, limiting access by others to their lives. In such an environment, family problems are more easily hidden.

Money is a metaphorical as well as physical barrier to scrutiny, for teachers, social service agencies, and police feel less inclined to interfere or take action when the family is rich and by extension, respected and powerful. Moreover, these agencies function much differently in poor areas than they do in wealthy areas. In low-income neighborhoods, for example, the primary purpose of the police is to monitor the activities of the residents, protecting them from each other, while in upper-income neighborhoods their function is primarily to protect the residents from outside intruders. Similarly, most social service agencies are specifically oriented to serving the needs of lower-income people. Outreach in wealthy communities is almost a contradiction in terms. Child abuse information posters appear in public schools and public health clinics with much greater frequency than they do in wealthy public and private schools or the paneled waiting rooms of pediatricians and family practitioners who cater to the middle and upper class.

It has been my experience as well that low-income persons have a much more sophisticated knowledge of how to deal with the police and social service agencies than other groups. The average upper-income person lives a life so divorced from public service agencies that approaching one for help is difficult even when the need is dire.

Discrepancies in the pattern of abuse reporting (especially sexual abuse) seem to confirm these assumptions: nationwide, the vast majority of sexual abuse reports concern low- and moderate-income people. Yet experts are unanimous in their agreement that sexual abuse is fairly evenly distributed in the population. Illustrating this underreporting, today adults who report sexual abuse as children are disproportionately middle- and upper-class white females.

In a bizarre twist of fate, middle- and upper-class abused children are perhaps *more* vulnerable than other abused children. While in all other respects they have a better life than lower-income children, their cries for help are heard least. I believe it is these differences between socioeconomic groups that explain in part why my clients are disproportionately middle and upper class. Because they live more isolated lives and are less able to take advantage of public social services, the opportunities for intervention are severely restricted, thus making the eventual explosion more likely than in a lower-income family.

After working on her case for six months, we still had no definitive proof that Cindy had been sexually abused. Though Henry subtly threatened and manipulated his daughter, it was Cindy's silence that was his insurance policy, a policy that continued in full force, ironically, after his death.

The police had done a thorough and, I thought, evenhanded investigation. They conducted detailed interviews with dozens of Henry Baker's business associates and friends, and with Cindy's friends and classmates. As they had found in their preliminary investigation, no one had observed, or at least admitted observing, anything that even hinted at his having an incestuous relationship with his daughter. Though one of the sex crimes investigators privately told me that she believed that Cindy was telling the truth, the department's official position was that Cindy was not the victim of a sexual assault.

Though what we found was not of monumental significance, we did uncover two pieces of potentially important corroborating evidence.

About three months after I returned from visiting Cindy, Halpern sent me copies of all Cindy's academic and medical records. There was nothing remarkable in her school records. The only fact I noted was that from the eighth through the twelfth grades, Cindy seemed to spend an inordinate amount of time at the nurse's office. During her last academic year, she had visited the nurse sixteen times, most frequently complaining of headaches and nausea. When I spoke with her mother about these visits, she told me that Cindy became easily stressed in school, which Mrs. Baker attributed to the fact that she was a high achiever. Her mother, however, was unaware how frequently Cindy had visited the nurse.

Mrs. Baker had also not known that, at fifteen, Cindy had been treated by a doctor for a series of urinary tract infections. When I spoke to Dr. Bailor, he said that the infections were not necessarily caused by sexual activity.

"Did you ask her if she was sexually active?" I asked over the phone.

"No, I didn't think it was necessary. Actually, it didn't cross my mind to ask," he said defensively.

"But it's possible that it was caused by intercourse, isn't it?" I inquired.

"It's possible," he said curtly. "But she never gave me any indication that she was engaging in sexual behavior."

While evidence of a urinary tract infection is not a positive confirmation of intercourse, in the absence of proof that the child had sex with any other male, its existence lends credence to the belief that sexual activity did occur. Cindy said that she had never had intercourse with anyone other than her father. And according to all the investigations (including that of the police), Cindy had only had one date in high school, and that over a year after she was treated for the infections. Coincidentally, it was the one date with Mitchell Clark that provided the other useful piece of corroborative evidence.

Mitchell met Cindy at the local library. She had just turned sixteen; he was a skinny seventeen-year-old with curly brown hair and wire-rim glasses.

When Cindy first told me about Mitchell, she was very blasé. "He was a nice guy, but I wasn't very interested in him."

"That's all?"

"Yeah. We went out once to some movie, but that's about it," she said offhandedly.

Clark's version of their encounter was slightly different.

"I spoke with her several times at the library. She seemed like a nice enough person, so I asked her out," he said. "It was all pretty innocent, until I dropped her off at her home.

"Her old man, the guy that she killed," he continued, "was standing in the front door when we drove up. . . . As I walked her up the walk, I saw he had this expression on his face like he was pissed off or something. She had this kind of scared look on her face as she went in. I said something like, 'I'll call you,' but she didn't even turn around. She just walked in with her head down. . . . Her old man slams the door. I stood outside for a second after they walked in. I was a little worried about her. Then I hear this yelling—'Well, was it good? Huh! Talk to me! Did he try to do anything to you? . . . I bet you screwed him! Did you screw him? Tell me what happened!'

"I split," Mitchell said. "I didn't know what was going on, but I wasn't going to call her again. Too, too weird."

Cindy denied that her father yelled at her: he was merely upset because she was late, she explained. I couldn't imagine that she was lying, but Clark had no reason to lie, either. Perhaps, I thought, Cindy had simply blocked out her memory of the incident because it was too painful. What I did know, however, is that it was common for sexually abusive fathers to become jealous of their teenage daughters' suitors. In most cases involving patricides like Cindy's, the daughters had been routinely berated or beaten by their fathers after they came home from dates.

Even without the medical records and the dating incident, our expert, psychologist Dr. Myra Anderson, was convinced that Cindy had been molested. Though she specialized in treating sexually abused girls, we chose the fifty-seven-year-old professor of clinical psychology to assist us because six years earlier she had created the evaluation program used by the local district attorney's child-abuse/sex-crimes unit. From time to time, in fact, she still conducted child abuse and sex crimes training seminars for the DA's office. By choosing someone from their own backyard, I hoped to blunt the effect of La Platta's inevitable attack.

Dr. Anderson was not bothered by the lack of corroborating evidence because she didn't expect to find any. She conducted six three-hour interview and evaluation sessions with Cindy, but became persuaded of Cindy's honesty and true suffering after her first interview. Anderson's primary finding was that Cindy suffered from posttraumatic-stress disorder and a dissociative disorder, specifically a depersonalization disorder.

"Often sexually (and physically) abused children and adolescents," she wrote in explaining the dissociative disorder, "disengage or remove themselves from reality in order to numb the emotional and physical pain of the abuse." Van der Kolk makes a similar, more general observation: "Dissociation is adaptive: it allows relatively normal functioning for the duration of the traumatic event and leaves a large part of the personality unaffected by the trauma."

While her father was having sex with her, Cindy "was able to in essence transport herself to another world, a safer place," Anderson wrote. "Cindy was aware of this ability and did it almost on cue when her father initiated the sex. In order to protect herself, she had to create two dads. One was the ideal dad, and the other was this evil man who made her his sex slave."

At the outset of the intercourse, Cindy could exercise some control over when she would drift off. "But as she got older and the sexual assaults increased, she was less able to control when she went in and out. . . . Towards the end, Cindy frequently felt an air of unreality about her life," Dr. Anderson wrote.

Aside from the specific clinical diagnosis, I needed Dr. Anderson to identify the immediate and critical circumstances of Cindy's life that led her to kill her father. Anderson pointed to two basic factors: Cindy's isolation and her fear on the evening of the homicide that her father was going to hurt her.

Dr. Anderson told me that she could not remember a patient who so "thoroughly loved and hated her father at the same time." Cindy was immobilized by her father's omnipotence.

Cindy idolized Henry, as a father and as a man. "Cindy's identity," the doctor told me, "was so wrapped up in her father's identity [that] she was convinced that to hurt him [by reporting him] was to hurt herself. His control over her was so absolute that all it took was one threat to silence her forever. . . . She never really rid herself of the illusion that she was daddy's little girl, and that he would never do anything to harm her."

Cindy was also very much aware that her father wielded immense influence in the community, and therefore she logically assumed that reporting him would do no good. However, this feeling of futility only fueled the fires of hate engendered by the actual abuse itself. Despite the ability to "put her mind somewhere else" during the sexual attacks, the pressure was steadily building in her each day. She found an outlet in running away, a healthy step, but her father's strong influence and her own fear pulled her back to him. It was not the fear of being alone in a strange place that made her get off the bus, Dr. Anderson thought, but the simple fact that she felt she needed her father.

Unfortunately, after her return, her isolation only grew deeper, as if giving in and calling him to pick her up brought out the essential hopelessness of her situation. "With no recognizable outlet for expressing her feelings," the doctor told me, "the pressure on her increased to a point where suicide seemed the only alternative."

On the evening of the homicide, "Cindy was in a heightened state of fear," Anderson said. As we saw with Tim and Mike, sexually abused and physically abused children often become aware that there is a pattern to their abuse and can predict how, when, and for how long they will be abused. This ability allows them to cope better with their predicament.

When Henry Baker forced his hands up his daughter's skirt, then cursed her when she fled upstairs, Cindy's coping mechanism was thrown off course. Though he had not touched her since she had come home from the hospital, she knew that this brutal screaming assault was not normal for him. He had never before grabbed her, nor had he ever accosted her when she told him that she didn't want to have intercourse. It was certainly the first time she had had to fight him off, and his curses only terrified her more.

The pattern had fundamentally altered, Dr. Anderson observed. "When Cindy ran up those steps, she literally could not predict what her father was going to do."

Based upon all of our evidence and Dr. Anderson's findings, we had two strong defense strategies. We could argue that Cindy was not guilty by reason of self-defense: under the circumstances as they appeared to her that night, it was reasonable for her to assume that her father was going to follow her upstairs and rape her. Based upon his violent assault downstairs minutes earlier, it was reasonable for Cindy to assume not only that her father would rape her, but that he would rape her inflicting serious bodily injury.

Alternatively, we could argue that Cindy was guilty of no more than voluntary manslaughter. The attack on the couch could be construed as adequate provocation, with the subsequent homicide committed during the heat of passion.

Fortunately, I did not have to test the strength of my theories, for the forces of nature intervened—Ms. La Platta got pregnant soon after Cindy's arrest and was forced to resign from the case ten weeks before trial. Assistant DA Don Brunswick got the case, and we soon discovered to our relief that he and La Platta were worlds apart in their thinking on the issues. Brunswick immediately let Halpern know that he was looking at the case through "new glasses." He wanted to interview Cindy with Halpern present and also to speak with Anderson to begin a reconsideration of the charges.

Three weeks after the interviews, we got together to discuss a possible plea bargain, meeting on a cold Friday afternoon in Brunswick's cramped office in the old wing of the courthouse. About thirty-six years old, with short, dark-red hair and a ruddy complexion, Brunswick turned out to be genial and open, refreshing in his willingness to listen.

The mounted bass and trout, the nature photos on his walls—these testified to his love of the outdoors. One photo, larger than the others, hung directly behind his cluttered desk, immediately captivated me. In it, he was standing next to his twelve-year-old daughter, who, with a proud smile from ear to ear, held a tiny fish on a line. "It's the way it should have been for Cindy," I thought to myself.

Though Brunswick could probably have persuaded a jury of twelve honest and true souls to convict Cindy of second-degree murder, he offered us a generous deal instead. She would plead guilty to manslaughter and then be sentenced as a youthful offender. Rather than being warehoused in an adult prison, this meant she could get specialized, therapeutic treatment at a state-contracted facility. Had she been tried and convicted of second-degree murder, she faced a *minimum* penalty of twenty years in prison. As a youthful offender, however, the *maximum* confinement would be four years—until her twenty-first birthday.

Brunswick went the plea bargain route, he told us frankly, for a single reason: he believed that Cindy was telling the truth. Before he was assigned to the homicide division, he had been in charge of child abuse prosecutions, five years spent prosecuting fathers for raping, sodomizing, and otherwise brutalizing their children. Abusers, he knew, came in all shapes and sizes; and he was particularly unimpressed by the size of a person's pocketbook or their reputation.

"Though I believe she was sexually abused," he said, reclining in his high-back leather chair, "I can't drop the charges any further. I don't think any of us will know what happened that night, but one thing is clear—there was absolutely no evidence of any rape. Something happened," he continued, "but whatever it was, it wasn't rape, and she should have had the presence of mind to think about what she was doing and put the gun away."

Yet something bothered him more than the specific circumstances of the crime. "I've prosecuted I don't know how many fathers, uncles, and cousins for sexually violating their relations. One of the last cases I had before leaving the unit was a guy who sold videos of himself having sex with his seven-year-old. A real scumbag . . . And I'll be the first to admit that I would have liked to flip the switch myself on some of these sons of bitches for what they did. But as evil as some of these guys are, we can't let the victims, no matter how cruelly they've been treated, take the law into their hands."

He expected a response, but I didn't bother arguing with him because he had given us a terrific offer. He had carefully considered the case, and I knew we weren't going to change his mind. Though we left that day telling him that he would have our client's response the next day, I'm sure he already knew the answer.

To my mind, what Cindy had done was not vigilantism. From her perspective, she was forced to act because her family, the community, and the law had not or could not protect her. Law enforcement and prosecutorial agencies do a fairly decent job of protecting banks from being robbed, but they do an absolutely abysmal job of shielding children from the criminal excesses of their parents. The family is, unfortunately for children, a veritable no-man's-land when it comes to law enforcement.

Avoiding trial was clearly a partial "victory" for Cindy, sparing her the stress that would inevitably accompany such an event. It was painful enough to tell her story in private to those who had her best interests at heart; she was petrified at testifying before a jury, let alone a full house of spectators, family, and friends. As well, if convicted of anything more than manslaughter, she would not have been eligible to receive treatment—something she urgently needed to survive.

Despite the fear, embarrassment, and insecurity, Cindy would probably have made an excellent witness. More than anything else, I knew, it was her emotional two-hour interview with Brunswick that persuaded him to offer the plea. Cindy's recall for specific detail was better than that of most children who have been sexually victimized, but this was a double-edged sword. While it proved invaluable in preparing her defense, it was also a curse because retrieving the past meant reliving the suffering.

In the months before the homicide, Cindy had had flashbacks and nightmares. The flashbacks were of sexual assaults that occurred when she was a little girl; after she was locked up, the flashbacks came more often and with more intensity. Sleep held no escape, and in the weeks following the killing, she soon had great difficulty sleeping at all, being terrified of the nightmares that pursued her.

In these nightmares, her father visited her at the detention center. "He walked in past the guards, right into my room. The locks couldn't stop him from getting to me. He would sit on the edge of my bed and say in a real angry voice, 'Why did you do it? Don't you love me? Don't you love me? You know I wouldn't hurt you.' "

The court heard the plea bargain on a cloudless afternoon, almost a year to the day after the homicide. Halpern and I met Cindy as soon as she emerged from the county sheriff's car. Though she knew what was going to happen, she was understandably very nervous. Halpern and I each took an arm, and together we climbed up the back steps to the courtroom.

It was not as full as I thought it would be. Perhaps the community's interest had waned in the weeks since word of a plea bargain had leaked out. Dierdre and several other old friends and classmates sat in the back row, but they were the only faces Cindy knew. Elaine, Kerri, and Nancy had chosen not to appear, something that I thought was inexcusable. The girl who had once had everything now sat alone with her two lawyers and whimpered quietly.

Judge Denton walked briskly into the courtroom, avoiding eye contact with us. It was obvious he wanted this to be over quickly. He did not even look up after he took his seat. After glancing at a paper, he turned to the bailiff and said, "Is the defendant here?"

"Yes, Your Honor," the rotund officer promptly responded.

"Call the case."

"*State* versus *Cindy Baker,*" the bailiff bellowed.

Cindy, Halpern, and I stood up. The judge cleared his throat and looked up for the first time.

"You are Cindy Helen Baker and your father was Henry Baker?"

Cindy wiped her eyes with the sleeve of her pale-blue cotton dress and softly said, "Yes, he was my father."

Cindy served two and a half years in a state reformatory for youthful offenders. When she was released, she voluntarily placed herself in a private long-term residential treatment facility for an additional year and a half. Today she lives in a modest home in a northern New England town, and she has changed her name. During the day she works as a telephone operator, and in the evening she attends a small state college. She is slowly mending the gaping holes in her life, one stitch at a time.

She went back to her hometown in Christmas of 1989 for one reason—to visit her father's grave and place a bouquet of flowers on his headstone.

PART III

SONS WHO KILL
THEIR MOTHERS

Introduction

> In our society any man who does not weep at his mother's funeral runs the risk of being sentenced to death.
> —*The Stranger,* by Albert Camus

Nero was one of the most powerful emperors of the ancient Roman empire, and Agrippina the quintessential overindulgent, controlling mother who refused to let him grow up. More than anything, Agrippina wanted her son to be emperor; he had no choice. Though she was only a consort to the reigning emperor, she plotted, connived, and manipulated until her son ascended to the throne. She had triumphed.

Or had she? Once crowned, Nero did not spend his remaining days thanking her, lavishing her with gifts and praise. Though she had borne him and put him in the most powerful position in the world with untold wealth and spoils, he despised her domination, especially since she still exerted her insidious control over him even after the garland was placed on his head. No longer the impotent youth powerless to escape her nefarious influence, his new authority stretched from Gaul to Judea and beyond and was certainly sufficient to throw her burdensome yoke off his shoulders. Yet Agrippina resisted his attempts in every way she could, undermining his rule, intriguing, desperate to take her former place beside him. History reports that she was so obsessed that she even tried to seduce him. Try as he might, Nero could not loosen her grip and so turned to a desperate solution: murder. Too intimidated by her to try it himself, he directed several members of his private guard to steal silently into her chamber and silence her forever. With drawn swords they willingly obeyed him.

Though Nero's story is a popular one, it is difficult to find a famous historical or for that matter literary figure who actually kills his mother. The mythological hero Orestes is perhaps the only other noteworthy figure who killed his mother. With his sister Electra, Orestes killed their mother, Clytemnestra, because she was responsible for the murder of their father, Agamemnon. Shakespeare's Hamlet appears to consider murdering his mother for similar reasons, after his father has been slain, but resists the temptation. "I will speak daggers to her, but use none," he promises himself. In fact, the ghost of his father seems to warn him away from such fantasies (". . . nor let thy soul contrive against thy mother aught"—*Hamlet*), and Hamlet himself says, "Let not ever the soul of Nero enter this firm bosom."

Orestes may be representative of mother-killing by sons in literature, but the motives and circumstances that brought about his mother's demise are found only in literature—not in actual, present-day matricides. Eerily enough, however, the psychological and emotional elements of Nero's story ring true, a pattern found in matricides by sons in our own time.

There is always a history of excessive domination and early physical abuse by the mother, which usually evolves into emotional and verbal abuse. The effects of such intense and prolonged maternal domination and control snowball until the boy's personality is nearly at the point of disintegration, never having had the chance to blossom and always beaten back by Mom when it threatened to do so. The motive is frequently murky—at least, to those who did not witness the boy's upbringing. It is extremely rare for these young men to be able to understand and talk freely about the abusive circumstances of their home lives to outsiders; they have a much harder time discussing their cases than do boys who kill their fathers.

This difficulty in communicating in large part stems from how the abuse perverts the special relationship between mother and son. Just how special this relationship is was brought home to me about twenty years ago on a trip to Europe. I was fortunate enough to spend two days in the last remaining walled town in England. Situated on the Tweed River in northeastern England, the village is composed of steep-roofed cottages and narrow cobblestone streets. I arrived late one evening and rented a room above the Hens and Chickens pub, and at about eleven that evening, I found myself talking with a craggy-faced, very drunk, old fisherman. Throughout the evening, I had been staring at a young lady sitting several feet away. "She's very pretty, isn't she?" I remarked quite innocently.

"I want to tell you something about women, and I want you to listen," he said with a riveting glance, roughly grabbing both my wrists. "You will *never* know in this life how much you love a woman until your mother dies." Though he was a grandfather several times over and his mother had died over fifty years earlier, the only reason he let go of my wrists was to wipe the tears that were streaming down his cheeks.

While psychologists may debate the whys and wherefores, few people would disagree that boys form exceptionally strong attachments to their mothers. It is when this intense bond is perverted not only by excessive control but by a domination with pronounced sexually provocative, seductive overtones that the boy becomes paralyzed, too humiliated and ashamed to reveal the situation.

Matricides by sons are the second most common form of parricide, averaging about one hundred each year in the U.S. Though society may understand or at least accept in the abstract that a boy could be led to kill his father, that he might have an equally legitimate (to his mind) reason to kill his mother is out of the question, unacceptable. To most, it is an abhorrent and inexplicable act, and judges, juries, lawyers, and journalists are no exception, demonstrating their bafflement and horror by lashing out in repulsion in their various arenas to punish the child heedless of motivation.

Perhaps most important of all, we regard mothers as saints and motherhood as inviolate. Sons are not only supposed to love and obey their mothers, it is their duty, as well, to protect them. Around the time a boy enters puberty he begins to get that message from his mother, father, and the rest of society: "You're the man around here while I'm away, son. Take care of your mother." His responsibility to her, he learns, is secondary only to his father's, and his teenage years are spent more directly training for the role he will ultimately assume as both husband and father himself. Despite the prevalence of wife battering and the relative frequency with which men murder their wives (the most common of all reported intra-family homicides), raising a hand to a mother, let alone murdering her, is the ultimate taboo, more heinous a crime, certainly, than if dad kills mom or the boy kills a stranger.

Because these cases are confusing and hard to comprehend, the community typically shows the least sympathy for these defendants. After such a murder, it is not unusual for the local press, after beatifying the murdered mother, to brand the son as alienated and unstable, a lost soul run amok. These are not like the cases that result from undeniable, forthright abuse—years of beatings, for example, or repeated rapes. They stem from the complex interplay of the mother's domination and emotional abuse; and sadly, they are heartbreakingly difficult to defend.

Steven

No matter *what* your mama does to you, you just don't shoot her.

—Lamont Green, local county sheriff

When the bullet hit her, I thought it would be like TV. I thought it would make a little hole. . . . I was frantic and I didn't know what to do. . . . I just stood there, thinking, 'I actually did it.' "

Steven had just shot his mother to death. Afterward the lanky, brown-haired boy, known by all of his friends to live in absolute fear of his mother, wrapped her lifeless body in a blanket and put it in the trunk of his car. He drove to a deserted spot off an interstate highway, where he dumped the body. Back at the house, he washed all the bedding and scrubbed the walls and floor. Because he had shot her twice in the head from close range, however, blood and tissue were everywhere. After cleaning up, he telephoned his best friend, Burt. Feigning great concern, he told Burt to rush over right away because his mother was missing.

Burt raced over, and immediately he saw telltale signs of blood on the floor. He ran and got his rifle, chambered in four rounds, and called the police. Then both boys went out into the blackness of the night to continue Steven's charade of hunting down the supposed culprits.

The ruse didn't last long after the police arrived. After a brief interrogation, Steven confessed to everything.

Roger Cratton, Steven's father, called me about six weeks after his son's arrest. A newspaper interview I had given prompted him to call.

In our first conversation, Roger haltingly sketched out the circumstances of the killing, unsure of the details. His uncertainty only increased when I asked him why he thought Steven had killed his mother.

He had divorced Ruth ten years earlier, he explained, and now saw his son only on holidays and summer vacations. As Steven had passed from adolescent to teen, so had the emotional distance between them grown. He just didn't know much about his son's relationship with his ex-wife, but what came crackling through the phone lines was his own unmistakable antipathy for her, undiminished even with her death. "[She was a] demeaning personality and drove me to the verge of insanity," he said. Yet Roger's reaction to the homicide was a sign of what was to come. Ruth had driven *him* to the verge of insanity, but even he, the boy's father, couldn't at first understand why Steven had shot her.

Though far from a wealthy man, Roger was willing to spare no expense to insure that his son had the best local legal talent. By the time he was informed of his ex-wife's death, however, the county court had already appointed an experienced attorney, Glen Cassidy. Roger did some research on his own, learning that Cassidy was considered one of the better criminal lawyers in the region. While he trusted Cassidy, Roger wanted me involved both because such crimes were my particular area of expertise and because Roger was also distressed by what he perceived to be Cassidy's initial pessimism. I could well understand Cassidy's outlook; from the little Roger had told me, there was rough sailing ahead, with a favorable outcome for Steven far from certain.

Glen Cassidy is the apotheosis of the understated, wise country lawyer. Soft-spoken and genteel, he knows the law. More importantly, after almost thirty years of experience as a prosecutor and defense attorney, he knows *how* the law is made and *who* makes it. These elements would prove crucial in Steven's case because of the conservative, old-fashioned values that prevailed in Steven's hometown, a place that had not had a parricide in recent memory, if ever. From our first hello, Cassidy was exceptionally cordial, but he also made it clear who would be steering the ship. He said he needed all the help an "expert" such as me could give him; in the same breath he let me know that taking the case to trial was a risk we could not take.

Considering the circumstances of the homicide, Cassidy felt that self-defense was out of the question; our best hope would be manslaughter. But he was not even optimistic about this prospect. Not only had Steven shot his mother while she slept, but according to all reports, including those given by Steven himself, nothing had occurred in their last conversation that could have engendered even the least bit of anger in him. What complicated matters even more was the apparent premeditation evident in Steven's admission to the police that he had thought about killing Ruth a week before he did it, going so far as to place the loaded gun beside his bed in readiness.

What troubled Cassidy deeply beyond the actual circumstances of the killing was that the "boy" (as he referred to Steven) never showed a glimmer of remorse. Not once during any of Cassidy's interviews did Steven cry or express any profound sorrow. And despite intense questioning, Steven could not give any specific reason for having committed the murder. Despite all his other experience, Cassidy had never before encountered a matricide by a son and did not know that the motive, though powerful, is most often not clear even to the perpetrator. From Cassidy's point of view, there simply was no motive; this meant that Steven might very well be a homicidal maniac, a danger to himself and others, especially to his father. Naturally, all this gave Cassidy little incentive to press for a trial.

Cassidy acknowledged to me that his investigation had revealed Ruth to be an "overbearing parent." Yet he was quick to point out that he had not been able to uncover any evidence that the treatment amounted to abuse. She demonstrated an active interest in her son's education and seemed to have given him anything he wanted. Moreover, Steven himself admitted that he never complained to *anybody* about his mother's treatment. Indeed, to the rest of the world, Ruth was an intelligent, resourceful, hardworking person, respected as a businesswoman, a senior buyer for a top department store.

Cassidy's family had lived in the county for five generations, and he knew its residents well. The average juror, he told me, would have no qualms about sending the boy to the penitentiary for the rest of his life. "You've got to understand that this [judicial] circuit is the number one law-and-order circuit in the state. Percentage wise, it has the highest [criminal] conviction rate." Although it was difficult for me to accept at first, Cassidy insisted, correctly, that whatever we could bring out in court about Steven's history of abuse, the community would have difficulty understanding and relating to it. Every mitigating factor, no matter how damning or conclusive, would be overshadowed by the single fact that Steven had killed his mother.

Cassidy's opinion was influenced in part by the psychiatrist he had retained to evaluate Steven before I became involved in the case. Dr. Jerome Lester conceded that Ruth was a "stern disciplinarian," but concluded initially "any healthy seventeen-year-old should have been able to handle" such treatment. Lester also believed Steven to have been sane at the time of the homicide, though suffering from some kind of mental illness. Still, Lester was unable to render a precise diagnosis because he had not yet spent enough time with Steven.

Lester had never before worked with an adolescent who had committed a homicide, let alone one who had killed his mother. Though he had substantial experience with abuse cases, he had always seen the youth as victim—not as aggressor. After speaking with him, I was concerned about his assumption that Steven's mental disorder was *not* post traumatic-stress disorder (PTSD)—the most common mental disorder associated with long-term child abuse, but something else. There was the real possibility that Lester would conclude that Steven's mental illness had absolutely nothing to do with his mother's treatment, a finding that would greatly complicate our defense. For unless Steven was insane, and all preliminary investigations showed this not to be the circumstance, a finding of any of these other mental illnesses would be unlikely to have any effect on reducing the charge from murder.

Luckily, Dr. Lester was a true professional, refreshing in his unabashed acknowledgment that he did not know every thing, and that he was especially unfamiliar with children who kill. He openly discussed the problems he had in evaluating Steven, and he eagerly pored over the research articles and other documents I gave him.

Few psychiatrists and psychologists are familiar with the research on children who kill, and even fewer have ever evaluated such children. Yet, unlike Dr. Lester, this inexperience does not stop them from rendering opinions that seal the fates of hundreds of teenagers every year. They obviously believe that mere possession of a relevant degree makes them competent to evaluate anyone a court or attorney may send to them. The fault does not lie entirely with these doctors, however, for as critical as mental health issues are in criminal cases, especially murders, most attorneys are profoundly ignorant of even the most basic psychological concepts.

Like law enforcement investigators, defense lawyers routinely become obsessed with how murders are committed and by whom, and not why they are committed. They are more comfortable operating in the secure and tangible world of ballistics, fingerprints, blood alcohol level, and hair and fiber analysis, than in the murky realm of a client's mental and emotional state.

As a result, most attorneys accept their psychologist's or psychiatrist's opinion carte blanche, rarely involving themselves in the evaluation process. In my work I cannot afford to be a passive player because the whole case hinges on the mental state of the adolescent. Typically, I spend more time reading medical and psychological research than legal literature.

From the start of Steven's case, there was an undercurrent of tension between Cassidy and myself. Despite his cordiality, he perceived me, I think, as somewhat of an interloper. Nevertheless, we worked together well and quickly agreed upon a division of tasks. I concentrated on preparing the psychiatric evidence as well as reviewing testimony of the out-of-state witnesses, those people who had known Steven before his mother had moved to this area. Meanwhile, Cassidy hired some private investigators and set about trying to learn everything possible about the mother's life that might shed light on the case.

In a way, the problems I had in formulating a coherent

defense strategy were not unlike the ones that Steven faced throughout his life: communicating that his living situation was much worse than it appeared to be. This problem typifies every matricide committed by a son that I have ever had anything to do with.

More than any other type of parricide, sons kill mothers under almost identical circumstances. The father is physically or emotionally absent; the mother physically abuses the boy as a toddler and up to puberty, when she switches, albeit unconsciously, to a pattern of emotional abuse, the centerpiece of which is complete domination.

Second only to victims of outright sexual abuse, these boys have the greatest difficulty in revealing their predicament to outsiders. After all, the beatings stop around age thirteen, and there is nothing concrete for outsiders to observe after that except incidents of public humiliation. Just as the particular circumstances of their suffering preclude disclosure before the homicide occurs, after it they are rarely able to admit to themselves, much less to their attorneys, what drove them to the act.

Steven David Cratton had the worst memory of any young person I had ever met. His childhood was a blur to him. He could not recall any of his favorite toys, the names of any childhood friends, nor could he even separate birthdays and holidays from the haze that made all the days of his childhood run together. The only Christmas he could remember was one on which his parents bought him some little cardboard bricks, but he was unable to place the year, even approximately. He had only the vaguest memory of the bad times, the good times, the sad times, and as brief as they were, the happy times.

Tragically, it was clear to me that Steven had blocked out most of his childhood. Later, with the help of the relatives, neighbors, and friends Steven had grown up with, we would uncover many horrifying details of the abuse Steven had suffered. It is virtually certain, though, that much of the abuse— probably the most severe part—never came to light. Most likely Steven was sentenced, as are most parricidal defendants, without the court's knowing the true facts of his family history, some of which will remain locked in his mind forever.

We all tend to forget the painful and agonizing experiences of life. If events are particularly disturbing or traumatic, we can wipe out not only the trauma itself, but everything else as well—losing the good times with the bad. Psychiatrists term this *psychogenic amnesia* and recognize that such blockage lets us cope with the present by protecting us from the debilitating effects of traumatic life experiences. A clear memory of severe trauma can immobilize us with the force of the colossal emotional disturbance it produces.

Steven did retain some things. He vaguely remembered his mother chasing him around the house with a wooden spoon and a thick, white ladies' dress belt. As Steven later said, "she hit me everywhere, on the shoulders, back, and legs. Everywhere." Though he remembers the implements his mother used, he can't recall how often she hit him, or even any of the specific instances when these "weapons," as his father scornfully called them, were used.

Ironically, it was only during the preparation of his defense that the seventeen-year-old boy discovered his childhood. At the same time, I had asked Roger to contact friends and relatives who could help us fill in the past through their written recollections.

From these old friends and neighbors, Steven learned, for the first time, what had befallen him as a child. Roger had been forthcoming, but he, too, appeared to suffer from partial memory impairment. Others, however, remembered much, responding with a motivation and empathy I'd never seen before. Some wrote to set the record straight; some wrote to assuage their guilt over not having interceded years earlier. Many simply wrote to express their sorrow. And still others wrote because they just felt they had to. Remarkably, most had not seen or spoken to Steven or Ruth in over ten years, yet they described the events as if they were yesterday:

> When Ralph and I were attending our daughter's wedding . . . we stayed in the same hotel as you and your family. . . . On the morning we were leaving for home, we went to the dining room for breakfast. At the table was Steven, and Ruth, and as soon as he (Steven) saw us, he sobbingly said, "Hello, Uncle Ralph." Naturally we asked what he was crying about, and Ruth, in a cross voice, said he had soiled his clothes. Steven was only two and a half years old. . . . When we were finished and

waiting in the lobby with the other relatives to say our good-byes, Ruth came out with little Steven still crying. She jerked and held his hand so high his feet could hardly reach the floor. . . . In about fifteen minutes they returned with Steven still crying and lugging a large, white plastic bag containing his wet clothes. Ruth told us he would have to wash them himself.

You and Steven are constantly in our prayers. . . . In the summer of 1970 (Steven would have been about four), I stayed in your home while you and Ruth went on a trip. . . . At the time, Steven was on medication for bedwetting. During the night he wet his bed, and in the morning his mother beat him with a wooden spoon. The first night I was with him, I got him up at two A.M. and took him to the bathroom. . . . All week his bed was dry. However, the night you came home from your trip, he wet his bed and his mother beat him unmercifully with a wooden spoon.

. . . Steven was a frail, quiet child. He was very timid. He was particularly anxious when speaking with his mother. He always seemed afraid of her. He had good reason. She physically pushed him around, punched his arms and shoulders, and slapped him. She often belittled him verbally. By the age of seven he was not being given the chance to grow into a healthy, confident boy.

Steven seemed to be the victim of harsh treatment by his mother, and there were times when I was quite concerned about that and wondered if he was being abused. In fact, I mentioned this to my son's pediatrician on one occasion, but he seemed uninterested in giving us advice as to what I should do about it [the pediatrician actually said it was none of their business]. That was in the 1970s when there was less awareness of child abuse and when it apparently was less appropriate than now to become involved. The situation that caused me to discuss Steven with the doctor was my observation, while helping him go to the bathroom, that he had noticeable bruises on his buttocks, actually the imprint of a spoon.

The letters showed that many, many people who knew the family were horrified at Ruth's treatment of Steven, yet no one ever intervened on the child's behalf.

In retrospect, several factors perhaps explain this tragic inaction. First, being solid middle-class citizens, they were reluctant to interfere in each other's domestic matters. It's okay to fix your neighbor's lawn mower, but to comment on how he treats his kids is verboten. The main impediment, however, seems to have been Ruth herself: everyone, apparently, was scared of her. One neighbor wrote that "Ruth intimidated both children and adults. Looking back, both my husband and I realize that we avoided any type of disagreement or confrontation with her. Disagreements were met with verbal attacks from her, usually in the form of public ridicule of the person involved." All were appalled by Ruth's behavior, but no one would dare to cross her.

One adult was even more intimidated by Ruth than all others—Roger. From the very beginning of their relationship, Ruth was in control. Though known as a confident, aggressive salesman by his peers, Roger cowered in the presence of his wife. All their friends and relatives knew it. That Roger himself did not even try to protect his son made it doubly difficult for them, as outsiders, to consider stepping in.

Roger was simply no match for Ruth. "She had a very demeaning type of personality," he said. "If you ever crossed her, God forbid, you would pay the price." And since he did not want to "pay the price," Roger found many ways to escape. "I'd grab a bottle and off I'd go; or I'd stay out in the bars, or I would be out with my buddies on the golf course." Unfortunately, little Steven was too young to get into a bar, and not big enough to swing a nine iron.

When he was at home, Roger noticed that his young son frequently had a bruised arm, a cut lip, or signs of a recent bloody nose. But because he was around so rarely, he accepted his wife's explanations that little Steven was simply "a clumsy kid." And even when Roger observed his wife being particularly brutal with his son, he stood idly by. Intervention, he believed, was useless.

After the murder, when he talked about the early years, Roger would cringe in sorrow, embarrassment, and disbelief at his own failings. Tears welled up in his eyes when he discussed the way his wife dealt with Steven's bed-wetting. "He got spanked either way. She'd ask him in the morning, 'Are you dry?' And if he made a little mistake, then he got spanked; and if he said he was dry and he wasn't, he got spanked. You know, he couldn't win. Unless he was lucky enough to be dry, which was very seldom."

Mealtimes were no different. Ruth couldn't stand to have a toddler who was a fussy eater. If Steven wouldn't eat something, "she forced him to eat it by stuffing it in his mouth," Roger said. "If he tried to spit it up, she tried to push it in again. Whatever he didn't finish or whatever he spit up, he'd get it cold again in the morning."

Ruth and Roger's marriage was, as could be expected, a divorce waiting to happen. When it did, it was particularly rancorous, even as bad divorces go. Four-year-old Steven became a pawn in the game of enmity and blame that followed. Ruth won hands down. She got custody of Steven and two years later moved to a Midwestern city two thousand miles from Roger. Now Steven was all hers, except for the occasional vacation to see his father. Sadly, the die had been cast.

The acrimony between the parents continued in the form of vituperative letters. Much of the mudslinging concerned Steven—his schooling, time he could spend with Roger, and the effects of Ruth's physical abuse during Steven's early childhood. Roger seemed to gain sufficient courage during this period to begin rebuking Ruth for her treatment of the boy. Perhaps divorce, the fact that Ruth now lived far away, and finally Roger's remarriage made it possible for him to start standing up to his former wife.

Apparently, trading accusations concerning Steven was not enough. Steven himself wrote letters to his father—letters that made requests on Ruth's behalf. Reading letters such as the one below, it is easy to imagine the circumstances under which Steven wrote them.

Dear Dad:

I'm writing this letter so you will get the idea! Dad, I have to get a new chest to put my clothes in. Mom is spending more than enough money on me, and not enough on herself. Mom does not say that you don't love me. And $1,500 is not enough to pay bills—electricity, gas and insurance.

Sincerely,
Steven

Ruth was certainly controlling and domineering, yet these same qualities made her passionately concerned about many aspects of Steven's welfare, especially his education. Not satisfied, as most parents are, to leave her son's education up to the teacher, she was intimately involved in all aspects of Steven's schooling. In this as in all other things, however, she clearly went overboard, passing from concern to obsession.

When Steven showed the least problem in school, for example, she immediately made an appointment with the teacher or hired a tutor. When his problems got serious, she placed him in a private school. What Ruth wanted for Steven was laudable. Unfortunately, her overweening control severely alienated her son; the harder she pushed him, the more he went out of his way to evade her influence.

Steven is extremely bright, with an IQ over 120, yet his academic performance was at best mediocre. Part of this was related to a mild learning disability, but his main obstacle was his mother. He quickly learned that, regardless of how he performed, he could never satisfy her. So he made it a point of honor *not* to satisfy her.

"Even if I didn't have any homework, she would make me do two hours of studying. So I would just open a book and daydream. I never did study," he told me during one of our first interviews. School became a game where, as Steven said, "I always tried to get by with the least amount I could, except for chemistry. I got A's and B's every time. I loved it." In most of the other subjects, Steven consciously tried to keep his grades just above passing, but he wasn't successful all the time. Even when he did manage to get above a seventy, he still lost, because Ruth had her own academic standard. If he received below an eighty, he would be punished. "She just wanted me to get all A's, [but] I didn't want to be an A student."

Food was another source of struggle. A child's health is paramount, and it is hardly unusual for parents to make and enforce rules concerning proper nutrition. Her "food rules," however, went far beyond what most parents would consider strict, much less practical or effective. Talking about his mother's obsession with his eating, Steven said, "She didn't like wasting food. . . . I just couldn't throw the food I didn't finish in the garbage. One time when I was about ten, I had thrown my peas down the toilet. Mom went out to the grocery store and bought a quart-size can of peas, and she made me eat them. . . . You know, the same thing happened with smoking. I was about the same age and she had gone out to the store. I smoked one of her cigarettes. She came home, smelled the cigarette smoke, and made me smoke two packs of cigarettes. I had to smoke them all. After that I just got into the habit of it."

She also maintained tight control of Steven's room. Every child considers his room his castle, yet, Ruth, like most parents, had a legitimate concern that Steven keep it clean and safe. "Starting when I was thirteen, she'd come in my room and say, 'It's time for inspection.' Then she'd go through my drawers to see if I had any notes from teachers or stuff like that. One time my room was real messy and she piled everything—clothes and games—in the middle of the floor. And then she put it all in a bag and put the bag in the trash. I got it right out and started coming back into the house, and she told me to put it back in the trash. So I ended up putting everything back in the trash."

As with everything else in his life, when Steven broke the "food rules," "neatness rules," or any of the other multiple house regulations, he got punished. During childhood, punishment meant beatings with the wooden spoon. By the time he was fourteen and was bigger and stronger than his mother, Ruth put the infamous wooden spoon into retirement. She did, however, continue to use her white belt as other than a fashion accessory. When she wanted to punish Steven, she grounded him—meaning he couldn't leave his home or watch television.

But being grounded was insignificant next to the vitriolic criticism. "She yelled at me every night of the week," he said flatly. These criticisms were always peppered with profanity; even after the homicide, Steven felt uncomfortable repeating those words. "She wouldn't even call me by my name, she just called me 'sneak' and 'liar' all day. Almost everything I did was wrong. . . . She said I was handy around the house, but would always come back and say I did it wrong—like the way I cleaned out the sink. I'd take an S.O.S. pad and clean out the stainless steel sink, and there would be something wrong with the way I did it."

Taken individually, each of Ruth's sets of rules may seem excessively strict—but they *do not* appear unmistakably abusive. To understand why Steven killed his mother, it is necessary to stand back and take in the entire pattern of his life.

In trying to comprehend a murder, we naturally want to find one clear, definable act that might have brought on such violence. It is the same urge that often makes one, upon hearing of a fatal car accident, ask immediately whether the victim had been speeding or perhaps had not been wearing a seat belt. In Steven's case, no single, undeniable provocation existed—a fact that complicated the handling of his case immensely.

Still, the events of Steven's life, taken in retrospect, clearly indicate that he was deeply troubled. When he was about twelve and a half, he went to live with his father for five months. Apparently this move was made against his mother's wishes, and it must have taken great courage for him to go. After the homicide, Roger's second wife described this interlude:

When Steven was thirteen years old he came to live with us for five months. He had been having problems in school in [the city where he had lived with his mother] and many of his schoolmates teased him. We were thrilled to have him and he blended into our family perfectly. While Steven was still wetting the bed when he arrived, after a few weeks it decreased in frequency. He seemed to thrive at [his new school] and met many new friends. When Steven first arrived he told us his mother had said to him that if he left, he could never come back. He was a very sad little boy when he got off the plane. We could see that he was filled with guilt and mixed emotions.

All of us, including my child, loved Steven and enjoyed having him live with us. When summer arrived, he thought he should go back for a visit to [his mother]. I clearly remember helping him pack, and when Steven saw I was putting in too much clothing, he said to me, "Remember, Mom, I'm only going to be gone for a week." We were truly devastated and shocked when we learned that Steven would not be returning. We were informed by my husband's attorney, who had received a call from Ruth's attorney. None of us could believe he would voluntarily return to such a negative environment. Since then we understand that Steven never stopped trying to win the love and approval of his mother.

Explaining "his decision" not to return to his father's house, Steven wrote:

Dear Dad,
I feel that it would be best for me to stay here. That doesn't mean that I don't love you. It's just that I feel it's a lot better here. With my friends outside and inside school. I love all of you, but this is where I grew up and I feel safe here. Don't think this was Mom's idea.

Love,
Steven

While staying with his father and stepmother, Steven began to see a psychologist. He saw the doctor for a total of eight sessions before his abrupt return to live with his mother. "A sad and tense youngster with underlying feelings of inadequacy, deprivation, and vulnerability," the doctor described him. "Apparently, over the years, Steven has developed a style of guardedness and caution and of not revealing much of his affect. . . . His relationship with his mother is intensely ambivalent, with much anger and guilt." Neither this psychologist, nor the one to whom his mother sent him after he returned to live with her, however, sensed the depth of the youngster's worsening problems. Neither is there any evidence that Steven revealed the abusive circumstances of his childhood to these doctors.

In fact, when Roger learned that Steven's mother had made arrangements for him to continue with a psychologist, a woman, he wrote her:

Are you aware of the fact that his mother physically abused him when he was younger? I don't know if that still goes on, but the mental abuse and constant degradation, I know, continue. I wanted to be sure you were aware of this in helping Steven overcome his problems.

The psychologist replied:

I must remain concerned about your last letter, which mentioned the home environment Steven has experienced. I had detected nothing in my work with Steven that would indicate that this is a continuing problem at this time, but as you know, Steven is defensive and at times does not always express himself fully.

Did the psychologist believe Roger? Or, since she was undoubtedly aware of the bitter acrimony between Roger and Ruth, and was being paid by the latter, did she chalk up Roger's allegations to postdivorce mudslinging? After the homicide, so many witnesses to the physical abuse came forward that no doubt remains about whether it occurred. But as the above exchange indicates, during Steven's adolescence, when professional intervention could have truly helped him and spared Ruth, Roger—the one person in a position to see what was happening to him—had little credibility in speaking out against Ruth.

The psychologists were not the only ones to whom Steven did not speak freely. He *never* complained to anybody, for there really wasn't anybody to whom he could complain. As he grew older, he grew increasingly alienated, too, and came to see his mother as omnipotent, beyond challenge. If his own father was unable to help him, who else could? Steven had few friends; he felt that no one liked him. And because he felt no one liked him, he never made an effort to seek the friendship of others. It was a vicious cycle that worsened each year.

Several times during this early adolescence Steven tried to run away. "The first time I ran away, I was heading back to see my dad. I wanted to be away from my mother, because she was bitching at me all the time. No matter what I did, I always did it wrong. I was always being told I was lazy. . . .

I was picked up by a lady, but she ended up calling my mom. I went home, but we never talked about why I ran. Things went back to the way they were, so a while later [about a year] I left again. I just started walking. I probably walked twenty miles. My feet hurt me real bad, and so I just called home. I just started crying and she came and picked me up."

Again, nothing changed for Steven, so he tried to run away a third time when he was fifteen. However, this time he tried getting away with somebody else's car. I asked him about this episode when I interviewed him after his sentencing:

> S: *I stole this lady's car, and I was caught by the cops. I told them I was running away from home.*
> P: *Did they ask you why?*
> S: *No.*
> P: *What would you have said, if the cop said why did you run away?*
> S: *I would have told him that I didn't like living at home.*
> P: *And what do you think the cop would have said?*
> S: *He'd probably laugh and shove me in the back seat and take me home. . . . Anyway, what did happen was that I spent ten days in juvenile. . . . I didn't like the feeling of the door being slammed behind me, but it was sort of a vacation.*
> P: *Meaning it was good?*
> S: *Yeah, it was away from Mom.*

Like Cindy and many other clients, Steven became convinced that if he couldn't run away, the only other way to escape was to kill himself. And though he tried only once, taking an overdose of pain medication and only getting sick as a result, he continually thought of suicide throughout his teenage years. The two scenarios he played over in his mind were jumping off a tall building and rigging up a gun so "all I'd have to do was pull a string."

As part of his probationary sentence for stealing the car, Steven was required to go into counseling. It was decided that he would simply continue with the psychologist whom he had by now been seeing continuously for two years, ever since his return from living with his father. This phase of therapeutic intervention was remarkable for its complete failure to discern Steven's increasingly serious problems. A great believer in empirical measures, the psychologist administered battery after battery of tests. To paraphrase Arlo Guthrie's "Alice's Restaurant," Steven was detected, inspected, and given every kind of test there was. Never once, however, was he directly asked why he ran away from home.

The psychologist's summary report focused on the superficial aspects of Steven's troubles: "He [Steven] doesn't like school. He doesn't spend money wisely. He feels nobody understands him and it is hard [for him] to talk about his problems." The report concluded by noting that Steven is "blocked in his feelings, but is not unduly resentful or angry." Most stunning of all, this woman postulated that "without sounding simplistic, much of Steven's problems can be traced to his addiction to television. Steven has kept himself young by continuing to watch a large amount of cartoons, particularly action cartoons. It is almost as if Steven is avoiding recognizing that he is growing up."

While this psychologist's clinical *observations* were absolutely correct, i.e., that Steven lacked self-esteem, was immature, etc., her conclusion that television was at the root of all of his problems was naive and tragically incorrect. Steven watched television to escape. Amazingly, in all the pages of reports and letters prepared by this therapist, there was not one substantive discussion of how Steven's personal problems, even his decision to run away from home, might have been affected by or related to his home life. His relationship with his mother was accorded little significance.

Unfortunately, it is not uncommon for even the most competent and thorough of clinicians to miss the important possibility of emotional abuse in evaluating youthful clients. This is especially true when mothers abuse sons. In Steven's case, it might have been especially difficult for the therapist to see the true situation. Not only was Steven completely unable to talk about the abuse, but Ruth, who hired the psychologist, gave the outward appearance of being overwhelmingly attentive to her son's welfare. Indeed, in the wider community, many saw Ruth as a concerned, vigilant mother.

Still, the progress reports and evaluations are somewhat startling in their supposition that all of Steven's problems had sprung, Medusa-like, from his own head. Perhaps the therapist's inability to understand Steven's problem was best illustrated by her concluding report:

"I wish all young people in my work showed the same progress and gains that Steven has shown in the last year. I have no reason to expect these gains not to continue." Six months later, the therapist's model patient put a bullet in his mother's head.

Ironically, the one person who could have shed light on Steven's plight was someone nobody would ever have thought to consult, because he was just Burt—Steven's best friend.

If there is an average American teenager, it is Burt. He sports a red, peaked cap with a Ford Motor Company insignia, and he plays on his high-school baseball team. He has a good relationship with his parents, a responsible after-school job, and he has never been arrested. Burt is the teenager you never hear about. But most importantly, he is also a loyal friend.

Steven and Burt met three years before the homicide when they were fourteen, and to this day their friendship has remained strong. Burt was the person Steven called to help him look for the "thieves" who supposedly killed Ruth. He had as much insight as anyone into Steven's life. Most importantly, he revealed things that Steven had forgotten or simply could not bring himself to discuss.

Burt, unlike most people, knew that Steven's problem was his relationship with his mother. Throughout my talks with him, he emphasized one thing: there was absolutely no semblance of a normal, caring mother-son relationship between Steven and Ruth.

"You never saw them hug or kiss or anything. You never heard them tell one another they love each other and stuff like that. Like . . . with my mom, if I'm going out, say I'm going to church or something, I kiss her, you know, tell her bye—tell her I love her and whatnot. But they just never seemed to do that. . . . She would constantly criticize Steven in front of me. . . . And she could fly off the handle at any little thing. She cussed at him and really made him look like a fool."

Even after the homicide, Steven was still trying to minimize the abuse to outsiders. "Sneak" and "liar" were the strongest words Steven said his mother called him. Yet Burt (and another friend) confirmed that Ruth regularly called him a "bastard," a "motherfucker," and a "son of a bitch."

Burt was amazed at how much criticism and punishment Ruth heaped on her son about chores and school. He shook his head incredulously, remembering. "She would leave these lists on little yellow slips of paper every morning for things for him to do. . . . One time she left two lists for him. He found one, but not the other, and she got real pissed at him. . . . [It was not] like a mother and son relationship; it seemed like a worker-employee relationship . . . it just wasn't right."

According to Burt, regardless of how she treated him, Steven never spoke back to his mother or showed even the slightest disrespect. Even away from her, he refused to speak against her or even to discuss his feelings. Burt tried a few times to get Steven to talk, but his friend wouldn't even acknowledge that a problem existed. "I had told Steven plenty of times, I wouldn't put up with that shit . . . [and] he just wouldn't say anything at all. What I was getting at was, 'Why don't you do something about your life, why don't you change it or something?' . . . It would have turned me against my mother . . . it makes you feel like nobody wanted you; just like you don't even have a purpose on this earth. . . . But Steven never said anything to me. . . . And he never said anything to make her mad. You know, teenagers they start growing up and they start back-talking at parents, you know. . . . Everybody, everybody [does that]. But not Steven."

In the six months before the tragedy, Burt observed that Steven seemed to be under unusual stress though Steven himself never hinted that anything was wrong. Burt's father and mother commented that during this period it was more usual for Steven to be "grounded" than not grounded. Everything Steven did seemed to draw his mother's reproach. But Burt and his family, despite being closer to Steven than anyone else during this time, only saw the tip of the iceberg.

At this time in his life, Steven's day would typically begin at six A.M. After he showered and put on his clothes he would go to Burt's house for breakfast because his own mother would scream at him if he woke her up while he was making breakfast. Aside from escaping his mother's wrath, he looked forward to breakfast at Burt's because it was the only real family meal he would have all day.

Steven was required to come home immediately after school. There, he would find little yellow notes stuck up throughout the house, directing him to do different tasks. If he finished the chores early, he would try to watch some television, always turning it off before his mother came home.

Right up until her death, Ruth believed, as did, not coincidentally, the psychologist she hired, that Steven did poorly in school because he watched too much television. So, starting when he was thirteen, she prohibited him from watching in the morning or right after school. But Steven loved television, especially adventure programs. Because of this passion for TV, getting around his mother's viewing rules became a bizarre game.

We had an old TV, so it would stay hot for a while after it was turned off. When my mom would come home, she would always feel the back of the TV to see if it was warm, and if it was, she knew I was watching it. And so I started [at about age fifteen] to take ice cubes and melt them on the back of the TV so that it would cool down. So a few times that worked, and she didn't know I was watching it. But other times, she had marked down the channel that it was on when she left the house, and if it was on a different channel, she knew I was watching it and [I'd get grounded].

Though Ruth trusted her son to do the chores when she was at work, she insisted he not do his homework until she returned. "She always had to be there to watch me," he said resentfully. "I would start at about eight and work till ten." Steven would then fix dinner for himself, usually something like macaroni and cheese, because she rarely ate with him during the week. Around eleven or eleven-thirty, he went to bed.

One unusual and revealing circumstance of Steven's life was that he had no privacy from his mother. He and his mother lived in a very large one-bedroom home. Ruth slept in the bedroom, Steven in the living room. Obviously, he had no place to go to get away—or just to be alone. Perhaps even more important, he was an adolescent male whose developing sexuality was painfully compromised by this arrangement.

"The place was nicely furnished," Steven said later, "but I was, well, a little self-conscious. I just changed my clothes in the corner of the living room, and my mom was always walking through, preparing for work." Embarrassed, he admitted that he often saw his mother partially clothed during these times.

In one of his early evaluations of Steven, our psychiatrist, Dr. Lester, had noted that "Steven's mother presented him with sexually provocative and stimulating situations which he was especially ill equipped emotionally to handle." In his final report, Dr. Lester commented that such behavior was "essentially provoking unconscious sexual conflict within her son. She in essence treated him in this regard as if he were a nonentity, a person with no capacity for feelings."

We had no evidence that in the months leading up to the homicide Ruth had actually treated Steven any different from in the past. Her heavy-handed criticisms continued, and she did occasionally slap his face. The last serious incident of physical punishment had occurred about a year before the murder, when Ruth had choked Steven during an argument. But what really changed was Steven himself.

Like every sixteen-year-old, Steven had begun within the previous two years to comprehend and define himself as his own person. Terrifically exhilarated, he could feel the winds of liberty blowing his way, could see the shimmering of a good, normal life outside his home. Mostly he saw it around Burt, who, with his mother and father, actually became Steven's surrogate family. Burt's father, Earl, would periodically take the two boys on weekend outings and sometimes hired Steven to work with him. Earl and his wife, Darlene, not only liked Steven, they trusted him. "He was a little immature," Earl remarked, "but [he was a] good and very trustworthy, responsible worker."

Despite these positive moments, Steven felt absolutely powerless to extricate himself from his situation. His past told him he couldn't successfully run away; and he was too embarrassed to seek help from anyone. "I felt really embarrassed, 'cause my mom wasn't like everybody else's mom. . . . When friends came over, they'd [always] ask me when my mom was coming home. I'd say, 'Around six o'clock,' and they'd say, 'Well, I won't be here then.' "

His solution was to crawl even deeper within his head, isolating himself from the rest of the world. Yet, regardless of his feelings, Steven was the dutiful son. Right up until the night of her death he bent over backward for her.

In that last year, as Steven became more his own person and began to imagine his own future, something else changed as well. "I started standing up to her, and she just slapped me for talking back. . . . I used to break down and cry, but when I got older, I would just stand there. I wouldn't do anything and she would get madder. I would just say, 'All right, if that's the way it is.' And that's when I started to realize how bad it was . . . how other parents were different from my mom. Like Burt's family—just an everyday, normal American family that love each other. They have problems, but . . . not constant ones."

"All right, if that's the way it is," was the credo Steven had lived by his whole life. Though he apparently began to question the wisdom of this approach shortly after his seventeenth birthday, too much damage had already been done to his personality to permit him to see the enormity of his problems, let alone seek help.

Initially, Dr. Lester, like Cassidy and others, had regarded Steven as emotionally unstable and Ruth as a controlling but not abusive parent. After reinterviewing Steven many more times and doing an exhaustive literature review, Dr. Lester's thinking underwent a remarkable change. Steven's situation, he recognized, was much more complex than he had originally thought. The fact that Dr. Lester, with extensive experience with disturbed youth, initially underestimated Steven's psychological problems simply emphasizes my own observations of the difficulty communities and judicial systems have in comprehending and dealing fairly and justly with boys who kill their mothers.

Ruth, Dr. Lester discovered, was far more than a strict, overbearing mother:

> She was . . . an imposing, powerful, dominating, and controlling woman who exerted her dominance over her son all his life, leading him to feel powerless to stand up

against her. She in essence had taken his identity from him, by never allowing it to develop. . . . Steven had become increasingly aware of his lack of identity with his repression of his long-standing rage against his mother beginning to break down, and as it did so, increasing pressure began to build within him to "get it over with once and for all." He lived in an environment where he was forced to repress normal psychosexual development, [which led him to be further confused about his identity]. Steven's three tries at running away from home, and one halfhearted attempt at suicide, were outward expressions of this. It had come to him that his only alternatives were to either commit suicide or destroy his oppressor.

In the end, the psychiatrist came to believe that the damage to Steven began almost the moment Ruth first laid eyes on her son. Infants don't need much: warm milk, a change of diapers, a safe place to sleep, and most of all, a loving bond with their mothers. Sadly, this last, crucial need was never filled in Steven's life. Through interviews with Roger and the vivid reports provided by early friends and neighbors, it seems clear that Ruth rejected Steven from the moment he came into her life. This may have been due to her own emotional problems, but we will never know.

Whatever the cause, there was, as Lester concluded, a "lack of goodness for fit" between mother and infant son. This early rejection became the polestar of Steven's doomed relationship with his mother.

Theoretically, if Steven's relationship with his father had not been in shambles, Roger might have helped. But Roger, still intimidated by Ruth and having surrendered emotional as well as physical custody after the divorce, was unable to protect his son. As each year passed, Steven fell more and more under his mother's control, at the same time becoming progressively more alienated from his father. "Steven described how Ruth would put his father down whenever he would call to talk to him," Dr. Lester commented in his report. "She would demand to know what they said and she would listen in on the other extension and afterward interrogate him about what was said and then criticize his father."

"She'd accomplished what she wanted to do," Roger told

me. "She drove a wedge between us. I just couldn't be myself with my kid, even when he was visiting me." Yet nothing Roger would say to me revealed his feelings about his son better than the letter he wrote Steven only two days after learning of the homicide:

Dear Steven:

I have never felt closer to you than I do now. What a shame it took a tragedy to bring us close, but God sometimes works in strange ways that we don't always understand. . . . As I told you over the phone, nobody understands more than I do why you did what you did. She totally dominated and controlled your life, and that is what you were revolting against. I couldn't live with her and as an adult I could leave. Unfortunately you couldn't. Steven, don't ever forget that what you did was wrong—in the eyes of the law and in the eyes of God. No one is ever entitled to take the life of another living being. But I do understand how years of first physical abuse as a child and constant verbal abuse which never stopped could lead to something like this.

Ultimately, Dr. Lester formally diagnosed Steven as suffering from posttraumatic-stress disorder, but he noted that a more appropriate name for Steven's condition would be "traumatized identity syndrome." What Lester meant was that Steven suffered from severe abuse of his identity. "[At the end] Steven was only able to focus on his mother's total control and domination of his identity. He thought continually about suicide but concluded that the only way he could gain his freedom would be to destroy his mother, his oppressor. . . . He saw no avenue of escape; the pressure piled up to a point where he couldn't live with it anymore. Another individual might have had the control to handle his mother, but not Steven."

Steven's psychological reaction to his mother's treatment was not unusual. Two years before him, for example, I worked on a case involving a fifteen-year-old boy, Morgan. Like Ruth, Morgan's mother maintained ironfisted control over her son. Not only did she constantly criticize and curse at him, but she even resorted to regularly searching his room. And like Steven, Morgan killed his mother by shooting her in the head. Amazingly, Morgan's psychological evaluation could have been substituted for Steven's:

> Morgan's identity—his sense of self—has been pummeled and pounded apparently since the day he was born. He grew up in a family that effectively taught him that he never did anything right. . . . His character and very essence have been maligned from birth. Prior to the homicide, Morgan was well on his way to developing some severe identity problems. . . . He holds his feelings inside and doesn't know how to mediate them. His feelings tend to overwhelm him, and he essentially gets debilitated by his emotions.

Though their crimes and psychological evaluations were virtually identical, Morgan was treated quite differently from Steven. Primarily because he was fifteen, Morgan was charged in juvenile court and sentenced to three years in a therapeutic facility. Steven was, however, not eligible for such enlightened treatment; because juvenile jurisdiction in his state ended at sixteen, he was tried as an adult. And despite Dr. Lester's diagnosis definitively tying Steven's mental state to his mother's treatment, developing a convincing defense strategy was a daunting task.

Our primary problem, one I'd faced in most matricides, was that each individual instance of mistreatment sounded trivial when scrutinized by itself. These murders are brought on by a constant, relentless barrage of relatively moderate abusive acts, which, even taken together, were not likely to spark immediate sympathy in judge and jury.

The second problem was that the state homicide law gave us little room to maneuver. Unlike most other states, where murder is separated into degrees, usually first and second, there was only one category under this state law: just plain murder, the charge on which Steven had been indicted.

When I had first spoken with Cassidy, he ruled out self-defense altogether. I was forced to agree with him. Even forgetting for a moment that Ruth was sleeping when killed (which did not in and of itself rule out self-defense), there were no circumstances reported by Steven or anybody else that suggested Steven would be in imminent fear for his life. In spite of these problems, I thought there was a slight opportunity, with Lester's abused-identity diagnosis, to argue "psychological self-defense."

For a traditional self-defense theory, you have to prove a person was defending himself against another's *physical* actions that were likely to cause imminent death or serious bodily injury. Psychological self-defense means the person is defending himself against any actions of another likely to cause grievous psychological injury. Extreme verbal and psychological abuse can lead to the metaphoric death of the personality [when the victim tumbles into insanity, for example], and sometimes suicide.

Charles Ewing, a psychologist and law professor at the State University of New York at Buffalo, describes this state of personality death in battered women quite compellingly:

> While these women may not be faced with a choice of . . . being killed, many are confronted with a dilemma just as dreadful. Unable to escape a battering relationship, they face the choice of . . . being reduced to a psychological state in which their continued physical existence will have little if any meaning or value. Whatever one chooses to call this state—"life without feeling alive," "partial death," utter hopelessness, chronic pathological depression, or "psychological infantilism"—the net result for the battered woman is a life hardly worth living.

If, in fact, Steven's mental state at the time of the killing was in such disarray that a total disintegration of his personality was imminent, we might have been able to argue the psychological self-defense. But *was* Steven at the point of such serious psychological injury? He had clearly been suicidal, had been growing progressively more agitated and isolated, and had become increasingly hopeless about being permitted to leave home at eighteen. Yet he had never disclosed his despair to anyone and not long before the homicide, had even sent a birthday-present list to his father, indicating that he had bright plans for the future. In sum, we had, at best, just a fair chance at making this argument stick. But after I mulled it over, I knew its success in such a conservative jurisdiction (or even a liberal one) was highly unlikely.

I was not much more hopeful about the voluntary manslaughter defense, which meant that we would have to prove that the homicide resulted from a "sudden violent and irresistible passion resulting from a serious provocation sufficient to excite such passion in a reasonable person." Burt had been the last person to see Steven and his mother together. "It seemed like a relaxed atmosphere," Burt said afterward. "His mother said he could go out that night after he did some chores for her. He had two beers [when we went out] and seemed in a good frame of mind. He went home at about eleven-thirty."

Steven told the police that his mother was watching television when he came in. Around fifteen minutes later, he said, both of them went to sleep. "I woke up at about five A.M. for no apparent reason. I got the gun [that he had put under his bed about a week earlier] and went into the bedroom and stood over her, [then I fired]." Everybody accepted Steven's version, except Burt—he refused to believe that Steven just woke up and shot her.

Instead Burt theorized it was much more likely that Steven was set off by an argument he had soon after coming in the door. Burt's notion was eminently more logical than Steven's, but it was irrelevant because Steven steadfastly stuck to his story. He was adamant that no argument had taken place that night. End of story.

I agree with Burt: to this day I remain convinced that something else happened that Steven has not revealed either because he consciously refuses to, or because, like his other frightful experiences, he cannot remember. As in Tim's case, parricide perpetrators are deliberately silent about certain events they find overwhelmingly shameful, even when they know that those revelations may be their only defense.

In my experience, when there is a large block of time that cannot be explained right before a parricide (in this case, eleven-thirty P.M. to five-thirty A.M.), it is likely that something happened, as was the case with Tim in Part I. I believe that Ruth was up when Steven came home and they had an argument. Perhaps Ruth grounded Steven for some trivial infraction, maybe she slapped his face. Of course, these theories are irrelevant because Steven denied that anything happened upon his return.

As reluctant as I was to admit it, Cassidy was right; the facts did not support self-defense or voluntary manslaughter, and a plea bargain was the only route to go. After the case was closed I went back to see Cassidy, and he explained one more time how he had arrived at this conclusion.

With lines carved in just the right places on his face, and his silver hair combed straight back, the country gentleman narrowed his steel-blue eyes, intent on making me understand his every word. Peering over his gold-rimmed bifocals, he said in a gravelly voice, "Steven was seventeen years of age, and basically people [here] grow up early. Seventeen is old enough to be out on your own and have a family; maybe join the Marine Corps. But he *didn't have to stay in the house and kill her.* He could have picked up his bags and left. . . . I don't think society is ready to say, unless it's sexual abuse [of] a father to his daughter, just kill your mother and let's forget about it. . . . A jury is not going to use [the psychological prison explanation] . . . as an excuse for turning a defendant loose. . . . Also, people who do wrong naturally tend to believe they need to be punished. I don't believe you will find anybody differs with that." Cassidy was right, of course; especially about the attitudes of his own community.

Cassidy got a plea offer primarily because Steven's psychological problems were obvious to everybody, even the prosecutor, and because of Cassidy's excellent reputation with both judge and prosecutor. Naturally, the plea must have been attractive to the opposition, too: nobody wanted this case to go to trial, which would inevitably have meant raising many unpleasant facts about family life in this otherwise halcyon community.

Because he was talking about killing himself soon after the homicide, Steven was placed in a state mental hospital for observation and evaluation. On the basis of a state psychiatric report that found Steven to be suffering from a mental disorder, the prosecutor offered a plea of "guilty but mentally ill." Ironically, this cursory diagnosis (made in ignorance of Steven's abuse history, but based on brief observation revealing that he suffered episodic psychosis) may have had more of an impact on the plea offer than Dr. Lester's lengthy and well-researched diagnosis—on which we had worked so hard.

"Guilty but mentally ill" is an obscure classification of homicide and is mainly used in the handful of states that have only one degree of murder. Its primary purpose is to restrict the defendant's use of the insanity defense when the defendant is mentally ill. An insane defendant cannot distinguish between right and wrong and functions under some delusional compulsion at the time of the crime that prevents him from understanding and controlling his actions. A person judged guilty but mentally ill, on the other hand, theoretically at least, knows right from wrong, but is suffering from mental incapacitation at the time of the murder.

The practical effect of this hybrid category is that the person is still found guilty of murder. The only benefit, and it is a theoretical benefit at best, is that the person has a better chance of receiving treatment than if convicted of simple murder.

After Cassidy had spoken with Steven and his dad about the plea offer, Steven decided to take it. The lawyer assured me that the plea was the most prudent course, giving Steven the opportunity to be treated by the state Department of Human Resources rather than by the corrections authorities. The plea also increased his chances for an early parole.

I was far from enthusiastic, but the prosecutor was adamant and would offer no other arrangement. Moreover, I knew that if we went to trial, it would be an uphill fight to sway the jury to my way of thinking. More likely, the jurors would respond as had the local sheriff, who had captured the feeling of the community in a single phrase: "No matter what your mama does to you, you just don't shoot her." As in so many of my cases, none of the options were satisfying.

Late in the afternoon on the day before the plea was going to be taken, Dr. Lester called me in great excitement. After much consideration, he told me Steven might be insane after all. He had previously told me that Steven was not insane, despite his seriously deteriorated mental state. However, in the three weeks prior to the plea's being taken, Lester became more and more convinced that though Steven knew right from wrong, he wasn't able to exercise the judgment to act on that knowledge. He had to get free from Ruth's dominance, and he was no longer able to control his compulsion to kill her. This final shift in Dr. Lester's position was potentially very important.

In my experience insanity has not been useful in parricide defense because most perpetrators are not, at the time they carry out their crimes, demonstrably unable to distinguish right from wrong. They usually maintain awareness that what they are doing is wrong, but they are unable to control the compulsion to kill the parent.

I knew that it was a long shot here, but nevertheless I immediately called Cassidy. I reached him late that evening, and the instant I told him Lester's insanity theory, I knew he would never agree. Withdrawing the well-prepared guilty plea at literally the last minute was the last thing Cassidy wanted to consider. "[Using the insanity defense here] was next to impossible," he said, "because this crime offends lay people. . . . If a psychiatrist comes in and says murder was the result of an irresistible impulse, then the jury will think she had it coming." He went on to say that if we went to trial, the state would not only bring in pictures of the mother with her head blown off, they would offer evidence of Steven's unsuccessful cover-up. He concluded by saying the plea was the best thing we could do for Steven. The matter was closed.

The plea was quietly taken at eleven-thirty the next morning.

Steven's father flew down. I wanted Lester at least to testify at the plea hearing, but Cassidy said his deal with the prosecutor was that neither side would offer any testimony. The judge did however receive Lester's final fifteen-page written opinion, along with letters from family members and friends who had witnessed Steven's treatment.

Our efforts were, unfortunately, in vain. Steven was sentenced to ten years to life, though his "guilty but mentally ill" conviction meant that he was to receive some sort of treatment. As of this writing, Steven has served over seven years at a maximum-security facility and has not spent a single hour in any nonpenal, mental-health facility.

On a warm spring morning six months after the sentencing, Roger opened the following note from his son.

Dear Dad: I can't cope with it anymore. I've been trying, but no more. Look at Exodus 21:15, (says "HE WHO SMITES HIS FATHER OR MOTHER SHALL SURELY BE PUT TO DEATH)

Goodbye and love, Steven

Roger immediately called the prison to inform them about the note, and Steven was put on a suicide watch. Remarkably, despite these attempts, he has received no formal psychological help at all. He does sporadically visit his counselor—a privilege afforded every inmate. My visit to see him in prison confirmed that the classification "guilty but mentally ill" was as meaningless as I initially thought.

The tragedy of Steven's present circumstance was even more cruel in light of Dr. Lester's warning in his final report against exactly this turn of events: "Inasmuch as his development is delayed and his identity is inadequately formed, he would quickly be influenced by the prison population and ultimately form a more disturbed identity, diminishing his chances of adapting to society in the future."

I left the case feeling profoundly frustrated because I had been unable to help Steven more than I did. A tremendous sorrow overwhelmed me—and not only for Steven. When Ruth wasn't being abusive, she was really trying to be a good parent. Yet her tremendous compulsion to dominate Steven perverted what she strove so hard to achieve. As a family friend wrote:

Ruth was always trying to force him with harsh words and physical punishment to meet her idea of what he should be. As I recall, Ruth repeatedly told Steven to "fight back"; "don't be a sissy"; "don't be such a baby"; "stand up for your rights." This kind of badgering was used on him when he was one to two years old. . . . It appears to me that Steven finally stood up to his mother and did what she was always trying to "force" him to do—and that was to "fight back" and be a "man." Tragically . . . [this] erupted in a violent, irrevocable act. I believe that Steven ultimately acted out of the fear and danger that must have been growing in him since he was a very small child. Steven was desperately attempting to free himself of what must have been a life full of nightmares.

Everyone closer to Steven had great difficulty accepting his chosen course to freedom. "You know, he thought he could never truly get away from her," Burt lamented. "Even my mom and dad said they wished he would have just run away or come to our house. You see, they told Steven before, you know, if things get too rough, all you got to do is come live with us. . . . I mean, it was a known fact, all Steven had to do was pack his clothes and come to my house and he had a place to live."

When I went to see Steven in prison, he seemed resigned to his situation. Like others convicted of parricide, he was not deeply bothered by the regimentation of prison. He sat across from me in his stark white prison uniform juggling a pack of cigarettes between his fingers. Nicotine seemed to have become his only therapy. "It may be prison, but I kind of like it—I'm on my own . . . I mean, I don't want to be in prison, but that's just the way it worked out. . . . I'm missing everything, but it's better than being with Mom. I mean, I'm locked up but I'm free."

After four years of reflection could he explain why he had felt he had no other option but to kill his mother? Did he know he could have picked up the phone and reported his mother?

"Yeah," he said, "but I didn't take it seriously. It didn't come into my mind. I never realized it was abuse. I thought it was normal. . . . I didn't realize until after I was [arrested] and spoke to Dr. Lester and got letters from everybody that knew me when I was a little kid."

This was the classic answer of the abused child, the young person who realizes only in retrospect that what he or she endured for so long was abnormal, abusive. Why, then, had he felt he had to kill her? He put the pack of cigarettes down and looked me straight in the eye, and said:

Probably it's sort of like when a mama bobcat sees another animal going after her cubs, but it was ass backwards with my mom. The cub should be afraid of the animal and be waiting for his mama to protect him; but I was always afraid of my mom. It's just ass backwards. I don't know if that explains it. . . . When I fired the shot, I just stood there. I froze, thinking, "I actually did it." I didn't think I would do it. I wanted to relieve the pressure in my mind. . . . I thought this was the perfect way. . . . I wouldn't have to come home always getting nervous in my stomach. I'd end up living with Burt's parents or my dad. I don't know why I pulled the trigger. I know I wanted to get rid of the shit that I get, but I don't know why I took the gun and shot her. I just don't know. . . . I knew there were kids who killed their parents, but I didn't think I would be one of them.

PART IV

DAUGHTERS WHO KILL
THEIR MOTHERS

Introduction

The title of the 1983 Academy Award–winning movie *Terms of Endearment* was ironic: For most of the film, the relationship between the mother and the daughter was anything but "endearing." From the day her child was born, the mother selfishly sought to control her, and in turn, the daughter was constantly resentful of her mother's domination. They tore huge emotional chunks from each other, wounds made worse by the fact that each knew the other's vulnerabilities, as only a mother and daughter can. Still, the movie struck a deep emotional chord in audiences because the strife was so real.

We all know that conflict between mothers and daughters is no less ferocious than between fathers and sons, but there is a significant difference. Mothers and daughters, and women in general, tend to "duke it out" with words, not fists. Statistics bear this out, for only 10 percent of all violent crime is committed by women. While cultural and perhaps biological differences between men and women may be responsible, we don't know conclusively why women kill so much less often than men. The fact remains that matricide by daughters is by far the rarest form of parricide, accounting for a minuscule four out of every hundred cases.

Before writing this book, I had only been involved in five of these cases, and in every one, the young girl killed in conjunction with at least one other person, one of whom was always a male. In two, the daughter killed her mother and father with the help of a brother; in the third, the child killed the mother with the help of a boyfriend; and in the fourth, the daughter killed her mother with the help of her sister, brother, and several friends. Because the participation of a boyfriend or brother is nearly always a significant factor, there is the lingering doubt that, but for the male, the murders might not have taken place. Patty Claremont's case is different from all of these, and it is also the single case in this book in which I was not contacted by the family or their attorney for assistance.

Patricia's story was one of several featured in a magazine about the "inexplicable" phenomenon of parricide. The author of the article, like so many who take on the subject, was writing from the perspective that seemingly normal kids, for some obscure reason, just flip out and kill their parents. Only several paragraphs were devoted to Patty's case, but they sparked my desire to explore it further, for Patty had killed her mom solely on her own.

This was not, however, the reason I ultimately decided to include the case in this book. Nor was it even the nature of the abuse, as bad as it was, that I found particularly fascinating or compelling. The brutal whippings that Patricia and her younger sister, Dionne, received from Deborah were horrifying, but the treatment was no worse than that visited on numerous children I have represented. The fact that Patricia had repeatedly been raped over a period of ten years by Deborah's live-in boyfriend, Billie Lalonde, was appalling, but again, not any worse than other cases I have had involving sexual abuse.

What distinguishes this case is that Patricia and her sister were not only abused by their parent, but that this abuse was allowed to continue by the very system that was supposed to protect them. For all Deborah's and her boyfriend's depradations and the lasting damage they did to the physical and spiritual well-being of her children, these paled in comparison to the contemptible, more reprehensible actions of the social service, mental health, and law enforcement agencies once the abuse was reported to them. Deborah severely abused her children, yet it was the blundering inaction of the county and state that ultimately created the environment that made her homicide possible. The true tragedy of this case is that the killing could so easily have been prevented.

Patty

Patricia grew up in a town nestled on one of the Great Lakes. Patty's lawyer, Eric Anston, describes the place as "a community woven through and through with family relationships . . . there is a strength within the community connected with family."

All of the life of the community of 200,000 flows out from the harbor. Head north from the harbor and you will find yourself traveling down beautiful wide avenues; on either side, sloping manicured lawns lead up to large homes. As you make your way south from the harbor, however, the houses are more modest, the yards smaller. When I first met Patricia, she was out on bail pending the resolution of her appeal. She was staying on the east side of the town, not far from where she grew up, in a four-bedroom home with her sister, Dionne, and Uncle Donald and Aunt Sally and their five children.

When I pulled into the dirt driveway, Patty and her cousins were sitting in a circle talking to each other. Her aunt and uncle, both in their late fifties, were the first to come over and greet me as I got out of my car. Patty was hesitant about saying hello and only did so after some prompting by her uncle, who since Deborah's death has become her legal guardian. Though Patty had just turned eighteen, she still looked like a young schoolgirl. She had a gentle face, with soft brown eyes and a slow, spreading smile.

We stood awkwardly in the yard, Patty looking everywhere but at me. Putting a comforting arm around her shoulder and hugging her to his side, her uncle Donald softly said, "She's kind of shy, and pretty nervous about this. But she does want to speak with you. You gotta understand, this will be the first time she's talked about it since her trial last winter. But it's important. People need to know what happened." Then he looked at Patty, whose eyes were welling with tears, and said, "Let's go inside, Patty, and talk with the man." Her head bowed, she hooked her arm around her uncle's neck and slowly walked with him into the house.

As I followed them, I felt my resolve to interview Patty wavering. The tears in her eyes had reminded me once again of all she had gone through in the last year; I certainly didn't want to cause her more pain. The brutal heat and humidity enveloping the dirt yard didn't help. I hesitated for a second, and then Patty's uncle Donald stuck his head out of the screen door. "You coming inside?"

"Yeah," I said, "I just forgot something in the car. I'll be right in."

He smiled. "Okay. I'll get you something cold to drink."

The four of us took our seats in an enclosed sun porch, Patty clinging to her aunt on a worn couch. For the first hour she couldn't bring herself to answer my questions with more than a yes or no or a shrug of the shoulders. Her aunt gently chimed in to help fill in most of the family history.

To the outside world, thirty-four-year-old Deborah Claremont was a paragon of virtue. A single parent, she had separated from Patty's father soon after Patty's younger sister Dionne was born. Deborah struggled tirelessly to support her two girls, leaving early every morning for her job as an office manager at a car dealership. When she finished up there in the late afternoon, she went to a second job, as a hospital receptionist. Often she didn't arrive home until past midnight. Sundays, however, were reserved for worship in the house of the Lord.

Deborah was determined that her children would have everything that she didn't. She bought them the best clothes she could afford, and her girls were *never* seen outside the house in anything but spotless, neatly pressed clothes. She taught them to respect her and all other authority figures, and they learned their lessons well. Deborah especially wanted them to do well in school so they could go to college and get good jobs. She was obsessively worried that her daughters might join the crowded ranks of black teenage girls forced to quit high school because of pregnancy. She knew how terribly difficult life was for a teenage mom: she had been one herself.

Mrs. Claremont was an inexhaustible little fireplug of a woman who never seemed to stop working. With her tireless energy and constant perfectionism, she impressed many people in her community as someone with an overwhelming desire to improve herself and the lives of her children. Patricia's high-school principal commented to the press that Deborah demonstrated unparalleled concern for the welfare of her daughters.

After the homicide, all of her coworkers at both jobs were understandably shocked and horrified and protested loudly that there were no problems between mother and daughter. 'It was just a happy family to me . . . ,'' one coworker said. Yet, even among her supporters, there was a tacit recognition of the fact that Deborah Claremont had run a tight ship. She had rules that her girls had to live by, and she expected them to be followed to a T.

Every parent has at one time or another gotten upset with her child for getting her clothes dirty. Deborah was no different, but she was obsessive in her insistence that Patty and Dionne always be clean and stay clean, clothes and body. Dirt was evil and getting dirty immoral.

Aunt Sally recounted to me what happened when the girls, even as very young kids, got their dresses dirty. "She would stand Patty and Dionne [at the time eight and five respectively] in the middle of the floor . . . give them both a switch and make them whip one another; when they got tired of whipping one another, she would turn around and whip them." The concern and vigilance that earned Deborah so much respect in the outside world became, behind closed doors, outright physical abuse.

Getting dirty was not the only sin Deborah cleansed with such ritual whippings. One relative who lived with the family for a short while said, "If she told them to do something, like if they didn't move fast enough, fast enough for her, then she'd whip them . . . with drop cords [electrical extension cords] and switches tied together."

Patricia described what happened once when she and her sister had stopped off for a soda on their way home from doing an errand for their mother and so were about a half-hour late.

"I think I was about ten," Patty said. ". . . Momma had come home early, and when we come up the road, we seen her in the yard waiting on us. . . . She whupped us so bad in our face people thought we had the chicken pox."

There was even an elaborate ritual about the way Deborah "whupped" her kids. She preferred an electric extension cord, and before she was going to hit them, she gave them the option of retrieving it and bringing it to her. Patty told me, "If we didn't find [it], she would get the nearest thing she seen, [like a] broomstick, yardstick—whatever was around her." She always made them take their clothes off, too, even their underwear, because, in Patty's words, "Momma said she won't whip us when we were wearing the new clothes that she bought."

After they had undressed, Deborah forced the girls to bend over a bed or rocking chair while she beat them. Patricia recited the litany that accompanied each beating, her voice singsong as she recited the words she knew only too well: " 'Turn round, because I'll whup your natural butt, and if you move, I'm hitting you in your face.'

"If you tried to turn over and put your hand back down [to protect yourself]," Patty continued, "she said, 'I told you to move your hand and you put your hand back down here.' Then she put down the switch or the stick and started hitting you with her hand. Then she'd say, 'I dare you to holler. If you make one sound, I'll hit you again. . . . And don't be sayin', "Momma, I'm sorry," or "How come you whupping me?" Don't say that because it's going to make me whup you more.' "

These thrashings continued right up until the night of the homicide. After Patty's description of the physical punishments, her uncle Donald broke into the conversation. He had been largely silent for the first hour, but now felt compelled to explain his sister's behavior to this stranger.

"Maybe it would help if you knew the story from the beginning. . . . My mother only had two kids, that was me and Deborah. We were raised in a one-family house. . . . Deborah kind of patterned herself after her mother. One night when Momma came in, she had been drinking, and she started in on us. And the only way we were able to skip a beating that night, 'cause we were beat all the time, was due to the fact that my uncle reached up and grabbed a shotgun and told my momma that if she hit us again what he was going to do. . . . Yeah, there was a lot of whuppings. In fact we got a whupping the same way that [Patty] got them. You know, extension cords."

"Right before this child here was born," Donald continued, "I'll never forget it. Deborah was already married and she was about seven months pregnant with Patty, so she would be about sixteen at the time. I came in and Deborah and Momma was fussing about something, and Momma told Deborah to take off her clothes. . . . 'I realize you're pregnant,' Momma said, 'but that still won't stop me from giving you a whupping . . . as long as I stay away from your stomach, I'm going to whip that butt.' And she made her strip down and she whipped her on her naked butt."

Almost immediately after Patricia was born, Deborah picked up where her momma left off. Relatives and neighbors saw what the outside world did not—that Deborah was abusing her children. Those close to the family did try to intervene, at least during the early years, but Deborah would listen to nobody. Ironically, Deborah's abuse of Patricia even became too much for her own mother, who became so upset with Deborah for beating two-year-old Patty (because the toddler soiled her Sunday dress) that she literally took Patricia away for about six months. Patty only went back to live with her mother when her grandmother died.

After the death of Patty's grandmother, Donald and several other relatives continued to try to persuade Deborah to change the way she treated her children. Their efforts were futile. And after the homicide, several of these relatives expressed sorrow for not reporting Deborah to social services as soon as they saw the first signs of abuse. While their guilt was understandable, remarkably someone *had* reported the abuse, and the authorities did "intervene." The physical abuse was reported by the only person whom Deborah would listen to—herself.

No one knows what precipitated the beating. It had something to do with Patricia's (then fourteen) leaving her younger sister alone at home one evening. When Deborah came home from work that night, she accused her daughter of "having connections with a boy." Patricia vehemently denied it. She was an attractive, gregarious girl, and other kids of both sexes liked her. She didn't have a boyfriend, however, and compared to most teens her age, actually had a limited social life. Maniacal in her fear that her daughters would follow in her footsteps and become single mothers, Deborah refused to accept Patty's protestations of innocence. The anger was strong in Patty's voice as she described what happened next.

"She knocked me to the floor and started whipping me. She said I had connections with a boy and I told her I didn't. . . . She kept beating me. And then she left and got Billie [Deborah's boyfriend] and told him that if he didn't stop her that she was going to end up killing me. She said she brought me into this world and she could take me out. . . . She called the police and told them they'd better come and get her before she killed me."

The local child protective worker called in by the police wrote in her report:

Mrs. Claremont admitted that she completely lost control and did not even know what she used to whip Patricia with. Patricia described a white pole with wires in the center. Mrs. Claremont stated that when she was on the verge of really hurting Patricia, she left and went to get her boyfriend, Billie Lalonde. He returned to the house with her and convinced them to go to the police department. . . . After conducting a private interview with Patricia, we determined that she was not really afraid of her mother, but that she believed that her mother might get angry with her again. We talked with Mrs. Claremont, Patricia, and Mr. Lalonde to decide what to do to insure protection for the child. Mr. Lalonde offered to stay with the family, and both Patricia and her mother readily agreed to this plan rather than to have Patricia go into foster care. . . . At the time of this investigation, Patricia was not felt to be in imminent danger as we did not substantiate a history of abusive discipline. Mrs. Claremont seemed to recognize her *mistake* [emphasis added] and was cooperative with agency involvement. Mr. Lalonde voluntarily agreed to assist the family and help prevent further physical confrontations."

During Patricia's eventual homicide trial, the caseworker described exactly how severely Deborah had beaten her daughter:

On her left forearm she had two raised one-by-two-inch welts; one bloody scratch a half inch long near her left elbow and one raised, red welt near her left elbow one by three inches in size; on the right forearm there were two raised, red welts about one by two inches and one small scratch; then on her left shoulder there were two red, raised welts one-half inch by three; and on her left front thigh two raised, red welts approximately one and a half by two inches in size.

The lackadaisical manner in which the Department of Children's Services handled this incident was typical of the way in which they would deal with the family over the next fourteen months. Because it is so rare that a parent has the insight and fortitude to call out for help when they see themselves going over the edge, this was an ideal opportunity to intervene to stop the abuse and get help for the whole family, Deborah especially. However, as so often happens, the helping hand of government struck with stupendous imprecision, leaving Patty in a worse position than if the abuse had never been reported.

The most blatant bungle was in the investigators' failure to do a comprehensive family history. As a department representative later stated, "we did not substantiate a history [of abuse because] that's one of the things that we do look for in determining the safety of a child to go back into the home." In other words, they didn't find substantial abuse because they didn't look for it. They regarded Deborah's beating of Patty as an isolated circumstance, a "mistake," and not part of any larger pattern. Later on, during the trial, Patty's defense attorney cross-examined the social service worker, asking her to explain how she arrived at that conclusion.

> Q: Did you look for any history of child abuse in this case?
>
> A: Yes, I did.
>
> Q: Did you talk to any of the family or anybody about it?
>
> A: . . . I spoke with Patricia herself and with Mrs. Claremont about whether there had been any prior incidents. . . .
>
> Q: Were you aware at that time that she had an uncle and he had a wife?
>
> A: No, I was not.
>
> Q: And that there were other family members who were familiar with the family situation?
>
> A: No, I was not.

Incredible as it may seem, these mistakes are not isolated events, but occur when caseworkers are overworked and insufficiently trained. Unfortunately, some child abuse investigators will accept the parent's and child's words at face value in the absence of an adequate understanding of the wall of silence that hides such crimes. They do not fully grasp the tremendous fear and denial that can keep both victim and perpetrator from admitting what is going on. In Mike's case in Part I, for instance, the same thing occurred.

And these deep-seated barriers are exacerbated by all the other problems most caseworkers must cope with: an overwhelming caseload, low wages, and inadequate guidance from supervisors. Patty Claremont's case, however, was handled with unusual ineptness.

There were numerous witnesses, many of whom testified at trial (when it was too late), who could have told the investigators that this particular beating was far from unique. Uncle Donald, Aunt Sally, and many cousins and friends knew the pattern of abuse that had begun from almost the moment Patty took her first breath. But nobody at the agency bothered to interview anyone but the girls and their mom.

Despite their benign conclusions, the beating itself was sufficiently serious that the agency opened a protective services file on the family, which meant that they would be monitored on a monthly basis. The first contact occurred only three weeks after the reported beating, and then Patricia confided to the caseworker that "her mother is physically abusive and loses her temper easily." Yet, even with this new information, no fundamental change was made in the monitoring of the family, nor were any steps taken to get the family therapeutic help.

In a pattern that was repeated again and again in this case, Patricia's word was simply not enough. The worker chose not to take action without physical evidence of the beating. Evidently the investigator did not understand the fundamental reluctance of abused children to reveal the truth and did not grasp that it was all Patty could do even to talk to her about the beatings. All the while, her mother was pressing her not to talk to the social service workers, later on even hiding in the closet during the visits to make sure that her children said nothing out of line.

Two months after the initial incident, Patricia reported that Dionne had been beaten with a belt, but no marks were left. The agency declined to act. Just eight weeks later, Dionne reported that "she had gotten a whipping two weeks earlier, and that marks had been left." Again, the caseworker did not act because she didn't see any physical evidence. Instead, she told the girls to report their beatings when they occurred and the marks were still fresh. From this, the girls got the message that it was somehow their fault that nothing was being done to help them. In reality, the girls were just too frightened to contact the social service workers themselves; they waited for the visits. And because they waited, it was as if the beatings had never happened. The concluding notation on the day that Patty reported Dionne's beating was: "No serious problems were evidenced." The caseworker didn't even bring up the incident with Deborah.

One month later Dionne again informed the caseworker that she had been whipped and marks were left. Yet, again the girls were admonished to report the abuse right away. Again, no one bothered to confront Deborah. Over the next three months, she continued to beat her children, but the caseworker judged none of the beatings sufficiently "severe" to warrant action. The caseworker, despite the girls' claims, was rather sanguine about the whole situation. The children and mother "were getting along better together," she wrote at the time.

Another enigmatic case note came seven months after the first report. "They [the girls] reported that their situations were fine," the worker blithely concluded, "no problems with their mother or discipline. Girls did indicate they got bored at home by themselves and seemed a little depressed." Apparently, the girls' depression was, to the case monitor, perfectly compatible with a "fine" family situation.

Predictably, things got worse as the months wore on. Though Deborah had set the state intervention in motion, she continually resisted efforts, as minimal as they were, to help the family. Her threats against revealing the truth to the caseworkers, and her hiding in the closet to enforce the prohibition, were parts of the pattern.

Her original call for help showed that on some level, she recognized that she had a serious problem. The solution, as she saw it, apparently did not include individual or family therapy. The same woman who had called the police to stop her from killing her daughter did not seem to think anything was wrong with her parenting skills. Once the crisis was past, she returned to seeing her problem as a simple one: Patty had disobeyed a rule and left Dionne alone. Therefore, to prevent her daughters from leaving the house again when she was working, she installed a complex lock system that prevented anyone from opening the door from the inside. And to further insure that they didn't have any contact with the outside world, she regularly took the phone with her when she went to work.

In many parricide cases, because of the tremendous psychological control exercised by the parents, the children, immobilized by fear and confusion and thus unable to escape, are often described as being *like* prisoners in their own homes. Patty and Dionne were not only confined in a metaphoric sense, but between three in the afternoon and midnight they were literal prisoners in their own home. Any slim chance they might earlier have had to reach out to others was then virtually extinguished.

In plain fact, the caseworker and the entire department seriously missed the boat with the Claremont family. As if the physical abuse weren't enough, it seemed that the agency had overlooked excesses visited on Patty of an entirely different sort as well, for a mere eleven months after Deborah reported herself, Patty finally told her aunt and a school counselor that her mother's boyfriend had been sexually abusing her since age seven.

"Two referrals received on the same date making allegations that Patricia had been sexually abused by Mr. Lalonde," the caseworker noted dryly. "Patricia had disclosed to school counselor after a suicide attempt. Field visit made to interview Patricia at school. Patricia indicated that Mr. Lalonde had been having sex with her for several years."

Several months before the sexual abuse report, when the caseworker had noted that Patricia seemed a "little depressed," she had been in reality acutely depressed, so much so that she tried to kill herself by swallowing a whole bottle of pain medication. In the hospital, she had been, like so many sexually abused children, too embarrassed to confess what was disturbing her. And the professionals charged with her care, also typically, were not sufficiently competent or sensitive enough to ask the right questions. Her problem, they said, was mere adolescent depression.

So, in the end, it took a suicide attempt before Patty broke her silence, but even then she did not break it willingly. Her aunt Sally had been the first to draw out the appalling truth.

"I was talking on the phone to my mother," she said. "My daughter came in and said, 'Patricia's crying.' So I got up and went in there and asked Patricia what's wrong. . . . And she come and told me about she was tired of having Billie 'fooling with me.' . . . She told me that it first started when she was seven when they stayed with him when their momma went into the hospital."

Aunt Sally was horrified and also certain that Patty was telling the truth. The next day she accompanied Patty to school and made sure that the girl repeated the story to her counselor, then insisted the school follow through and actually report the allegations.

Speaking softly, in a voice laden with pain, Patricia would later take the stand in the fifth day of her trial for killing her mother, to tell the jury about the "first time."

> *P: Mama went in the hospital to have surgery, and she asked Billie to stay overnight with us. Me and Dionne was sleeping in Mama's bed. In the middle of the night I woke up and he was on top of me.*
>
> *Q: Did you know what was going on?*
>
> *P: All I know he was on top of me.*
>
> *Q: Did he say anything to you?*
>
> *P: He told me not to tell, and if I do, he'd do something to Mama. . . . [Later] Mama called, and I told Mama that when I woke up, Billie was on top of me, and she told me that I had a bad dream. . . .*
>
> *Q: But did you try to tell her what he did?*
>
> *P: Yes, but she just said I had a bad dream. I told her I bled; she told me that I may have hurt myself and that I should put a little Vaseline on my body.*

Patty testified further that Billie had then forced her to have sex about twice a month, and that this had gone on for the next seven years. She tried several times to tell her mother what Billie was doing to her, but Deborah refused to hear her daughter's words, no matter how vague. Billie was after all, in Deborah's oft-repeated words, "like a father to my children," and simply beyond reproach. Well, almost. Deborah apparently trusted Billie with her children, but she also knew that she couldn't completely trust this surrogate father to be faithful to her with other women outside the family.

Several nights a week it was the same routine. Billie came in at three or four in the morning, and Deborah accused him of being with another woman. Billie protested loudly, saying that he had been playing cards, a usual outing for him. One night Deborah had had enough. With twelve-year-old Patty in tow, she followed Lalonde. He did go to his card game, but on the way back, he stopped at another house first where Deborah caught him in bed with another woman.

Even though her suspicions were confirmed, she wanted to keep him. But how could she keep tabs on Billie and at the same time hold down an evening job? The answer was simple—Patty. Her daughter would accompany Billie to his evening card games. Surely with Patty present, Billie would never attempt to fool around with another woman. And if he did, well, Patty would be her faithful reporter. Even better, while

Patty watched Billie, Billie would insure that Patricia would stay out of trouble while Deborah was at work. It was a perfect solution.

While such an arrangement served Deborah's personal needs, it had devastating consequences for Patricia. Before this, Billie could only force himself on Patty when her mother was not at home and Dionne was sleeping. Now there were no buffers. He could sexually assault her whenever he wanted, and he did—usually in the back seat of his car down some deserted dirt road or in a cheap motel.

Soon after this, Deborah forced her daughter to go with Billie on all his trips, even during the day, regardless of the destination. Like the obedient child she was, she did exactly what her mother told her to do. But Patty was churning inside. She hated every moment with the man; and it was impossible for her to accept that her mother didn't know that something was going on. "Every time he'd [want to] go somewhere she said, 'Patricia, go with him.' I told her that I didn't want to go, and she used to make me go in case he's going to see another woman. . . .

" 'Momma, when am I going to do my homework, and I got to eat,' I'd say to her; and she would say, 'It will be here when you get back, so you better go with him.' And when he would bring me home at three, four in the morning, she asked no questions, no questions."

Even if her mother had asked, it is doubtful that Patty would have told her mother the truth, especially since her mother had so steadfastly refused to believe her the first few times. As Patty would drive home late at night with him, Lalonde would threaten to hurt or kill her if she talked, then reminded her that he kept a gun under the driver's seat. He would also "do something to Momma" if she told anybody about the sex.

In addition to the threats, Lalonde also told Patty several times, "It won't do no good to tell anybody, because they won't believe you." These words proved correct. In fact, what occurred following the formal filing of the sexual abuse report was so appalling that I refused to believe it when Eric Anston, Patty's defense attorney, first told me about it. Only after I reviewed the police reports and sworn trial testimony did I become convinced of the dismal truth.

Lalonde was brought into the police station, and initially he denied any involvement with Patricia. However, after several hours of police interrogation, he had a change of heart. The following trial testimony is his version of events as told to the court during Patty's trial. The only variation was that he originally told the police he had had sex with her four to five times, while in court he said it was three times. The interrogator is Eric Anston:

> *Q: Tell us how that [the first sexual incident] took place.*
> *A: I was in bed and Patricia just climbed in. . . .*
> *Q: I believe you told Lieutenant Moreau when you talked to him about it that you woke up and she was wriggling all over you. Is that right?*
> *A: That's right.*
> *Q: So you just couldn't fight her off?*
> *A: Well, I did push her off after I woke up and seen it was her.*
> *Q: After you woke up?*
> *A: And seen it was her.*
> *Q: But it happened anyway?*
> *A: Well, she was putting it in.*
> *Q: Pardon?*
> *A: She was putting it in.*

(The court reporter notes that there was an outburst of laughter in the courtroom.)

> *Q: You couldn't stop her?*
> *A: I was asleep.*

(The court reporter notes another outburst of laughter.)

> *Q: Mr. Lalonde, did you say to her, "Patricia, this is wrong, you can't do this"?*
> *A: Yes, sir. I told her to get out here, and she did.*
> *Q: What was the next time?*
> *A: The next time I was in the kitchen in there sitting in the chair waiting on Deborah.*
> *Q: And what happened?*

A: She came in there and sat on my lap.

Q: And it happened again?

A: Yes, sir.

Q: Did you say, "Patricia, get out of here, we can't do this"?

A: I just kept pushing her and told her this was wrong. She said, "Well, I just need it."

Q: Where were you the next time it happened?

A: The next time it just didn't take effect. I stopped. And that was it.

At the time Mr. Lalonde was "sexually assaulted" by fourteen-year-old Patricia, he was fifty-six years old.

What happened when Deborah heard the news was equally fantastic. Upon her arrival at the police station, the assistant police chief informed her of the allegations against Lalonde. She couldn't believe it because Billie "was like a father to Patricia." Of course, it had to be Patty's fault. After briefly speaking with the assistant police chief, Deborah asked if she could speak privately with Mr. Lalonde. The principal investigating officer testified during Patty's trial as to what happened next.

Q: What was Mrs. Claremont's attitude toward the situation when you investigated it?

A: After she talked with Billie Lalonde, she decided that she did not want him prosecuted for anything. She thought that the sexual contact by Billie Lalonde and Patricia was Patricia's fault.

Q: She blamed it on Patricia?

A: That's correct.

Q: Did Mr. Lalonde make any admission to you?

A: He admitted that he had sex with Patricia Claremont.

Q: Did he also blame it on Patricia?

A: Yes, sir, he did.

Q: Now, you did not take any criminal action against Mr. Lalonde at that time. I'm going to ask why you did not.

A: Well, for two reasons. The main reason is Deborah did not want him to be prosecuted; the second is the in-

*cident was reported as a child molestation. At the time of
the incident Patricia was fourteen years of age. By Billie's
own statement the times he said he had sex with her she
was also fourteen. Therefore it was not child molestation.*

*Q: Did you make any investigation or try to find out
whether or not it had gone on at a time before she was
fourteen?*

*A: Nothing other than interviewing Billie Lalonde,
and . . . Patricia's statement . . . was that Billie Lalonde
had had sex with her for the past six or seven years.*

*Q: Is there any particular explanation why that infor-
mation was not acted upon by the police?*

*A: Nothing other than the fact that by Billie's own
statement . . . What it boiled down to was his word against
hers.*

Following her discussion with the detectives, Deborah took
her daughter by the hand and left the station. Billie Lalonde
drove them home, just as he had done a little over a year
earlier when the social services people had agreed that his
living with them would be an ideal solution to help prevent
further physical confrontations. No criminal charges were
ever filed against Mr. Lalonde, nor did the county charge
Deborah with child abuse or neglect.

Did Deborah truly believe, as she claimed, that the sex was
"Patty's fault"? One psychologist involved in the case found
her reaction "not characteristic of her personality. Based on
her history with the girls, it would have been more appropriate
to exhibit an emotional outburst and punish Patty severely.
Also, after having been intimate with Billie for years, upon
finding that he had been having sex with her daughter, she
only felt 'sad.' The probable explanation is that she had been
aware of the exploitation for a long time and that she tacitly
encouraged and abetted it."

We will never know whether Deborah, in fact, knew about
the sexual abuse. But she was the one who decided, firmly
and immediately, not to bring charges against Billie. Obviously, she wanted the incident forgotten as quickly as
possible.

Despite what Deborah may have wanted, however, what
should have happened did not. Patty's claim of sexual abuse

before she was fourteen, the legal cutoff in that state for that crime, should have caused the police to launch a full-scale investigation. But as in many parts of the nation, the tendency is still to take the word of an adult over a child.

Patricia's age at the time, fourteen, complicated matters as well. Fourteen is the age at which a person is deemed mature enough to give informed consent to sexual activity with an adult and is thus the cutoff age for child molestation and statutory rape in Patricia's home state. Thus Billie could only have been prosecuted for those crimes if, and a big if it was, the officers had chosen to believe Patricia that the abuse had begun years earlier.

The only applicable crime, in the police department's eyes, was rape, which would have required evidence that Lalonde forced and otherwise intimidated Patty into having intercourse. For some inexplicable reason, not only did the police believe Mr. Lalonde's version of events, they didn't even deem it necessary to ask Patty if she wanted to file charges, instead turning to Deborah to make that decision. The only plausible explanation for this turn of events was that the police thought Patty, though old enough to consent to sex, was not competent enough, because of her age, to make the decision to prosecute. After all, the thinking probably went, she's not yet eighteen, so we should leave such a critical decision to her mother. Deborah, as her behavior unmistakably demonstrated, wanted the whole incident forgotten, and that's exactly what happened.

In a system of true and equal justice, even if the police didn't accept that Lalonde had sex with Patty before she was fourteen, the decision *at least to file* a rape complaint should have rested solely with Patty. The police department should have conducted an in-depth investigation and then, if they found probable cause, gone to a magistrate for a warrant, or referred the case to the DA for prosecution. Despite the lack of any physical evidence (not an uncommon circumstance in these cases), Lalonde's alibi alone should have lent credence to Patty's version of events.

Deborah's wishes, her good name—these should have had nothing to do with the decision to get an arrest warrant or prosecute. The DA can consider the *victim's* desires, but must also weigh heavily the public's interest in justice. What happened to Patricia in that police station was not only a travesty of justice of the highest proportions; it was also a quintessential example of the law's naive and myopic treatment of abused youth.

Because of society's almost pathological desire to maintain parents' control over their children, it has created a different standard of justice to deal with one of its darkest secrets. Rape has been illegal since biblical times, an offense which has historically carried the strictest of penalties; in our own time, it used to be punished with the death sentence in some states. Yet this ultimate penalty was meted out only if the female was raped by a stranger. Under the law, rape by a family member has always been regarded differently. Though incest laws are generally more strictly enforced today (*if* the incest is reported, and *if* the report is believed), up until the late 1970s the enforcement was less than vigilant. And on those rare occasions when a father was prosecuted, he usually received a comparatively light sentence.

When it comes to fathers and stepfathers who rape their daughters, we as a society have historically exhibited a strange double standard, as if the crime were of a fundamentally different nature from rape and the perpetrator somehow deserving of understanding. It is often believed, or at least claimed, that the daughter initiated or wanted the sex. Of course, rapists frequently make this claim. Given what we now know about the dynamics of sexual abuse, however, it seems shockingly illogical to blame incidents of sex between adult fathers and female children on the children. Nevertheless, this attitude has been around for a long time. The story of Lot in the Book of Genesis provides one ancient example.

After fleeing Zoar, Lot lived with his two daughters in a cave in the hills. Lamenting their isolation from prospective husbands, one evening the older sister said to the younger, "Our father is old, and there is not a man on earth to come in to us after the manner of all the earth. Come let us make our father drink wine, and we will lie with him, that we may preserve offspring through our father." The daughters carried out their scheme over the next two evenings, and nine months later two babies were born.

The story's implication was clear: incest was the daughters' fault. Poor drunken Lot was taken advantage of by his scheming children. Times have changed, but sadly some attitudes have not.

The department had already been "monitoring" the family for over a year, and they accepted Lalonde's version of events. Like Deborah and the police, they saw Patricia as the cause of the problem. Consequently, their efforts were desultory and largely ineffective. But Deborah did have to make some temporary arrangement to keep Patricia away from Mr. Lalonde, so she sent Patty and Dionne to live with relatives in another town. It was as if she were protecting him from the attentions of Patty, as if she were just another sexually precocious teenager who would initiate sex if left alone with her mother's boyfriend.

The alternative living arrangement was short-lived, however, because two months later Deborah discovered that Patty and Dionne had gone to a birthday party at the home of a person of whom she disapproved. She insisted they come home. After their return, the department continued its involvement for another five months, though contacting Patty and Deborah only twice. Apparently, they were under the impression that things were improving.

Besides separating Patricia and Billie Lalonde, the agency also recommended therapy for Patty, which she received. Following the first counseling session, Dr. Parks, a local psychologist, noted in his intake report, "Client seems sad and feels that situation is hopeless—has made suicide attempts in past (when questioned about suicidal feelings now says her feelings are upside down) . . . mother seems suspicious of client, especially regarding sexual issues. From client's report she and mother are both angry."

The sessions that followed revealed no surprises, just the same problems that had been plaguing Patty for the past year. Dr. Parks did not discover anything new, but he witnessed the progressive deterioration of the relationship between mother and daughter. Unfortunately, like the police and the family services workers, Parks did not appreciate how desperate Patty's predicament was becoming, though his interview notes present a subtle but chilling documentary of the situation.

Patricia seems to feel that her mother is suspicious and restrictive because she fears Patricia becoming sexually involved. Patricia says that since her mother's boyfriend has been having sexual intercourse with her since she was seven or eight, "I don't see that there's anything else for me to learn." Mother for the most part avoids this issue, only alluding to her position by saying, "Why didn't she tell me about this when it first happened if this was going on." . . . Deborah feels people (mostly family) have expected her to respond differently [to the sexual abuse incident]. Says they think she should be angry, but she just feels sad for everyone involved. . . . Talked with mother today [who] . . . feels she cannot trust her daughter and this is why she can't allow her to go places or date. Expresses fears about "what might happen."

Later, Dr. Parks would be questioned on the witness stand. A small man with mousy hair and a wisp of mustache, he nervously pleated his trousers as he spoke. During his testimony he painted the relationship between mother and daughter as even worse than his notes reflected. "I did not speak to them together because there was some real difficulty with them, but that was certainly what I was working toward, helping them communicate, and trust [each other], and hopefully deal with issues in a better way. She indicated to me that her mother had a temper and became abusive. . . . [She would] fly off the handle and start hitting them with anything in sight. . . . She portrayed her mother as being impulsive in her anger and hitting and just kicking with things like cords."

Despite the fact that Patricia had repeatedly told him in their sessions that the beatings continued, he chose to do nothing with this information, not even informing the people at the social services department who had referred the Claremonts to him. When defense lawyer Anston challenged Dr. Parks for his silence on the continued abuse, Parks responded rather strangely, that he had not chosen to focus on the beatings but rather on the emotional problems that arose between mother and daughter as a result of the sexual abuse.

"I was aware that the caseworkers were working with them . . . so I kind of left all that up to them. Not that that wasn' an issue. It was. But I was more concerned about how thi child was feeling . . . and to help her work on some of her depression."

The so-called "therapy" lasted about five months before Dr. Parks terminated his assistance. In court he described the last session: "Patricia looked better, and by that I mean she was able to smile a little more, although things were not going perfectly at home, things were somewhat improved. . . . She said her mother was still seeing Billie Lalonde, but he wasn't coming around anymore . . . [however] I don't think she felt totally safe."

Three months after Dr. Parks terminated therapy, the department also declared a victory. "After 18 months our agency felt there had been sufficient progress within the Claremont home and our child protective services case was closed," their final case note read.

Tragically, little had changed for the better in Patty's life; in fact, the same things happened all over again—even Lalonde turned up again. During my interview with her, Patty said, "It got worse. Mama wouldn't have anything to do with me . . . she never spent no time with us no more . . . [and] I told her I was tired of Billie staying at home and she knowing what was happening to me, and then she slapped me and she told me she's going to make me suffer. . . . Even after everything had came out in the open . . . she still made me go [with him in the evenings]."

Patty had been in the last semester of eighth grade when the sexual abuse incident was reported. For the next year she did quite well considering the circumstances under which she was forced to live. She had always been a hardworking, courteous student. In fact, in tenth grade she was nominated to a nationally recognized academic club for being the most improved student in her class.

Like many abused children, Patty was able at first to distance herself from her feelings so that she could focus on schoolwork, her ideal escape. By the time she entered the eleventh grade, however, she could no longer pretend that "nothing was wrong." She began to arrive at school late, and her grades dropped. Unlike the previous year, when she had been known as a student who could accept criticism without a problem, now it made her angry and belligerent. In the spring of her junior year, her grades dropped dramatically, from an A to a C average. It was also during this period that she made another attempt to escape by trying to kill herself with pain tablets. There was a compelling logic to her decision to end her life: "I did it 'cause she let him come back in the house and stay with us. And that's about enough to have to live with, so if you can live with that, it's no more to live for."

It was the day after Patricia's seventeenth birthday. Things had actually been going well for a few weeks, so much so that Deborah had bought Patty a dozen red roses for her birthday. Both children were full of anticipation and excitement for the big summer vacation that they were going to take the next day, their first trip to New York City.

At about ten P.M., Cindy Gradson, a neighbor who watched the girls when Deborah worked, called Deborah at the hospital reporting that Patty and Dionne were having a loud party. Deborah bolted out of the hospital. When she arrived several minutes later, she saw a strange car in the driveway of their little green, frame house. Her rule about visitors was strict and simple: No visitors—especially of the male variety. She was blind with anger when she slammed open the front door. In court, Patricia related what happened next:

> She told [the boys] that she ought to call the police on them for being there at her house when she wasn't there. And she told Dionne to go in the back room and take off her clothes, including her underclothes, 'cause she wasn't whipping the clothes that she spent her money on . . . and she told Dionne to find her an extension cord and that she was going back to work and coming straight back home to finish whatever she was going to do. . . .
> [After she left] I was walking the floor thinking about all the whippings that she gave us. . . . My sister said we should get our clothes on and run. I told her I tried it before, it wouldn't work. If she caught us, she'd still beat us. So we had decided to go ahead and take it. And I was saying in my mind that I couldn't let her do us like that. That's when I got the gun which Mama kept in the closet. I was walking the floor and I had the gun in my hand and it went off. . . . [Then] I backed out of it; I

said we was to go ahead and take the beating. So I hid the gun. . . .

Soon Mama came home and she started whipping Dionne with the yardstick. And she was sitting there telling Dionne, "Put your head down on the bed and I dare you to cry. . . . I'm going to whip you till the blood comes." And she was sitting there beating Dionne with the yardstick. I was standing there thinking of her, now why she beating her like that. And I got the gun and I was holding it out . . . and something kept going through my head saying don't do it, and before I knew it, I had shot her . . . I really didn't hear the gun go off. . . . I seen Mama when she fell. Dionne was still laying on the bed with her head down. She wasn't crying 'cause Mama dared her not to cry.

Patty and Dionne then ran across the street and told a neighbor, "Somebody done shot Mama." They couldn't call for help from the house because Deborah kept the phone locked in the trunk of her car.

When the police arrived, Patty and Dionne told them that they had come home from the supermarket and had found their mother dead in the bedroom. Did the girls have any idea who could have killed their mother? Billie Lalonde, they said. Three days earlier Lalonde and Deborah had gotten into a ferocious argument, and Lalonde had packed and left. The police immediately picked up Lalonde but released him just as quickly after confirming his alibi. With Lalonde out of the picture, the investigators turned their attention to Patricia and Dionne, interrogating the sisters separately and obtaining solid confessions from each. Because she was the eldest and had pulled the trigger, the prosecutors focused their efforts on Patty. Indicted for murder, she was transferred to adult court. Dionne, only fourteen at the time of the homicide, was put into the hands of the juvenile court, which would ultimately place her on probation.

Understanding better than anyone else the motivation behind Patty's actions, Uncle Donald and Aunt Sally felt tremendous compassion for their nieces. They managed to bail out Patty and Dionne and brought the girls to live with them while they waited for Patty's trial.

Meanwhile, the state prepared its case. The prosecution theorized that the sisters wanted to kill their mom to be free from the legitimate restrictions that she imposed upon them. Deborah they saw as a hardworking, single parent who only wanted the best for her children. According to the state, she was not at all abusive; on the contrary they believed she was a good, responsible parent. And, their scenario went, when Deborah rushed home that night, she had embarrassed her children so much that they decided to kill her on her return from work later that night. The gun had not gone off accidentally the first time, but rather Patty had test-fired it to determine how hard she would have to pull the trigger.

At first glance, this interpretation seems shockingly unfair to Patty, yet the prosecution apparently did not have any "officially" substantiated evidence that Patty was abused. The original report of physical abuse had been written off as merely an isolated mistake in judgment on the part of the mother. As for the sexual abuse report, the position was predictable: no molestation had taken place since Patty had been the initiator of sex with Lalonde. After the county agency terminated its involvement with the family, no reports of physical or sexual abuse were received. From all this, it was concluded that everything must have been fine at home.

The trial opened in April and the courtroom was packed with Deborah's friends and co-workers, all intensely interested in discovering why she was taken from them. A half dozen of Patty's relatives sat in the front row, immediately behind her and Eric Anston.

The prosecutor, Frederick Welder, established that Patty had actually shot her mother, and then he set about trying to prove that Patty had never been abused. Friends and neighbors willingly testified that they had never seen Deborah strike any of her girls; nor for that matter had they ever heard Patty complain about her treatment at home. The prosecutor's following examination of a neighbor was typical:

> Q: *Did [the girls] ever indicate that there was anything abnormal going on in the house?*
> A: No.
> Q: *And you lived next door to them?*
> A: Yes.

Q: Did you ever see any evidence of any bruises or anything like that on either one of the children?
A: No.

It was excruciating for Patty, who had to sit day after day and listen to witness after witness swearing that her mom had been a saint. Coming to court each day in the same simple yellow dress, she spent most of the trial with her head cradled in her hands like a young child. When Billie Lalonde took the stand, it was simply too much for her. It is extremely rare for a defendant to be excused from the courtroom because she is offended by a witness. Patty, however, became so distraught that the judge permitted her to leave. As Lalonde was sworn in, all eyes in the courtroom followed a tearful Patty as she slowly strode down the center aisle and out the heavy oak door.

Lalonde's testimony, excerpted earlier, speaks for itself. It is sufficient to note that twice during Mr. Lalonde's description of the first time Patricia "forced" herself on him, the judge had to admonish the courtroom audience to refrain from laughing. The spectators, in a sense all expert witnesses on sexual behavior, knew Lalonde's version was too fantastic to be true. Equally outrageous, the prosecutor actually found a doctor willing to testify that Patty had not been abused—physically or sexually.

As with all the individuals in this book, I have changed the doctor's real name. But because his testimony still eludes my comprehension, I shall call him Dr. X. The following is an excerpt of what Dr. X had to say—under oath.

I examined all the documents sent to me in very great detail, looking for what I would consider to be evidence of physical and sexual abuse. Quite frankly, I'm not of the opinion—and I'm going to give you my reasons why I'm not of the opinion—that she was either physically or sexually abused. . . . To start with I was given the interviews . . . of all the teachers that she'd had for the last couple of years. There is not a single indication from the teachers of any physical abuse . . . and I'm of the opinion that teachers know very well what's going on

259

with students. The principal describes the mother as being an ideal parent.

    . . . Let me talk about the sexual abuse thing, because I don't quite frankly think it happened. I don't deny that Mr. Lalonde had intercourse with the girl, but when you have to make up your mind about whether sexual abuse was taking place, you've got to decide: Are you going to believe the girl or are you going to believe Billie? . . . The girl was fourteen years of age. Okay. . . . Fourteen years of age is the legal age to give consent to have sex, and that's the law. I may not like it. You may not like it. This man was not her stepfather. He was not her biological parent."

Despite the prosecution's efforts to disprove abuse, there *was* more than sufficient evidence to prove that Patty had been physically and sexually abused. However, the defense still faced the formidable task of proving how that abuse had affected her actions the night of the homicide. Testifying for the defense, Dr. Jean Lasty, a psychologist who specializes in the treatment and evaluation of battered women, described Patricia's mental state the night of the killing:

    In Patricia's mind there was a sense of hopelessness and feeling that this violence is going to continue and continue. . . . And then there was her depression, which influences a person's ability to create options for herself, particularly optimistic options . . . [At the time of the killing there was] a whirlwind of feeling and a very rapid-changing emotional climate within that home and within each of those individuals. . . . This time it was different in fundamental ways. The mother's agitation was higher than it had ever been before, and Patricia's depression and emotional state was worse than it had ever been before. . . . There is a great deal of evidence to suggest that at the time Patricia fired the gun she was very much dissociated from her action. I say that because she wasn't sure which hand the gun was in . . . whether it was light or heavy . . . she repeatedly said she didn't hear the gun go off. All of that suggests to me that at the time Patricia was in a dissociated state . . . [meaning] she was not part of it. In cases of extreme threat, like in victims of rape, we see dissociated states when they feel their life is being threatened. They feel themselves as observers from the corner of the room.

When it came time for the defense attorney to explain to the jury why Patty had failed to get through to the police or social workers, Dr. Lasty provided a compelling yet very common-sense answer, which also led the jury to an understanding of Patty's motives in covering up the homicide. "Patricia had never been helped by the police before by telling the truth," Dr. Lasty began. "[And] when she realized that her mother was dead, she didn't believe that the truth would function for her in any useful way, because it hadn't in the past. . . . She told the things that had happened to her in what she believed was a truthful manner, and the authorities did not move to help her or protect her."

Dr. Lasty's most dramatic testimony came as she was cross-examined by the prosecutor on the sexual molestation issue. Welder wanted Lasty to distinguish between "sexual abuse" and what he termed normal "sexual activity." I was not in the courtroom, but it is not difficult to hear the tremendous anger and offense in her voice.

> *Welder: And so there again we get into a terminology. Could a happening [sex between an adult and a person under eighteen] be sexually abusive or could it just be an instance of sexual activity?*
>
> *Lasty: Sir, even if you're making the distinction that Patricia was fourteen years old, and if you assume and totally negate the previous incidents that she reported, [namely] that the relationship occurred since the age of seven. I mean even if you make those assumptions, for her to engage in sexual activity with a person that had been in that home and acted as a caretaker since age seven, that would be sexual abuse by any clinician's standards. Whether it meets the definition of the law and whether it's prosecuted, it is every bit as damaging. . . . The legal ways in which we try to dissect the human experience do not account for the amount of human pain that is the result of that kind of treatment.*

But perhaps the saddest moment was a description of Patty's current emotional, psychological state: "She is very regressed," Lasty said. "There are times when she curls up in a fetal position, and she's also highly perfectionistic and has a compulsion for neatness. She plays with things which are not what we would consider age-appropriate—dolls and toys and younger children are much more comfortable companions for Patricia than children her own age. . . . Patricia, in every dimension that we were able to measure, presents herself as a person who has suffered intense physical and sexual abuse."

The jury took about eight hours to deliberate, returning a verdict of voluntary manslaughter. It was not an easy case to decide. As Anston told me, "They wrestled with this thing. They sent notes to the judge; they wanted questions answered. . . . They wanted to know how the hell they could get the legislature to pass a law against a man having sex with a fourteen-year-old."

The verdict meant, in purely legal terms, that the jury believed the homicide was committed during "a sudden violent and irresistible passion, resulting from serious provocation sufficient to excite such passion in a reasonable person." Anston's more human appraisal was a little different. "I'll tell you, there was one little item of evidence that was really very devastating and may have been the thing that caused her to get a conviction at all—it was the fact that [the jury thought] she test-fired that pistol."

Though they found her guilty of manslaughter, the jurors displayed a great outpouring of emotion for Patricia, even asking the judge to be lenient in sentencing. Patty's plight even affected Dr. X, who, despite his rather incredible findings, had recommended in a letter to the judge that Patty be placed on probation rather than be sent to prison even if she was found guilty.

As happens in so many of these cases, the judge chose to ignore all pleas for leniency based on the history of abuse. "A life has been taken without cause in my opinion and justification," he said. Then he sentenced her to the maximum term of fifteen years in prison.

Though I entered Donald's house that summer morning as a neutral observer, I was no longer impartial when I walked out some six hours later. It was not just Patty's treatment at the hands of her mother and the boyfriend that engendered me and engendered my sympathies; rather, what set my blood boiling was how Patty had been revictimized and violated by the very system designed to protect her. Though the appeal process was already underway, I told Patty and her family that I wanted to help in any way possible.

Patty was allowed to remain free on bond pending her appeal. As soon as the trial was over, Patty began therapy on a weekly basis. She also returned to school and found a part-time job. Not only did she finish high school, she also began taking junior college courses.

During this period, her uncle Donald tried on several occasions to persuade the local prosecutor to reopen the child-molestation/statutory-rape case against Billie Lalonde, but the request fell on deaf ears. The powers that be steadfastly maintained that no crime had been committed because there was no evidence of sexual contact between Patty and Lalonde prior to her fourteenth birthday. Any sexual contact after that time, the prosecutor insisted, was consensual; it was simply a case of Patty's word against Billie's, and they chose to believe Billie.

Eight months after my interview, I received the depressing, but definitely not surprising news that the Court of Appeals had upheld the conviction. Patty's bond was revoked, and within seventy-two hours she was sent to the state prison for women. Several months later the state Supreme Court unanimously upheld the decision of the lower appeals court.

Following the action by the state Supreme Court, I joined a local attorney in preparing a clemency petition to the governor. People from Patty's community have been mobilized for this effort. As of this writing, the petition has not yet been filed. Patty remains incarcerated in state prison.

Some people will say that Patty Claremont was a girl who fell through the cracks in the system. I disagree. She was pushed. And when she fell, there was no safety net to catch her. At the end of my interview with Patty and her relatives, Uncle Donald summed up the situation perfectly: "I feel sorry for my sister, you know, and I miss her. But you see . . . I don't blame Patricia, I blame the system. When the system stepped in there . . . if they just would have acted accordingly

. . . For instance, like they can see that the momma and daughter couldn't get along, why not separate them for a while? . . . You know Patty's been *forced* to deal with it. She tried the police department; it didn't work. She tried running away, it didn't work. . . . You know she's tried to take her own life; it didn't work. What else could she do?"

PART V

CHILDREN WHO KILL
BOTH PARENTS

Introduction

Lizzie hated Mrs. Borden, planned to kill her, and carried out that plan; but when Lizzie . . . came downstairs and saw her father, it occurred to her that he probably would discover what she had done and disapprove of it. So on the spur of the moment, she had to kill him, too, even though she hated to do it.

> —from the closing argument of Hosea Knowlton, the district attorney who unsuccessfully prosecuted Lizzie Borden

I once represented a fifteen-year-old boy who killed his mother, father, and a two-year-old cousin. I greatly respected and admired the psychiatrist who worked on the case because he was so honest.

"No doubt the boy was abused by his mom in some fairly sadistic ways, and the motivation for her homicide is directly attributed to the relationship she had with her son," he said to me several weeks before trial. "But as for an explanation of why he killed his father [who was basically a bland, non-offensive person] and his younger cousin, I can't be very sure. Basically your client flipped out, snapped after killing his mom. . . . Perhaps he had an acute psychotic episode. . . . But at the present time I can't detect any thought disorder."

"Doctor, if I put you on the stand, you're not going to say he flipped out, are you? You'll be more precise, right?" I said apprehensively.

"Of course I will. I have a medically based opinion, but the bottom line is that I can't tell you precisely what happened in his mind after killing his mother."

Though we have few statistics on the relative numbers of double parricides, or "familicides" as I call them, they occur with sufficient frequency that I see about three to five a year. These cases are infinitely more complicated to understand (and thus to defend) than a patricide or a matricide because they involve multiple homicides, and thus they are exponentially more shocking than a single death. The child has killed not only both parents, but frequently a sibling as well.

Given the absolute horror of such a situation, the average person (including the defense attorney) concludes that the child had to be insane or at least temporarily psychotic. Though such cases involve a higher percentage of severely mentally ill children than other parricides, the reality is that the majority of these teenagers are not legally insane.

These cases follow a fairly predictable pattern where one parent, usually the father, is the primary abuser, while the mother is frequently a co-conspirator in the abuse. Though in the worst cases the mother visits her own brand of mistreatment on her children, most often she abuses her children by actively condoning the father's mistreatment: informing on her child and taking absolutely no steps to protect him or her from the wrath of the father.

For these children, there is never even temporary refuge from the storm.

Byron

Today, he lives in a massive, five-story building of dark stone about two miles outside a sleepy little Southern hamlet. The turn-of-the-century edifice sits on twenty-five acres of what was once some of the richest cotton-growing land in the world. If you look closely, your eye will quickly detect the heavy mesh wiring covering every window; it keeps the sunlight to a minimum inside, even at noon. The huge front yard is surrounded by a double Cyclone fence thirty feet high, topped with curls of razor-spiked barbed wire. Just outside sit, at regular intervals, towers thrice as high again, each the roost of a man armed with a semiautomatic rifle, whose job it is to stop anything or anyone going out—or in—by whatever means necessary.

After pushing open the heavy wooden front door, I entered the foyer, then passed my attorney's identification card through the small opening of a bulletproof-glass window to an individual in a crisply pressed blue uniform. My identification was checked, then rechecked by the intake officer's supervisor. I proceeded to another checkpoint where my briefcase was inspected, and I was patted down, then was ushered through an airport-size metal detector to a barred gate, which opened before me.

Finally, I made my way down yet another dimly lit hallway, coming to the last cell-like gate. I pressed an orange button, and the bars creaked slowly to the left. Before me was a large room painted a noxious yellow-green. It holds only a dozen small Plexiglas-enclosed cubicles, and it is here that my host receives his few visitors.

Conscious that my every move was monitored by two television cameras and by a single officer perched on an eight-foot-high platform to one side, I walked to a tiny cubicle in the far corner. I sat down in one of the two cheap plastic chairs and waited for him.

He lives upstairs in one room with about twenty other men, his bunk sandwiched between two others with a mere two feet of space between each. His personal belongings he keeps in a locker at the foot of his bed and also in a larger one that stands next to the head of it. The tops of both lockers he uses as bookshelves.

There is one washroom in his dormitory with four sinks and four toilets. He eats in a cavernous main dining hall along with three hundred others: breakfast from four A.M. to six A.M., lunch from ten A.M. until one P.M., and dinner from three P.M. to six P.M.

His "housemates" number about one thousand, and they are considered to be the most dangerous people in the state. They have killed grocery-store clerks, robbed and beaten elderly pensioners, kidnapped children, and raped young boys and women. Many are members of violent gangs that distribute drugs and carry out murders for hire. He counts some of these men as his friends, but knows the bottom line here is brutal indeed: his life can be bought and sold for no more than a pack of stale cigarettes.

He doesn't look or act like a hardened, street-wise criminal. There are no tattoos on his arms or chest praising some long-forgotten girlfriend or criminal syndicate. He is a stockily built young man who keeps his clothes neatly pressed and speaks in soft, emotionless, measured tones. When I first met him that day, I saw an average-looking guy with short-cropped, wavy, auburn hair, his posture as straight as a Marine's. He reminded me of the earnest kid you always see playing tuba in the high-school marching band.

He doesn't like the fact that he will have to live here for at least the next thirty years, but he accepts it as he must. Yet, in spite of *all this,* of what his life has come down to, when I asked Byron Grant, Inmate Control #423769-H55A7, to compare his existence at the State Reformatory for Men to the life he led with his parents at 3682 Milton Lane, he didn't pause a second.

"I have more freedom in here than I did when I was home.

"The rules are less stringent and I even have more friends. But primarily, I don't feel the threat, the constant threat that something is going to happen to me, so I can basically walk around here pretty much with ease. Sometimes there are tense situations, but most of the time I can relax."

Ironically, even though he had never even been in a fistfight, let alone spent a night in jail, before the incident that landed him in prison, he is perhaps better able than most inmates to cope with the perilous life here. For he carries around inside an early-warning device he developed in childhood.

Byron can smell an attack coming. Psychiatrists term it hypervigilance—the ability to discern preaggressive behavior in others. Byron's past has taught him how to sense, from certain behavioral cues, that another person is preparing to harm him. It was this sensitivity to impending violence that saved his life several months before I came to see him.

"A particular guy was saying things and making gestures that said he was going to try something," Byron said. The inmate was about five foot five, Byron's height, but he was much heavier and stronger.

"For several days I watched him very closely. Then it happened," Byron said excitedly. "I was walking along an upper tier and saw out of the corner of my eye that he was running up at me from behind. No doubt about it, he was going to throw me off."

To fight the man would have increased his risk of falling or being thrown thirty feet to the concrete below. Instead, just as he had planned, Byron dropped to the floor and grabbed hold of the steel railing. His attacker did exactly what Byron had predicted.

"He tried in every way he could to throw me off," Byron said. "He banged my fingers and punched me everywhere he could, but I was glued to the railing." After kicking Byron viciously in the head and body, the inmate gave up.

Byron survived this attack and one other because he went through a hell worse than any prison before he came to this place. In fact, by the time he entered the State Reformatory, he had already been in prison for over seventeen years.

I did not get the call to help in Byron's case until after he had been convicted of murder and his case was being readied for appeal before the state Supreme Court.

Tom Alan, Byron's court-appointed attorney, called me about two weeks before his brief was due. He had read about my work, and would I be willing to work on an appeal of a double parricide? Pro bono? State funding guidelines would not cover my fees, and he had long ago exhausted his own funds on the case. Because of my financial circumstances at the time, I had to refuse, always the most distressing aspect of my private practice.

The next day I awoke feeling guilty. I thought I had learned how to turn down cases without much emotion, but it was difficult to let this one go. Typically, my torment in declining a case usually centers on thoughts about abandoning the child. Here it was different. While I was immensely sympathetic to Byron's plight, what drew me just as strongly to the case was Tom Alan's utter passion, his devotion to the boy, something I had never seen before.

Most attorneys maintain an antiseptic relationship with their clients and prefer it that way. As hired guns, their first concern is whether they win or lose; only secondarily are they concerned about how winning or losing affects their clients. To the outside world, attorneys want to give the impression that they are the defenders of the kingdom of justice; the actual truth (something I believe is apparent to most Americans) is that most value their egos and pocketbooks over the interests of their clients. But Tom Alan is not like that.

About forty-five, Alan is soft-spoken, almost demure, a man of great gentleness belied by the fierceness of intense gray eyes and bushy, dark-blond eyebrows against a ruddy complexion. He is the son of working-class parents and still lives in the town where he was born. He has two young children who mean the world to him, and a third child whom he visits once every three months in the confines of a Plexiglas enclosure.

From our very first conversation, it was obvious that the case had dramatically affected him. Unlike most attorneys, he was brutally honest with me about his feelings; in fact, he berated himself for not doing a better job. With only two previous murder cases under his belt, insufficient funds to hire an investigator, and an ignorance of child abuse, Alan had been completely overwhelmed by the time of the trial.

"It was one of the most devastating experiences of my life, very emotional. . . . I've been heartsick over [the] results. Just literally physically and emotionally sick," he confessed. "Byron has . . . written me a couple of beautiful letters about the fact that he doesn't want me to be worried too much about him. . . . It is an amazing thing—with all the people in your life who take and take and give you no room to breathe, and if anybody is in a position to be entitled to take something and demand something, it's him, and yet he is telling me take care of myself."

Several days after our first conversation, I called Alan back and told him that I would send him some support material and that I would review a draft of his brief. As we spoke several times over the next week, I became progressively more enmeshed in this legal and emotional maelstrom. Even after the brief was filed and we could do no more than await word of the date of oral argument, Tom and I kept in regular contact.

After thoroughly reviewing the case, it was clear to me that Byron would have been hard-pressed to find another attorney anywhere who could have done a better job than Tom Alan had. Byron sat in prison not because he had an incompetent attorney, but because, like Patty, the legal and child protective service's system failed him.

This was *not* a parricide case in which there was any question that Byron and Anne had been abused. The only real issue was to what extent, and what consequences the constant batterings and threats had on Byron's young psyche.

Stanley Grant was a brute; and his wife, Juliette, actively aided in her children's oppression.

A burly truck driver with short, tightly curled, dark hair and a jowly face, Stanley was about five foot ten and tipped the scales at just over 270 pounds. Even at seventeen, Byron weighed at least 150 pounds less than his father. Juliette was built like her husband, except that she weighed more. Short, stocky, and with thin, dark-auburn hair that she always kept in a tight bun, she had graduated from the same high school as her husband and was a housewife.

Stanley served his country in Vietnam, a seemingly regular Joe who went to church, paid his taxes, and kept a roof over his family's head. He belonged to a local men's community-service club and even played for their summer softball team. He and his family lived in a modest seven-room home on a country road.

Grant was no Jekyll and Hyde—his reputation, even among friends, was that of an aggressive, boisterous person. This is how a man who had known him from childhood described him in a letter to Tom Alan:

"Most of those who knew him were familiar with his violent nature and the emotional undercurrent which seemed like a time bomb constantly threatening to go off. . . . He was the most violent person I ever knew. As a youth most of the fellows were afraid to play football with Stanley; as an adult, his violent nature was even more threatening."

Bill Dix, Byron's maternal grandfather, had perhaps more contact with his daughter and her husband than any other relative. When he took the stand in his grandson's defense, he painted a stark, unforgiving picture of the Grant home. In a voice heavy with pain and disbelief, the white-haired old farmer told the packed courtroom, "You have to understand my son-in-law to be able to know what was happening. I don't know whether it was the Vietnam thing or what, but the house was run like a military post . . . he would scream at the kids, and they would have to run up in front of him, including my daughter. And from there on, he would give them another direction, another order to do whatever he wanted them to do."

Dix's other daughter, Byron's aunt Denise, echoed the military analogy. "Stanley was this general," she testified, "and everyone was under his control. . . . He would say their name one time and they would run from wherever they were in the house and stand in front of him to see what his orders were. . . . If they wanted a drink of milk, they would have to ask their parents. If they wanted to take a shower, they would have to ask their parents. . . . They had name tags on the towel racks in the bathroom, and their towel was hung there.

And they had their name on a cup in the bathroom and that was their cup to use."

His grandchildren would never under any circumstances even *attempt* to disobey their parents, Dix told the court. Submissiveness, silence, and withdrawal had been the order of the day since they were born. Disobedience never even crossed Byron's mind.

"I was driving down the road one very rainy afternoon and I saw Byron [who was thirteen at the time]," Grandpa Dix said. "I stopped and asked him what he was doing out there. He said he forgot to deliver one paper, and his father told him, 'For doing that, you walk there and you walk back.' " Dix told his grandson to get in the car, and he would take him to deliver the paper. Though his father was several miles away inside the house, Byron steadfastly refused his grandfather's offer; the rain-soaked boy only agreed to get in the car after fifteen minutes of begging. After delivering the paper, Dix brought his grandson back to his house, dried him off, and gave him a cup of hot cocoa. Knowing his son-in-law's penchant for meting out severe punishment for the slightest infraction, however, he knew better than to drop Byron off at Stanley's front door. "I dropped him off about five houses from where he lived so he could continue his walk and be wet when he got home."

Like most children who kill their parents, Byron's story is the familiar amalgam of unceasing violence and silent, intimidated witnesses. And like most of the parents you have read about, the Grants, though they may have screamed loudly about instilling respect and moral values in their children, were not remotely interested in their children's well-being. Stanley and Juliette did not care about raising independent, secure, and caring children; all they wanted were two warm bodies to do their every bidding, bodies on which they could vent their frustrations and anxieties.

Stanley assaulted his children in almost every conceivable way. Throughout his life, Byron and Anne were punched, pinched, and slapped about the face and body; kicked in the head; dragged and thrown by the hair; and threatened with one of the many guns in Stanley's arsenal. But far and away, Stanley's preferred tool of destruction was what the children called the "board," but what Stanley proudly and affectionately referred to as his "persuader."

To know the board was to know Stanley. In fact, the board was the embodiment of the abuse, and no further description of his abusive behavior is really necessary after one understands the twisted ideas that lay behind it. Stanley and Juliette revered the "persuader." Indeed, it was such an integral part of life in the Grant home that it took on the significance of a religious icon. It had a history known by all those who knew the family, and there was even a specific protocol for its use.

Byron was about seven or eight when the board was born. His father cut it out of a one-by-four-foot piece of oak on the jigsaw. As Byron recounted its history to me that day in prison, the suffering was still evident in his eyes.

"It had a little pattern to it," he said. "Basically it went out and then it tapered in. . . . He sanded it and varnished it. . . . It wasn't that much of a threat to me as I watched him make it, but after he started using it, it was definitely a threat. I was scared to death of it."

The board occupied a hallowed place—its altar was the top of the refrigerator. Though Stanley would often get the paddle himself, he preferred to have the children retrieve it for him. Byron could not reach the board until he was twelve. Before that, he had to make a rather precarious climb to the top of the refrigerator, all the while sobbing and trembling: "I [would] open up the cupboard, step partially inside, and get up on the counter; then I would reach the top of the refrigerator from there."

After getting the paddle, Byron respectfully handed it to his father, as a defeated general hands his sword to his conqueror. Before he hit Byron, Stanley, with a smile on his face, would tell his trembling son, "People say that this is supposed to hurt me more than it hurts you, but it's not going to hurt me at all."

Byron would then "assume the position"—bending over to grab his ankles. "And if I didn't grab my ankles or if I came up, he would add more swats for coming up," Byron told me sheepishly. "He hit me with full force. . . . He'd kind of place his teeth together and just basically give it all he had. . . . Up until about the time I was sixteen and a half, I got hit at least . . . every other day."

And for committing what opprobrious sins did Byron and his sister get the board? "Forgetting or not bringing the newspaper in on time. Chores that we had forgotten to do . . . Bringing conversation up at the table; not finishing a meal within what he thought was a reasonable time or with the rest of the family . . . or chewing with our mouth open."

If they missed a chore one day, the usual punishment was a full week of the board. But being the enlightened parent he was, Stanley allowed his children to choose when they got whacked. But if they forgot to bring the paddle to Stanley at the appointed time, another week of the board was added.

If Stanley discovered a single infraction, the merest deviation from his orders, after the children had gone to sleep, he would wake them up for a beating.

The children's aunt Denise told the jury a typical "board" story: "Byron spilled some juice. And Stanley brought him back into the kitchen. He held on to the top part of Byron's arm and swung back very, very hard . . . maybe six or seven times."

As could be expected, Byron and his sister cried and screamed while they were hit. When he got older, Byron told me, "I would usually try to go up in my bedroom [after a beating] where I could hide my face in a pillow and let some of my tensions out. I could scream in the pillow and it would muffle it and Dad couldn't hear it."

Stanley had, however, an insatiable passion for witnessing his children's pain. "I would be on my way upstairs and he would say, 'Oh, no, you don't. You come down here and sit by me.' . . . If I continued crying for very long, he would tell me to shut up, 'unless I wanted something to cry about.' And [he meant that] he would either give me the board again or take me out in the backyard [and beat me with his fists]."

After several years of almost daily use, the board began to crack and splinter. Because of his great love for his persuader, Stanley could not simply throw it out and make a new one. Instead, he wrapped it in duct tape, and its reign of terror continued. By the time the board was admitted into evidence in the case of the *State* versus *Byron Grant*, yards and yards of new and worn tape barely held it together.

Much of the physical punishment was tied to the performance of chores. And regardless of how he performed his chores, Byron was continually criticized. "He would give me something to do, and if I did it wrong, he said, 'Why didn't you ask?' . . . And if I did ask, he'd call me stupid for asking."

Often these were just typical household chores such as getting the newspaper, splitting wood, or washing the dishes. Often, however, the line between the chores and the punishments got so blurred as to make the two indistinguishable.

Stanley liked a clean yard, so he would send his children out for hours at a time in the hot sun or in the darkness of a cold night to pick up the tiny sandburs that were strewn over the grass. A next-door neighbor told the court that she would often see the children in the yard in the dead of night, Anne holding a flashlight while Byron picked the burs off the ground. And in the winter when there were no burs to pick up, the children were ordered to collect rocks that the snowblower had thrown into the yard and put them back on the driveway.

In most families where the father is as ruthless as Stanley, the mother is often unable to protect her children effectively. She, too, is often the target of abuse and thus helpless to protect herself, let alone her children.

Though Stanley often screamed at his wife, the mistreatment she endured was minuscule compared to that visited upon her children—there was no evidence, for example, that Stanley beat Juliette. If she had acted like the typical passive mother in these situations, the children would have been lucky. Instead, Juliette was an active confederate in her children's abuse.

All her relatives and friends agreed Juliette never stood up for her children; in fact, no one ever even tried to protect them. Juliette did not merely sit idly by while her husband repeatedly assaulted her children; she often joined in screaming at them while her husband beat them. And while Stanley was not home, she was his eyes and ears. As soon as her husband walked in the door after work, she reported their behavior to him with full knowledge of the grievous consequences.

An active as well as passive contributor, she also tried her hand at "persuading" them. Though she didn't possess her husband's strength, the children still wailed when she smacked them with the board. "My mother hit me with her full force," Byron said. "It hurt a lot, but not as much as from my dad."

Like her husband, Juliette was more disposed to mete out the punishment when nobody but her husband and children were around. But there were certain things she did to Byron that she didn't want anyone, especially Stanley, to find out.

It started when he was about fourteen and continued for four years almost daily. When Byron discusses his physical abuse, there is anger and resentment in his voice. When he talks about "it" he is still so embarrassed that he can barely speak above a whisper.

"It basically started out as pinching my pimples. . . . But then [within several months] it graduated into her wanting me to come into her bedroom and lay in bed with her. She would take off my shirt, or robe. . . . She would lay between my legs, like you would do to—to make love to a person. I was always on my back, and my mom would spread my legs apart and lay between them and pinch my face and chest. She'd rub my groin with her groin. . . . Sometimes she would pat and rub my bottom and inner thighs. . . . And when she would do it, she would get angry at me for not holding still. But it hurt, [and] I didn't want her to touch me. And she would also come into my bedroom in the morning, lay in bed with me, and pinch my pimples."

Byron was not only confused and angered by his mother's sexual assaults, he was also deathly afraid that his father would discover what his mother was doing. Since the sexual abuse, which also included Juliette's watching her teenage son in the shower, occurred almost every day before and after school when his father was out of the house, Byron was terrified of getting caught. "I did not want my dad to find out for fear that he would hurt me or kill me, because he would blame it on me," Byron said.

While Juliette occupied herself with her son, her husband was off pursuing his own, equally bizarre sexual adventures. Not only an avid collector of hard-core porno films and magazines (left out on the dining room table for the children to see), he commonly spent his evenings and sometimes days prowling strip joints and whorehouses.

When Byron got his driver's license at sixteen, one of his chores was to be his father's "bar chauffeur." "Because he didn't want to drive intoxicated, I would drop him off [at a bar] and go to high school, and then I would pick him up," Byron told me. "On the weekend I was out with him till three or four in the morning. . . . He would buy corsages for the women—the strippers—in the bar on holidays sometimes. . . . One time he came out of a strip bar and he was intoxicated. He wanted to be my friend and everything. . . . He asked me if I would say anything to my mother if I saw him with another woman." Grateful for these crumbs of affection and equally frightened of disobeying his dad, Byron never revealed his father's wanderings.

Ironically, in this life so woefully devoid of any semblance of "normal" family interaction, Byron has fond memories of being his dad's chauffeur. "Those were actually some of the better times," he told me wistfully. "Sometimes he would take me to a place to get a bite to eat, when it was real late, and he'd talk to me like he really wanted to be a father to me."

What a pathetic scene, I thought as he told me about these "good times." The stories of the board were grisly, yet I was long used to hearing them. But the image of this meek teenage boy sitting behind the wheel of the car on a cold, rainy night with the garish light of a cheap strip joint illuminating his face seemed more tragic still. Most sons look forward to going fishing or to a baseball game with their fathers; Byron looked forward to his father's emerging, stone drunk, from a brothel, so that they could then go get a cup of coffee at an all-night diner together.

Many might say what Byron should have done was drop his dad off one night and just keep on driving. Actually, Byron entertained the idea himself. When he was fifteen, he even got to the point of secretly drawing up detailed escape plans. But he felt he couldn't leave. Aside from the fact that he believed he would not be able to take care of himself, he feared for his life.

Though there were many things about his father that Byron could never understand, there was one thing he knew absolutely: his dad *always* made good on his threats. So, when Stanley told fourteen-year-old Byron that if he ran away, he'd kill him, Byron believed it. Byron can still hear the admonition: "You had better hope that the police find you first and put you in jail, because you'll be safer there than if I find you."

Like most teenagers, Byron knew that if the police found him, they would hold him only for a short while before returning him to his parents' custody. He was correct: it is virtually a universal policy for law enforcement agencies to return runaways to their parents, despite any protestation the adolescent might make.

Such death threats were an integral part of the control that Stanley maintained over Byron, more important, even, than the board. They started when the boy was about eight years old. After almost every beating, Stanley would tell his son that if he didn't straighten up, the next time he would take Byron out into the backyard and kill him. The threats were very specific and backed up with grisly props, such as Stanley's loaded .357 magnum or a baseball bat.

The most common death threat, however, didn't involve any weapons. Byron choked up as he repeated his father's words to me:

" 'If you think you're enough of a man, we'll go out in the backyard and [it will be] no holds barred. We will fight until one of us is unconscious or dead.' "

Also preventing him from leaving was fear for the safety of his younger sister. Byron had a tight bond with Anne, forged by their shared abuse. During his trial, Byron testified that he had to leave the room when his sister got the board because he couldn't stand to see her harmed. "It would hurt me because I knew what she was going through. And I was scared and my stomach would get tight. . . . I was angry at my parents and I wanted to grab her and run away with her, but I couldn't."

At home, he absorbed the brunt of his father's angry and vicious assaults; if he left, he knew it would fall on his sister. And his love for her was too great to let that happen.

Though paralyzed by the fear of retribution if he ran away, Byron did make an absolutely valiant attempt to protect himself and his sister. Lamentably, this effort only resulted in reinforcing his growing pessimism, robbing him of any hope that he would *ever* be saved.

"I was in my seventh-grade reading class and I was having

trouble concentrating," he said. "My teacher approached me and asked me what was wrong. I said I just had troubles. Then she asked, 'What kind of troubles?'

" 'Troubles all the time,' I said.

" '[Did you have trouble] yesterday?' she said.

" 'Well, yes, I had gotten yelled at and smacked a couple of times [with the board] for not getting the newspaper,' I said. She thought that that was not right, so she made an appointment for me to see the guidance counselor, Mrs. Deardon."

Mrs. Irene Deardon was thirty years old and had obtained a master's degree in guidance counseling years earlier. In addition to her academic training, she was a state-certified guidance counselor and had passed an exam qualifying her to be a "nationally certified counselor." Along with this experience, she was a certified teacher, and a "mandatory reporter."

One of the most significant legislative advances in the identification and treatment of child abuse in recent years has been the enactment of mandatory-reporting laws in the late 1970s. They were developed in recognition of the fact that most child-victims won't report abuse and neither will their parents, relatives, friends, and neighbors.

A mandatory reporter is a person who, in their official capacity, is likely to have direct or indirect contact with abused children. Doctors, dentists, nurses, paramedics, commercial film processors, and of course, teachers are just some of the professionals likely to be mandatory reporters. These individuals are required to report to the appropriate state agency any incident of child abuse or neglect that they have actual knowledge of or reasonably suspect to exist. All fifty states have such laws, and the failure to report an incident of child abuse is a misdemeanor.

Byron saw Mrs. Deardon about twice a week for about three and a half months, during which time he told her frequently and in detail about the verbal and physical punishment, keeping the sexual abuse to himself. At Byron's trial, Mrs. Deardon read from the notes she took during the counseling sessions. Her testimony provides an eerie oral history of Byron's ordeal:

November 3: Father beat him for not cutting his fingernails.

November 8: Father has added the penalty of working an extra hour when Byron and sister don't get their regular jobs done. Work six hours and get five dollars. Works at night with flashlight. The children work on the weekends nonstop, except when they went to church and did an activity. . . . Mother spanked him for forgetting something his father was going to work on. He couldn't remember what it was or where it was in telling me about it. Nine o'clock bedtime through the summer as report-card penalty instead of ten P.M.

November 14: He asked to see me early in the school day. We had ten minutes. He forgot to give his father a phone message about some boxes. His father said, "You're going to get whacked. And it won't be just with the board, and it will be every day for a week." Plus [write] fifty sentences, "I will not forget to give messages." Father is waiting to catch him in a mistake of some kind or other.

November 15: He asked to see me again. He said he had done the sentences at school. Showed them to me. Got three extra whacks with board for forgetting something else.

November 18 & 19: Asked to see me. I wasn't able to.

November 21: Father skipped the board for the last three days of punishment. That was Friday. Saturday and Sunday made him do the writing. Moved three trees. Byron dug the holes. Father yelled at him for taking so long. Said he would have to work at night with a flashlight. They both worked, and sister held flashlight. Continued next day as well.

As a junior high–school guidance counselor, Mrs. Deardon's responsibility was to assist Byron in resolving his problems. The following, elicited on direct examination by Tom Alan, was Mrs. Deardon's advice:

Q: Did you have any discussions with Byron about being able to avoid abuse in the home? What he could do to get away?

A: ... It fairly quickly came out that Byron didn't have a lot of places to go or a lot of ways to avoid what his father was doing. ... He really seemed to want to talk about what was going on at home. And I perceived my role vis-à-vis Byron as his school counselor to really be there and be someone who would listen in a nonjudgmental way even though there was nothing I could do about the situation.

Q: Did you have a discussion with Byron about what could or could not be done in terms of any intervention?

A: Yes. I do recall bringing up to Byron what would happen if we made an official, formal report to the authorities. I explained to him what I thought would happen. I had not reported a child abuse case before, so I didn't know exactly what would happen. ... I told him that I would report that I felt abuse was going on, and an investigator would go to the home and try to talk to the parents. I didn't follow through for two reasons. Number one, I never saw any physical evidence on Byron's body in terms of bruises or marks or anything. ... Number two, I felt that in my counseling with a fourteen-year-old as opposed to counseling with a six- or seven-year-old who might have come in with marks, I felt Byron had a real part in this decision because he was going to have to live with the circumstances of that report. And I don't think I ever would have made the report without his knowledge and consent because I feared for his safety.

Q: In 1983, you were aware that there was a mandatory child abuse reporting law, is that right?

A: Yes. ... But as far as I knew, none of the counselors that I worked with had to that point been involved in an actual reporting case. I was aware of the law, but I wasn't real clear on the details. ... In my mind, I realized that if I had seen marks, then I would really have had to report. ... It would not be a matter of consulting with a client ... but in terms of the knowledge of [Byron's abuse] I couldn't know that I had the specific information at that time [to report].

> *Q: You did conclude, did you not, that Byron was a victim of child abuse?*
>
> *A: Yes.*
>
> *Q: Did you discuss the dangers of reporting with Byron?*
>
> *A: Yes. . . . We talked about the fact that . . . a good amount of time would elapse between the initial report and whatever actions might be taken on the part of the authorities. I think Byron sensed that reporting would put him in more danger than he already was in. . . .*
>
> *Q: And were you [yourself] afraid of a report being made?*
>
> *A: And I was as well, yes.*
>
> *Q: On the basis of those discussions that you had about the possible intervention, including those dangers, did you come to a final understanding about whether there would be a report?*
>
> *A: I think we agreed together that I would not make an official report to the authorities. . . .*

Certainly, reporting the abuse to the Department of Public Welfare could have exacerbated Byron's predicament, as it did, for example, in Mike's case. Being obsessed with his own power, especially that which he exercised over his children, Stanley, it is safe to assume, would have reacted with hostility to any social service investigation, and he would most likely have coerced Byron into recanting his allegations, using among other things his persuader. And it is entirely conceivable, based upon what I know about the "Stanleys" of this world, that he would have threatened Mrs. Deardon.

If there is one thing that experts agree on, however, it is that pathologically abusive parents such as Stanley and Juliette don't get "better" on their own. Contrary to popular perceptions, *effective* law enforcement or other official intervention such as diversionary counseling usually does not aggravate family violence, but rather ameliorates it.

This fact has been clearly demonstrated in studies of wife assault, especially one conducted by the Minneapolis Police Department in 1982. In this study, researchers found that wife beaters who were arrested and put in jail, even for a night, were much less likely to batter their spouses when once again in the home. As a result of the success of the experiment and other research, laws were changed around the country to require law enforcement officers to arrest male batterers.

Intervention does not, however, always stop battering. Incompetent treatment such as Patty (from Part IV) was forced to endure is not uncommon, and incidents of abusive husbands who kill their spouses after being released from jail or prison unfortunately occur. Though I am not aware of any case in which a child was killed by a parent after a report was made, it is entirely conceivable that complying with the mandatory reporting law could have resulted in Byron's murder. Infanticide is a very real problem in our nation—with an estimated five thousand children killed by their parents every year; however, it occurs when child abuse goes unchecked, when no one responds to the screams. Nevertheless, it is undeniable that the fear of reprisal is legitimate for an abused child; but if teachers and other mandatory reporters become imprisoned by these fears, then the child abuse protection system and the children and the families they serve don't have a chance.

By the ripe old age of thirteen and a half, Byron had given up all hope that anyone would or could help him and Anne. He limped along with his sister until he turned seventeen. With each year the beatings, sexual abuse, and verbal assaults increased in frequency and intensity. Byron, however, pegged the most dramatic escalation of his torment to the early fall of his senior year.

He was to turn eighteen that October, something he looked forward to with heart-thumping anticipation. In his diary he put a giant "1" on his birthday, signifying, as he said later, the first day of his freedom. Stanley, however, was not so willing to unlock the cell.

If, after Byron left home, Stanley found out that Byron had either quit school or had done anything wrong, he would hunt him down and bring him back to the house, he threatened. After that, he continued, he'd put a lock on Byron's door and handcuff him to his bed until he finished school. During the trial, Tom Alan asked Byron if he thought his parents would really let him leave home.

"I don't think so, no," he said despondently. "If he would have, I think he would have come and found something because he needed something to punish or hit. And I don't think my sister could have totally satisfied his needs."

During the months following his seventeenth birthday, Stanley even told his son that things would worsen for Anne when he left. Even in prison, Byron shuddered when he repeated his dad's menacing words: "Anne is getting as bad as you. She'll get her share."

If there was a straw that broke the camel's back, it was the "soda incident."

> One day after I came home from school, he said, "I want you to help me do something." I changed shoes and I followed him outside.
>
> As I followed him into the backyard, he suddenly turned around like he had forgotten something. Then he started swinging punches at me wild and hard. . . . He hit me in the head, shoulders, and back. I had a sore spot in my left temple for about a week and a half.
>
> "What did I do?" I said.
>
> "Next time I find a can of soda in your room, you son of a bitch, I'll *kill* you!" he said. He found two cans in my closet that I wasn't supposed to have.
>
> . . . We went back into the house, and he started yelling at me. He lectured me for a couple of hours about how I wasn't living up to his expectation; I wasn't doing well in school . . . I thought this was the start of something . . . that it would lead to more and more occasions out in the backyard and eventually my death or disappearance.

Though it did not seem possible, the situation worsened soon after that. Stanley tightened his iron grip as the boy's eighteenth birthday approached. "He would keep track of my mileage before I left home, but not tell me. If I went anywhere out of my way or anything, he was sure to catch me. He would travel to the places to mark off the miles."

Byron first thought about killing his parents three weeks after the soda incident. The death threats that Stanley had made since Byron was eight had suddenly taken on a new and more perilous meaning. The incident frightened him in a way others hadn't, because, as he told me, "it was just a couple cans of soda in my room, and he said, 'Next time I'll kill you.' I just didn't know what was going to set him off next."

Byron approached his twelve-year-old sister on a Saturday morning when they were cleaning the yard. "I asked what she thought about me killing our parents. At first she said yes, then a couple of days later she said no. Then a few weeks later I told her I was leaving home when I turned eighteen and that I didn't want my parents following me. I couldn't take her with me . . . and it might get worse for her. She said yes at that point." From that day on, Byron would ask his sister every day if it was still all right with her to kill their parents. Each time Anne said she wanted them dead, and that she wouldn't tell anybody about their discussions.

One Sunday morning in mid-September Byron came into Anne's room as she was reading a book. "I'm going to do it today. . . . Do you think I'll really do it?"

Anne looked up and wiped the bangs away from her eyes. "I don't know. You talked about it before and you didn't do anything," she said. "But if you do it, I won't say anything."

Soon after, Byron left to help his father prepare for a family gathering taking place later that afternoon. He always dreaded these events because his father seemed to regard them as forums to ridicule him. As the family got in the car to go to the party, Stanley discovered that Byron had forgotten to bring a case of soda.

"You stupid son of a bitch, you can't do nothing right! It was right there on the counter," Stanley yelled. Before leaving home that afternoon to go to the dinner, Byron had taken a double-bladed ax from the garage and placed it under his bed. Though there were numerous guns in the home, he chose the ax because a gun's report would attract the attention of the neighbors.

Around four that afternoon, Stanley ordered his son to go back to the house to get a bottle of whiskey. When he got home, he took the ax from under his bed and placed it in some bushes just outside the kitchen.

When he returned to the party twenty minutes later, he took his sister aside.

"I want you to think about what we talked about this morning. I want you to place it in your mind what I'm going to do. Is it still okay?" Byron whispered.

"Yes," Anne replied softly, then she went back to play with her cousins.

"My father went to bed about ten," Byron later said. "Then I went down to the kitchen and let the dog out." Byron was in his underwear because he wanted his mother to believe he was going right to bed.

My mom was in the living room, and I told her to come to the kitchen [door] because I saw something outside. We talked a little bit and . . . I picked up the ax and hit her in the back of the head and she fell backwards. . . . She was still making some kind of noise, and I didn't want her to suffer like that, so I hit her in the back again. And then the noise stopped and I wanted to make sure, so I hit her in the head. . . .

Then I went up to my room to get some headphones for Anne to wear [in case] I messed up and he got up or something. I didn't want her to hear anything. I left the ax in the hallway and went into my sister's room.

[When] I . . . went in and said that I had done it to Mom, she kind of backed away from me a little bit. . . . I gave her a hug and kiss. . . . I asked her to put the headsets on and play some music or something so she didn't hear anything. And then I slowly went into his bedroom.

"I didn't see him. I went basically by his shadow and his breathing. . . . I hit him in the head seven times. When I was hitting him, not much was going through my mind except that I had to do it."

What was going through his mind after the killings, I asked. He let out a deep breath and said, "I was scared, but I was kind of relieved. I was scared because I still had to try to attempt to get away with it, but I was kind of relieved, it was over, they were out of the way. I just wanted that part of my life gone."

Immediately after killing his father, he took a shower to wash the blood off his arms, legs, and the ax. After getting dressed, he and Anne ransacked the house to make it look as if a struggle or robbery had occurred. Then they jumped in the family car, the plan being to call the police from a roadside telephone and tell them they had just returned to find their parents' bodies.

"Before I could get to a phone the police pulled me over for speeding. My sister started crying immediately, and I told the officer that I thought my father killed my mother, but I wasn't sure."

Though nervous and frightened, Byron, unlike many children, was relatively lucid before, during, and after the killings. He took his parents' lives after careful reflection on the choices he had before him. He reasoned that if he resisted his father during one of the beatings, Stanley would kill him.

For six days, Byron and Anne steadfastly denied that they had any knowledge of who had killed their parents. On October 27th the police formally arrested him. Throughout the morning he continued his denials. Then the police brought Grandfather Dix to the station. The police transcript of the interrogation reflects that Grandfather Dix went into a room with Byron at 5:18 P.M. and that they emerged together at 5:33 P.M.

"Are you willing to talk to us now about the case?" the investigating officer said.

"Yes," said Byron.

". . . If there's something important that you have to tell us, we need you to tell us," the detective said.

"I killed my mom and dad."

Byron was charged with two counts of first-degree murder. His sister, Anne, was never charged.

From the moment of his arrest and confession, prosecutor Ken Ellerbee's position was that Byron was exaggerating the incidents of abuse, and when he wasn't exaggerating, he deserved the punishment his father gave him. The prosecutor contended that Byron had wanted to leave home early against his father's wishes, to escape the rigid, though not abusive discipline.

Shortly before the trial, Tom Alan sat down with the prosecutors to discuss the possibilities of a plea, but he discovered that they had absolutely no sympathy for Byron. "Ellerbee told me that whatever thoughts they had about extending leniency to Byron were extinguished after they read his account of his mother's alleged sexual advances . . . ," Alan later said to me. "They didn't believe it. They thought he fabricated it, and they thought it demonstrated what kind of kid he was, and why he needed to be prosecuted."

Aside from the usual assortment of cops and forensic experts, several of Stanley's friends testified for the state. By their accounts, Stanley was a boisterous and opinionated man, but not an abusive one. He was a strict disciplinarian because he was a perfectionist. And he was very concerned about instilling the values of thrift and responsibility in his kids. Yes, he gave his children numerous chores, but he paid them for their efforts. The state also established from several friends that they never saw Stanley or Juliette physically punish the children.

"Juliette was a good parent," one of the family friends testified. "She made sure that her children were provided for. If they had a problem or something, she tried to talk to them about it. I felt she was loving to them." This friend also stated that she saw Mrs. Grant squeeze her son's pimples on occasion, but hadn't detected anything sexual in her actions.

Ellerbee also called Mae Simpson, Byron's high-school guidance counselor. He had stopped seeing Mrs. Deardon when he left junior high. Simpson, who had over thirty years' experience, told the court that she had only spoken with Byron on two occasions, two months before the homicide.

"He told me he would really like to be on his own as soon as possible," Simpson said. "He said he considered running away, or thought about leaving or running away from home. And I discouraged this as I always do, because he was a minor. I cautioned him that if he ran away, he would start a juvenile record, and I didn't want that for him.

"I recommended," she continued, "that he would soon be eighteen, and that I would do everything I could for him once he could be emancipated. . . . I really wanted him to stay with his family until he was eighteen."

"Mrs. Simpson, did the defendant report to you any abuse?" Ellerbee inquired.

"No," she replied forthrightly.

"Mrs. Simpson, was the defendant's request about moving

out of the home different from any other request that you have had [from other students]?" said Ellerbee.

"Many [of them] have conflicts with their parents. And so I have dealt with several runaways. . . . It isn't unusual," she replied.

There were good reasons why Simpson didn't know about the abuse. In what can only be explained as an effort to protect Byron and herself from what she perceived as the dire consequences of an official investigation, Mrs. Deardon never made her progress notes part of Byron's official junior-high-school file, nor did she ever speak to any other counselors about Byron's problem. Byron's secret became her secret.

After Deardon had told him that there was nothing she could do to help, Byron not only quit seeing her, he resolved not to tell anyone else about the abuse. Byron went to see Simpson later solely because he wanted to find out his rights when he turned eighteen, specifically, could his parents force him to finish school. Byron was drowning in such despair and confusion, he could not reveal the truth.

Tom Alan's trial strategy was that Byron acted in self-defense and in defense of his sister against the life-threatening acts of both parents. "Stanley Grant possessed," he told the court, "a cold, deliberate, calculating, constant, and insatiable appetite for mistreatment." Though not as vicious as her husband, Juliette was, in her son's eyes, every bit as injurious.

The abuse was well documented for the jury through the testimony of several relatives, close family friends, Mrs. Deardon, and Byron. Despite this, Alan was unfortunately hampered in his efforts by the fact that Anne was advised not to testify for her brother. Though no charges had been filed against her, her attorney was afraid that, if she took the stand, thus waiving her Fifth Amendment privilege not to incriminate herself, she could make certain damaging admissions and be indicted. Had Ellerbee granted her immunity from prosecution, she could have testified.

Though the Grants left a significant estate, Byron was not able to use any of the money for his defense. Because he could not afford to retain an expert witness, the court appointed two psychiatrists—Dr. Pernell and Dr. Voslau. These psychiatrists did not work for the defense, but were chosen by and worked for the court. The scope of their appointment was limited: Was Byron insane and could he aid his attorney in his own defense? Their role was not to determine if he had been abused, nor how the abuse might have affected his actions on October 21, or why he killed his parents.

After speaking to Tom about these doctors and reading both their reports and trial testimony, I came to the conclusion that they were, for practical purposes, almost useless to the defense. First, the parameters of their appointment prohibited Alan from working with them on a confidential level. They were literally the court's experts, and thus Alan could not even regard them as part of his defense team.

Under the law, an expert witness is a person who, because of his experience and/or education, can explain facts or concepts that are beyond the understanding of the jury. In these cases I look for a psychiatrist or psychologist specializing in adolescent behavior who has preferably treated abused as well as delinquent youth. And ideally I want someone who has experience working with teenagers who have committed homicide. If an expert has these qualifications, a lack of courtroom experience is typically not a problem.

Though both men graduated from accredited medical schools and had been in practice for at least thirty years (which included work on hundreds of court cases), neither was an expert in child abuse, family violence, or adolescent homicide. This lack of expertise obviously didn't bother the judge. I can only surmise that he thought any psychiatrist, regardless of his experience, is qualified to be an expert witness. In their defense, however, I must say that both were sympathetic to Byron's plight. They believed that he was abused, but really contributed no more to the jury's understanding of Byron's actions than Byron's aunt or grandfather.

Dr. Pernell was clearly more compassionate and understanding of Byron's ordeal than Dr. Voslau. In fact, Tom Alan told me that when he had first met Pernell, the doctor hadn't even said hello: "He just said, 'Those people should have been hung by their toes and beaten until dead.' "

Pernell's report consisted of two, two-page letters to the judge (by contrast Tom's psychological evaluation ran almost thirty-five pages). He concluded his first letter by writing that

293

Byron was sane and in good contact with reality at the time of the homicide. In the second he wrote, "No doubt Byron has been damaged by the abuse he endured through the years. . . . This was not an impulsive act; on the contrary he was clear, calculative, and rational every step of the way. His motive was by no means bizarre and made more sense than the senseless cruelty he had to endure all his life. I believe the major reason for this crime was not hatred or revenge, but rather the only way he could find to free himself and his sister from abuse and oppression."

Dr. Voslau's report ran three pages and contained six lines of analysis: "It is my opinion that while Byron Grant (if the information given me is valid) was certainly abused and very badly abused, it is my opinion that at the time of the alleged offense, he did not suffer from a mental disease or defect such that he lacked a substantial capacity either to appreciate the wrongfulness of his conduct or to conform his conduct to the requirements of the law."

On the stand Dr. Pernell characterized his experience working with abused children as "very little, very little." What he knew about child abuse, he said, came principally from what he had read. Still, Pernell stated categorically that Byron had been physically and emotionally abused by his father. He characterized Stanley Grant "as a man drunk with power [who] wanted to destroy this kid." He also stated that Juliette's treatment of Byron constituted rape because "it was sexual behavior against his will." And he described Byron as a submissive, passive, nondangerous person.

The jury didn't need a psychiatrist to tell them that Byron was abused or that he was a passive person. What they did need was an expert who was well versed in the effects of abuse on a child's mental state. They particularly needed a psychiatrist or psychologist to discuss how the abuse affected Byron's perceptions of danger. Unfortunately, they got neither.

Byron was relatively calm throughout Tom Alan's four hours of questions. He described incident after horrifying incident as if he were a news anchor reporting on someone else's life. Perhaps the most poignant part of his testimony came in his responses to Tom Alan's last four questions:

Q: Byron, how do you feel about what you did?

A: I feel sorry that I did it, sorry for family and friends, that I felt I had to do it.

Q: Have you thought about what alternatives you had, things you could have done to make things work out?

A: Before or after?

Q: After.

A: After, I thought about it while I was being here in jail. And the only alternative I would have had was to make several copies of a note stating the situation at home and how bad it was and how bad I thought it was getting, sending it to my grandparents, friends, relatives . . . and then committing suicide, and I felt that would have got Anne out of the house. Someone somewhere would get Anne out of the house.

Q: Have you ever thought of a way you and Anne could get out of the house alive?

A: No.

In an effort to discount the abuse allegations, DA Ellerbee asked a number of compelling cross-examination questions of defense witnesses that focused on their inaction. To Aunt Denise, who testified that she saw numerous incidents of physical and verbal abuse, Ellerbee inquired:

Q: Did you tell Stanley or Juliette how you felt about any of the physical reprimands?

A: Only one time I can remember, and that was with the snapping to Byron's head. I said, "Don't do that" [to Stanley]. . . .

Q: Is it not a fact that at the time you observed these things, they did not move you enough to say anything to Stanley or Juliette Grant and that it's possible now, in hindsight, that you feel the way you do?

A: No, that's not true. I never—

Q: If you felt differently about it, why did you do nothing about it?

A: . . . It was not my household. I feel like everybody disciplines their children differently, in different manners. I had . . . learned their ways very early with the children. I felt like if I interfered, that I would be either told to mind

*my own business or that I would be pushed away from
the household to where maybe I would not get to see my
sister or the children again by Stanley, because what he
said went.*

It is debatable whether Ellerbee made points with the jury
with this and similar examinations. By his tenacious cross-
examination perhaps Ellerbee convinced some jurors that
Aunt Denise was exaggerating the abuse because she now felt
guilty that she hadn't intervened. On the other hand, if she
was really interested in protecting her image, wouldn't she
say she didn't intervene because the treatment was not that
harmful? Where I believe Ellerbee did succeed, however
(though I am sure unknowingly), was in illustrating starkly
one of the major problems we face in eliminating child abuse:
relatives, friends, and *even* people such as Mrs. Deardon are
extremely reluctant to involve themselves in the family affairs
of others even when they know the child is being abused. In
fact, after reading the testimony of friends and relatives, I
wondered what punishment, short of Byron's murder, would
have moved any of them to intervene.

Ellerbee continued to press the witnesses on the severity
of the abuse, conducting a particularly relentless cross-
examination of Byron. The primary intent of his inquiry,
which was often bitingly sarcastic, was to prove that Byron
was exaggerating his fear. Though most of his questions were
intelligently crafted, his zeal to break Byron often led him
into the mundane.

*Q: Mr. Grant, was there ever a time when you were
not fearful of your father?*

A: No, there wasn't.

*Q: Were you fearful of your father when you were
bowling?*

A: Yes.

*Q: And how was it that you were fearful of your father
when you were bowling?*

*A: He was always criticizing my bowling and several
times he would grab me and yank me where he wanted
me to stand to throw the ball.*

Q: Were you fearful of your father when you would roller-skate?

A: No.

Ellerbee's brutally unforgiving attitude toward Byron was best illustrated toward the end of his examination when he picked up the murder weapon, which was leaning against his table, and approached Byron.

Q: If the court please, we'd ask Mr. Grant to step down for purposes of a demonstration.

Q: Mr. Grant, I hand you State's exhibit No. Thirteen and I ask you if you can identify it?

A: Yes, that's the ax.

Q: Would you take it in your hands, please? Would you put down your handkerchief on the table, step out here please in the middle of the room? Would you face the jury and show the jury what you did with this ax that night?

(Pause in proceedings)

A: I can't. I swung it.

Q: How did you swing it, Mr. Grant?

A: At my parents.

Q: How did you swing it at your mother? . . . Mr. Grant, is there some reason that you cannot pick up the ax?

A: I'm not proud of what I did. I'm sorry. [Byron then resumed his seat.]

At the conclusion of all the testimony, the judge instructed the jury on the specifics of the law they could consider in deciding the case, explaining in detail the various definitions and nuances of each possible verdict. Tom Alan requested the court to give the jury a self-defense instruction, asking them to find that Byron was justified in using deadly force because he reasonably believed he and his sister faced an imminent threat of death. He contended that, because the abuse followed a continuing, chronic, and escalating pattern, it was reasonable for Byron to expect that abuse would occur in the very near future, as it had throughout his whole life, and that it would be life threatening. The judge rejected this position outright.

Since neither Stanley nor Juliette was assaulting either of their children at the time of their deaths, Judge Lemaster reasoned, Byron could not claim he was acting in self-defense. Though the judge believed that the children were victims of serious child abuse, he was presented with no evidence of assault at the precise time of the homicide. Therefore, he prohibited the jury from even considering whether Byron acted in self-defense, limiting them to consider only verdicts of murder, guilty but mentally ill, and not guilty by reason of insanity.

The guilty-but-mentally-ill statute in effect here was similar to the one in Steven's case (in Part III). And as in Steven's case, because there was a guilty-but-mentally-ill statute, the state had no classification of second-degree murder, a charge that encompasses ideas of diminished capacity as a mitigating circumstance, thus implying less culpability.

What is odd about this "verdict form" is that it is a basic maxim of American jurisprudence that jurors are restricted to deciding only the degree of culpability. Almost every state, including Byron's, specifically prohibits a jury from deciding a person's sentence (except in cases of the death penalty), for that is the judge's legally mandated responsibility.

The "guilty but mentally ill verdict" form is insidious because it leads jurors to believe erroneously that, by voting for it, they are in effect determining sentence—namely, that the individual will be *treated* rather than *punished* by the system. However, a person found guilty but mentally ill in this state, as in Steven's state, is sent to the same institution as a person found guilty of straight murder.

Despite the two psychiatrists' assertions that Byron was *neither* insane nor suffering from any mental disorder at the time of the homicide, the jury found Byron guilty of murder but mentally ill. One can only assume that, faced with a limited set of options, they chose what they thought was the most humane. On another level, the verdict reflects a popularly held belief that a severely abused child who kills his parents is, despite expert testimony to the contrary, a disturbed person.

The jury foreman, a tall, soft-spoken man in his early fifties, did not look up at Byron or anyone else when he read the verdict. As comprehension dawned, Byron looked down suddenly, took a long, deep breath, and sat down. He had no tears. Sobbing, Tom Alan held Byron to him for several minutes, then the deputies took the impassive youth away. "The only [composed] person I saw in the courtroom was Byron," Alan later told me. "I guess he never expected any breaks in his life."

Any experienced trial attorney will tell you that explaining a jury's thinking is virtually impossible. But in this case the job was made a little easier. After the verdict, several jurors sent letters to the judge requesting him to be lenient in his sentencing. One reveals, at least in part, the jury's logic—or perhaps their confusion:

> Dear Sir:
> . . . Every one of us [on the jury] had great compassion for Byron Grant. There wasn't a single person on the jury that night that wanted to see Byron go to jail. Our only wish was to see that he gets the proper psychiatric treatment he needs—but not in prison. It would defeat the whole purpose of our mentally ill verdict. [The] decision came this way only after convincing [ourselves] that the verdict meant little or no jail sentence, but a proper and fair amount of psychiatric help.

After the verdict the judge was also deluged with letters urging him to be lenient in his sentencing. The letters came not only from friends and relatives, but others as well: students at Byron's high school; strangers who sat through the eight-day trial; elderly people who read about the trial in the local papers.

> Your Honor:
> . . . I know the killing of your parents is not a solution to a problem, but it really seems no one wanted to help this youngster. . . . If someone lives in the kind of environment that the Grant children were subjected to, I am very surprised that he didn't kill his parents sooner.

Judge:

. . . Hasn't he suffered enough? . . . He tried to get help but nothing worked. His parents seem to be more of the criminals in this case than the children. I'm not saying what he did was right, but when you're desperate there is no accounting for your actions sometimes. I think he's paid for what he did—eighteen years worth.

Dear Judge:

Never in my life have I felt so compelled to write a letter. I don't know Byron Grant, [but] don't you think he has suffered enough? I really feel very sorry for what he has done, but I don't feel he had any other way out. . . . Anybody that would treat their children or anyone's children like they did deserved to be axed to death. There is far too much child abuse in this country.

Honorable Judge:

. . . While you may say Byron Grant showed his parents no mercy, I can truthfully say he was driven to commit the crimes due to the fact he could no longer endure their cruel treatment. . . . I am now past eighty-one years of age, a widow, maintain my own home, not senile, and a nurse by profession. . . . My mother expired last year at the age of one-hundred-two-and-a-half. I was the oldest child of a family of twelve. My mother hated me from the day I was born until the day she died. . . . If I was a little slow in getting my chores done, she would take both hands and pull my hair and shake my head like a dog shaking a rat. . . . I think the worst whipping ever was when she hit me with Dad's buggy whip. . . . During those years, I [knew] . . . if I did anything to her, I would suffer much worse. . . . If you must give this young man a sentence, please be lenient; if any member of the jury would have had to endure punishment and resentment as I have told you, they would never have said he was guilty.

One thing is sure: letters did not stream in calling for a harsh sentence. If Stanley and Juliette's defenders were out there, they were not making themselves known. Ken Ellerbee, however, was unaffected by the outpouring of support. He had to defend the memory of Stanley and Juliette and all *good* parents. Ellerbee demanded that Byron be sentenced to the maximum term of sixty years on each homicide, the sentences to run consecutively. As he told the court in his sentencing memorandum,

> Premeditated murder of two human beings, particularly one's parents, is a terrifying unacceptable example of criminal conduct within our community. Parents and children throughout this community were carefully watching as this case unfolded, and the evidence upon which the State based its case made it clear that the allegation of abusive treatment supposedly suffered by Byron Grant was unsupported except by his testimony and the testimony of a member of his family."

Tom Alan made an impassioned plea for leniency during the sentencing phase. His pointed characterization of Byron's options was especially moving:

> Are we saying that he should have honored his father and mother by running away and becoming involved in child prostitution? How did the State think that Byron would survive if he ran away, particularly if he ran away with his sister? These children were not criminals; they could not make their way in the world by selling stolen goods or drugs. They would have made their way by selling themselves through acts of intercourse, sodomy, and fellatio. Those are the plain facts.

Somewhat moved by Alan's plea and the tremendous outpouring of support for Byron, the judge sentenced Byron to serve forty years for the death of his mother and thirty years for the death of his father, with the sentences running concurrently. He could have taken the prosecutor's lead and sentenced Byron to the maximum of one hundred and twenty years.

When Tom first contacted me, his brief was due in sixteen days; by the time I told him I wanted to help him, the filing date was only a week away. At that late date, unfortunately, all I could do was help him flesh out his argument and provide moral support. Though he repeatedly expressed to me his dissatisfaction with his efforts, I could only see a persuasive and passionate piece of legal writing.

The principal grounds for appeal was that the judge should have submitted the self-defense instruction to the jury. Though Tom's appellate brief ran forty-five pages, the gravamen of his argument was that the judge confused the word *imminent* with *immediate*.

As we have already most graphically seen in Michael's case, to be justified in using deadly force to protect himself or a third party, a person must have both a reasonable belief of being seriously harmed or killed and a reasonable perception that the threat of that attack is *imminent*. In his brief Tom argued that "attacks and threats that are constant and continuing are by definition imminent. . . . *Imminent* has been defined as 'near at hand; mediate rather than immediate; close rather than touching; impending; on the point of happening; threatening; menacing; perilous.' "

Sadly, defending Byron took a great toll on Tom. Soon after he filed the appeal, he had to take an extended vacation. About a year after I first spoke with him, I received the following letter:

> Dear Paul:
>   Enclosed is the extraordinarily bad news.
>
>   Tom

In its infinite wisdom, the state Supreme Court affirmed the conviction and sentence, unanimously agreeing with the trial court judge that Byron was not entitled to a self-defense instruction because *imminent* meant instantaneous.

"That defendant was a victim of an abusive or violent ongoing relationship does not," the Court wrote, "support the giving of a self-defense instruction. . . . We find that the absence of imminent or impending danger presented by the victims in this case, as evidenced by the remoteness in time between the murder of the victims and the last physical abuse, and by the fact that the father was asleep and the mother was in a nonthreatening disposition on the night of the killings, precludes the successful assertion of self-defense or defense of others."

In essence, the high court ruled that Byron's perception of imminent danger was, per se, unreasonable; he could *only* claim self-defense if he was assaulted immediately prior to the homicides. The fact that there was clear evidence at trial that Byron was slapped, hit, or otherwise brutalized on a regular basis in the month immediately preceding the homicides, meaning that he went to sleep with the expectation he would probably be beaten the next day, was irrelevant to the court.

The members of the Court ignored a fact on which all child abuse experts agree—attacks visited upon a child are qualitatively different from the violence one adult perpetrates upon another. Severe long-term child abuse has a profound effect on a child's understanding of reality, and thus on their perception of danger. Children and adolescents like Byron live in a heightened state of fear and agitation, not knowing when the next punch or whack will result in their death; nor do they know when their parents will make good on their oft-repeated threats to kill them.

While there was little the expert witnesses said that could have enlightened the Court about Byron's mental state, one of the letters written to the trial judge explained Byron's dilemma simply but eloquently.

[Except] for close members of the family, there was perhaps no one who saw the whole picture [of abuse] at the time. . . . As adults we realize this does not mean that the community supported Stanley's use of force or discipline. Yet a child might not view things similarly. In light of Byron's knowing since he was a child that neither the neighbors, Sunday school teachers, nor relatives were going to defend him, it is unrealistic to believe that he could be expected to look for help from the outside.

Obviously, the state Supreme Court had not evaluated the reasonableness of Byron's perception of danger in the light of years and years of physical, sexual, and emotional abuse and the toll this had taken on his psyche. Rather, they used as a measure a normal adult male.

In the eyes of the legal system Byron's case is closed. The only recourse is to seek clemency from the governor. Though I was not able to help Byron during his trial, I will be working with Tom on the clemency petition.

Pleas for clemency or commutation of sentence are essentially political solutions to legal problems. In domestic-violence cases they have been successfully used about a dozen times in recent years to circumvent narrow-minded court decisions. Specifically, governors have granted clemency in cases where state courts either disallowed the use of self-defense or limited the defendant from putting on expert testimony as to the effects of abuse. Of all these cases, only a handful have been parricides, the remainder being battered women who killed their husbands. The first was Richard Jahnke, whose case is discussed in the prologue. Another was James Bresnahan, whose case bears a striking resemblance to Byron's.

On August 4, 1964, fifteen-year-old James Bresnahan of Silverton, Colorado, stabbed his parents, William and Laurel Bresnahan, to death while the family was on a camping trip. James, who had never been arrested before, pled guilty and was sentenced to two life terms. Bresnahan's appellate attorney, John Kane, now a federal judge, tried unsuccessfully for eight years to get his client's sentence overturned on the grounds that the trial court in sentencing did not consider the fact that Bresnahan was physically and emotionally abused. Bresnahan, whose father was a physician, was not decimated by the failure of his appeals. He took college extension courses at the University of Southern Colorado and graduated first in his class.

In 1975 his plight came to the attention of Colorado governor Richard Lamm, who commuted the sentence to twenty-four years. The next year Bresnahan was paroled and following in his father's footsteps, enrolled in medical school. Dr. Bresnahan, who has devoted his medical practice to serving the needs of migrant laborers, made application for a pardon in 1987. In support of his petition, Judge Kane stated, "Of all the people that I have sentenced or that I have heard about or read about, I don't know of any that even come close to this story of triumph."

"The pardon is not to absolve me of blame," Dr. Bresnahan said. "It's more in recognition of what I've done since. The pardon just gives me back all the rights and responsibilities of a citizen." On May 8, 1987, Governor Roy Romer granted Bresnahan a full pardon.

Though these petitions often fall on deaf ears, I am encouraged that Byron will have a fighting chance. Not only will he undoubtedly have the support of those moral persons who stood by him after his conviction, but Byron has Tom Alan, a man who, until he dies, will refuse to stop fighting the conviction.

Tom Alan is no longer fighting just for Byron Randall Grant. He is fighting for all abused children. Though he was devastated by the outcome of this single case, it was a dramatically eye-opening experience for him. Six years after the verdict, he is still railing at the injustices represented by Byron's treatment by the system. "It's just amazing how we treat kids in this society," he told me. "We treat them violently and have a very dismissive attitude towards their pain. We think because they are little they have little pain."

More than the people in his community, Tom Alan, or me, the strongest advocate Byron has is himself.

Since he entered the state reformatory almost four years ago, Byron has not once been permitted to see a psychiatrist or psychologist. His entire treatment program has consisted of a meeting every couple of months with a prison counselor. Though he has been denied therapeutic treatment, Byron has come a long way from the person whom Tom Alan once described as "a nonentity, a vapor who could barely talk."

Over my two-day visit, Byron and I spent about fifteen hours together. Today we currently speak about once a month. From our first conversation, it was obvious to me that he was different from most of the people I have represented. He is one of the few who has developed a relatively sophisticated understanding of himself and is able to articulate his needs.

Most of my prison interview was spent talking over the facts of his case. Toward the end of the evening, however, we began to explore new territory, things he told me later that no one had ever asked him.

"Some people have a concern that people who are abused will do the same to their children," I said forthrightly.

"I know that," he acknowledged, nodding. Though I never discussed it with Tom, I had a hunch that Stanley had been victimized by his father.

"Your dad was abused, wasn't he?" I said.

Byron raised his eyebrows, his expression saying, How did you know? "I found out a little about his childhood after his death," he answered slowly. "He was abused by his stepfather. . . . I guess he hit [my dad] with a cane and got angry at him. I have no idea how often, just that he was hit with a cane. I also remember him talking a lot about what was expected from him when he was young. . . . My mother once told me of an incident when my dad's stepfather came home drunk and struck my grandmother a couple of times. My father jumped in the middle and told him that if he hit his mother any more, he was going to kill him."

"Tell me how you think you wouldn't continue that cycle with your children."

"I think abuse is carried on from generation to generation only when it is not recognized as abuse. . . . Abused kids think it's normal, and then they do that to their kids," he said.

"What do you mean by 'that'?"

"Now, like there were so many years that I thought what I was going through is normal, and you know, this is the way that most children are raised. . . . After a punishment I always asked myself what I did and looked at the situation and tried to see if it was really my fault, if there was some way it could have been avoided. . . . Now I know what it is. I can recognize it, and I read about it. . . . You have to recognize that something is wrong before you do anything about it, or even make any corrections in your own life about it to deal with it."

Stay safe, Byron.

PART VI

CHILDREN WHO
HIRE OTHERS TO KILL
THEIR PARENTS

Introduction

Our society generally holds that murder for hire is one of the most heinous forms of killing. Involvement in a murder-for-hire scheme is one of the few categories or "special circumstances" of homicide for which the death penalty is mandated in those states that have this severest of punishments. The penalty applies to those who get paid to kill as well as to those who hire the killers.

No one knows how many people are killed by hired assassins each year, but it is safe to assume that the figure is an insignificant percentage of the total. Given the unusually intense emotional dynamics common in parricides, to say nothing of the gross inexperience and meager financial resources of the average teen, it is rare indeed to find a parricide where the homicide was committed by a hired killer.

Actually, we know little about hired killers in general. News reports tend to focus more on the results of their efforts—"A man was found slumped over his steering wheel this morning, the obvious victim of an organized-crime slaying . . . no suspects have been identified"—than on who they are. In fact, most of what has been written about the hired assassin has largely been concocted by novelists and scriptwriters. *Day of the Jackal, The Hit, The Godfather,* and *Prizzi's Honor*—from these and other films we have come to know him (and in the case of *Prizzi's Honor,* her) as embodying the words *cold and calculating.* Even the euphemisms used to describe what he does, have a mechanical ring—*hit, terminate, eliminate.* He is efficient, knowing his intended victim's schedule as well as the victim himself. He moves in the shadows, wearing dark clothes and sleek-fitting leather gloves, leaving no trace.

When I first became involved in defending a parricide where the perpetrator had hired another to kill, I looked to the abuse as somehow distinguishing the case. But after three more similar cases, I was forced to conclude that the abuse was no worse than in other patricides or matricides, and that the only difference is that these kids used someone else's finger to pull the trigger.

Parricides involving hired assassins are anything but carefully executed murder schemes carried out by shrewd, ruthless individuals. Rather, driven by abject desperation, they tend to be sloppy, chaotic efforts. This was certainly true in the most famous murder-for-hire parricide case in recent history, that of Cheryl Pierson. What makes Pierson's case even more fascinating is the complex interplay of media and public opinion that resulted in a very different outcome from most other cases in this book. The only reason I use her real name, in fact, is because of the inordinate amount of press attention the case has already received.

On November 7, 1985, the topic of conversation in homeroom 226 at Newfield High School in Selden, New York, was Beverly Wallace, a woman who lived in a nearby community and who had been arrested for hiring someone to kill her abusive husband.

"Who would be crazy enough to do that?" said sixteen-year-old Cheryl Pierson to classmate Sean Pica. A diminutive boy with cascading, dark-brown hair, Pica had sat behind her for several months, yet oddly enough those were perhaps the first words she had said to him all year. At school they hung out with completely different circles of friends. Cheryl was a popular student, co-captain of the junior varsity cheerleading squad, and had a college-aged boyfriend. Sean was a loner and an avid Boy Scout.

"I'd do it if the money was right," Sean retorted.

"Oh, yeah, how much?" Cheryl said, upping the ante.

"A thousand bucks," said the boy who had never been arrested and whose father was a retired cop.

This idle classroom chatter grew more serious over the next few months and came to a head on a cold February morning as Pica sat crouching behind a tree in front of Cheryl's home at six A.M. Sean was no seasoned criminal, but he was a good enough shot to make the first bullet count—Jim Pierson, a recent widower and wealthy plumbing contractor, tumbled to the ground with a bullet in his head. To make sure that he'd done the job, Sean walked up to Pierson and emptied the remainder of the clip into the back of his lifeless body. Then he headed for school. Even though he had just killed a man, he did not want to be late for homeroom. Sean Pica was not a kid who broke the rules; in fact, he was only a few merit badges away from qualifying as an Eagle Scout.

Cheryl and Sean were arrested shortly after the homicide and indicted as adults for second-degree murder and conspiracy to commit murder. Rob, Cheryl's boyfriend, was indicted for solicitation to commit murder. During her confession, Cheryl revealed that she had hired Sean to kill her father because he had been sexually abusing her since she was thirteen years old.

New York is a city so jaded by violence that evening newscasters report stories of gangland slayings with about the same nonchalance as they do automobile accidents. Cheryl Pierson's arrest, however, created a veritable feeding frenzy among members of the print and electronic media.

The New York press, which has a penchant for creating its own sensational shorthand names for notorious criminal cases (Bernhard Goetz, the "Subway Vigilante"; Robert Chambers, the "Preppie Murderer"), immediately dubbed the Pierson case the "Homeroom Hit." Scores of newspaper articles and television stories blared out not only painstaking details of the plan and the murder, but also gave detailed descriptions of Cheryl's abuse along with daily progress reports on the legal proceedings. The press interest was so intense that, even after she was sentenced, articles provided the public with a description of the schedule Cheryl would have to follow in the county jail, complete with mealtimes. Eventually, the case spawned a book, *The Deadly Silence,* by Dena Kleiman, the reporter who provided in-depth coverage of the case for the *New York Times,* and a television movie by the same name.

What is of special interest here and what was not covered by the press was how the case was essentially driven to resolution by the media itself. Cheryl, like all abused children and adolescents, was paralyzed by the fear that her ordeal would be made public; yet ironically it was the publicity of her plight that became her ultimate salvation.

Though an intense legal effort was expended on Cheryl's behalf, what I believe most affected the ultimate disposition of this case was the media coverage of the case.

Though it may sound cynical, the reality was that Cheryl's story was perfectly suited for the press. As her local attorney, Paul Gianelli, reflected, "[S]he was a little girl . . . [and when she was arrested,] she had on a red-and-white cheerleader's jacket. She looked like the kind of kid that you had seen hanging out at a pizza place. She looked very, very ordinary, and here these extraordinary things had happened to her."

On television and in the newspapers, the public saw an all-American girl with dark-auburn bangs shading her eyes and a cute button nose. She lived in an all-American small town with an all-American dad. She went to an all-American high school where she was co-captain of the junior varsity cheerleading team. And at this high school in homeroom 226, she found herself an all-American hit man. Cheryl's story begged to be told.

For his part, Gianelli found a thoughtful reporter in Dena Kleiman, who, in her early stories for the *New York Times*, demonstrated that she was understanding of Cheryl's plight. As Paul later said to me, "The [other newspapers'] stories ran with headlines like 'Homeroom Hit.' . . . I wasn't comfortable with 'Girl in Homeroom Hit Plot,' and I got to know Dena Kleiman from the *New York Times*. Her stories were so much more sensitive, and I think they had a lot to do with educating [the public] about this particular case."

Because of the rapport she established with Gianelli, Kleiman was soon afforded wider access to Cheryl than other newspaper reporters. The result was a thoughtful, extensive article that appeared in the widely read and highly influential Sunday *New York Times Magazine*. The article appeared on September 14, 1986, one day before the trial was originally scheduled.

Gianelli retained me to assist in the development of the

defense strategy. Though there were ongoing plea negotiations, I treated the case, as always, as if it were going to trial. Painstakingly, all the efforts that I use in preparing a parricide defense were set in motion. In retrospect, however, it was the conversations I had had with a producer for ABC's investigative news show "20/20," several weeks before becoming involved in Cheryl's case that proved to be my most important contribution. For some time prior to the Pierson case, the producer had been interested in doing an in-depth segment on parricide. Shortly after I began working on the Pierson case, she called me, expressing interest in doing a show on it.

Agreeing to cooperate with the media is always a crapshoot for an attorney, especially when it is for a television news show. Journalistic impartiality aside, it is difficult to gauge what slant the story will take. For shows such as "20/20" or "60 Minutes," hours of videotape must be distilled into a piece only seven to twelve minutes long. The situation is even worse for the national network broadcasts, where sometimes two hours of tape must be condensed into a forty-five-second piece.

The crucial issues of who and what will be edited out are something that interviewees don't know until the actual airing of the segment. Sometimes the line producer (with whom one has been working for four or five months) will not even know what will end up on the cutting-room floor until the day of the airing. Yet all of this must be balanced against the enormous educational and consciousness-raising value of twelve minutes or even twelve seconds on a national program televised at prime time. Even a poorly rated national television news show reaches millions more people than the most popular daily newspapers and magazines.

After several hours of conversation with her, I concluded that she would produce an objective but appropriately understanding piece. It was particularly important that the producer stated frankly that the show intended to focus solely on Cheryl's story. I then spoke with Gianelli, who had been deluged with requests for television interviews, and he agreed to allow "20/20" to interview Cheryl.

Deciding to permit Cheryl to do the "20/20" interview *before* the sentencing hearing was one of the most crucial judgments of the case, other than accepting the plea bargain. The television interviews were conducted over the spring and summer of 1987, but the segment did not air until two weeks before her sentencing hearing. The first and only television interview Cheryl Pierson ever gave aired August 27, 1987, at ten P.M. It was given the simple but sensational title "She Wanted Her Father Dead." Ironically, it aired with another story entitled "The Best Chance Yet"—discussing new medical techniques to enable infertile couples to have children. I'm sure the programing decision was accidental: one story about a child's taking a parent's life balanced by one about parents creating a new life.

Whenever "60 Minutes," "20/20," or any other long-format news program focuses on a particular court case, the primary benefit for the public is educational. The specific results can range from letters and phone calls of encouragement to legislative hearings. But in the case of the *People of the State of New York* versus *Cheryl Pierson*, the result was the stuff of a defense attorney's dream.

Millions of Americans watching "20/20" that hot August night were moved by Cheryl's story, and one of them was Jay Fleckenstein. He was so moved that he called Gianelli the next morning. Not just any interested viewer, Fleckenstein was Cheryl's maternal uncle.

As Gianelli later told me, "Fleckenstein was appalled at seeing the grandmother and the aunt trying to bury Cheryl," trying to portray James Pierson, Sr., as a docile person "who could not have done this sort of thing." Fleckenstein hadn't thought that there was any doubt, any argument at all that Cheryl had been molested and abused by Jim Pierson. "[And so] he was silent. . . . He felt that his testimony, his recollections, would not be particularly helpful. . . . [Besides] she [Cheryl's mom] had sworn him to silence."

Fleckenstein's story was a bombshell that provided critical corroborative evidence that could blow the sentencing hearing wide open. Though there were numerous witnesses who thought Jim Pierson might have sexually abused his daughter—one neighbor testified that he saw Pierson massaging and pinching his daughter's rear end, saying things like "Doesn't she have a nice pair of tits"—there was no definitive proof other than Cheryl's statements. It so happened that once

Cheryl's mom had called Fleckenstein and asked him to drive her to the doctor's office. Along the way, she told him that Jim Pierson had beat her up because she had suspected or had found out that he was having sexual relations with Cheryl. She had heard him leave her bedroom at night and go into her daughter's bedroom. Jim Pierson had really beaten her quite severely, and she didn't know what to do . . . she had her brother promise that he wouldn't say anything.

I couldn't believe what Gianelli was telling me. "Did it ever occur to him to report anything for Cheryl's sake?" I asked.

"Nope. He didn't feel that Cheryl was in any kind of peril of being convicted. He took [the dying promise] seriously. He felt that there were people around who would be watching and that Cheryl would be protected. He felt that even the grandmother and Marilyn would be supportive of Cheryl. But when he saw [them] deny it, he felt compelled to call."

Two weeks after the "20/20" piece was televised, the sentencing hearing was held before Judge Harvey Sherman. In the intervening weeks the judge had been deluged with letters of support. Though he did not reveal the contents of those letters, they were probably no different from the ones sent to Gianelli's law office.

The letters ranged from that of the seventy-year-old lady who sent Cheryl a check for two hundred dollars because she herself had been a silent victim, to a lady who wrote that after her sexually abusive uncle died she went to his grave and overturned a bucket of urine on it, to another who offered to reimburse Cheryl for the ammunition used to kill her father.

When Cheryl took the stand, she didn't reveal much that most people, including the judge, hadn't already known. Her testimony, however, made banner headlines in *Newsday* and the *New York Post*. In fact, to anyone who had been closely following the case, there was really only one surprise in the eight-day hearing—Jay Fleckenstein. Fleckenstein confirmed what the others had thought but had been too afraid or too ashamed to say: his sister Cathleen knew for a fact that her husband was having sexual relations with her teenage daughter, Cheryl.

Judge Sherman wrote the closing scene on October 5, 1987. As tradition and the law demands, he first asked Cheryl if she had anything to say before sentencing. Cheryl, in a white dress, with tears streaming down her cheeks, stuttered, "I know what I did was wrong, I'm sorry." Then she collapsed and had to be revived with smelling salts. No longer able to stand, Cheryl sat in a chair as the judge delivered his sentence.

Because Cheryl pled guilty to voluntary manslaughter, the sentencing hearing took on the trappings of a trial itself, with the entire focus revolving around whether Judge Sherman would grant Cheryl youthful offender status, under which she would be eligible for parole. Each side was given the opportunity to make an opening argument, present and cross-examine witnesses, and make a closing argument. The majority of the spectators already knew the essential details of the story. For many, the sentencing hearing would be an extended version of the "20/20" segment. The only difference was that Judge Sherman would have the final edit.

Judge Sherman granted Cheryl youthful offender status, but sentenced her to serve six months in the county jail and ordered her to receive therapy upon her release. In a sentencing memorandum, Judge Sherman acknowledged that Cheryl had been sexually abused by her father since she was thirteen years old. "This Court," the judge wrote explaining the jail time, "must encourage victims of domestic violence to seek other alternatives than the path taken by Cheryl Pierson. . . . This Court cannot countenance a planned homicide, albeit planned and carried out by teenagers suffering emotional distress; society has the right to condemn and the duty to punish such conduct."

Cheryl was whisked away to the Suffolk County Jail in Riverhead, where, because of time off for good behavior, she was released in a little over one hundred days.

The newspapers covered her release in the same detail as they had the rest of the case. The photo in *Newsday* showed Cheryl leaving prison and entering a white stretch limousine with her brother and Rob Cuccio. Cuccio, who had pled guilty to second-degree solicitation and was given probation, asked Cheryl to marry him later that day.

As sensational, however, as the Cheryl Pierson case was, the case of the Carter brothers (if these matters can even be compared) was even more remarkable, though it received almost no media attention.

The Brothers Carter

$\overline{\overline{}}$

Veteran defense attorney Mel Taylor does so much court-appointed criminal work that the county jail attorney room is like a second office to him. And until he had interviewed seventeen-year-old Douglas Carter, he thought that he had truly seen everything. Two minutes with Carter made Taylor realize his error.

Before Taylor even had the opportunity to introduce himself formally to the stout teenager with light blue eyes and a freckled face, Douglas declared, "I shouldn't be in here, my father should." Douglas was polite, but he didn't let Taylor finish one question. The interview was more like a rambling monologue. Douglas told Taylor stories of physical and psychological torture so ghastly and bizarre that Taylor at first thought his new client was either lying or crazy or both. The only reason Taylor didn't totally dismiss his client's story was that the crimes with which Douglas was charged were as outlandish as his stories of abuse.

Taylor called me about two weeks after his interview with Douglas to ask me to assist him on the case; what he had to say shocked me profoundly. Though in my line of work, I routinely hear weird stories, this was beyond belief. Despite my intimate familiarity with the dark side of family life, these stories of malevolence were simply beyond my comprehension. It was only after I met Taylor at his office and listened to Douglas's confession that I knew I was entering a legal Twilight Zone. I replayed the following section of the taped confession three times to make sure I heard it correctly.

> *Douglas:* *If my father finds out that I hired people to kill him, he'll kill me. . . . You're not gonna tell him?*
>
> *Detective Glaser:* *Well, he's gonna have to be told obviously, but we'll tell him in a certain way that if anything ever happens to either one of you, we're gonna hunt him down, like we hunted you guys down. . . .*
>
> *D:* *I don't want my father to find out about this.*
>
> *G:* *Well, he's gonna find out. . . . We have to tell him. On the other hand, too, obviously the guy needs some help. He's driven his own sons to this point. . . . You're talking serious crime here. . . . You hired someone to kill your father. You had him stabbed. You had him injected. And you hired a policeman tonight. Let's face it. It's not good. . . .*
>
> *D:* *What kind of protection do I get for myself?*
>
> *G:* *Well, you're gonna be in jail now. That's all the protection you'll need. Nobody's gonna harm you there. . . .*
>
> *D:* *Well, what if my father bails me out?*
>
> *G:* *Well, you can go with him if you wanta. . . . You want to stay in jail until this goes to court?*
>
> *D:* *Yeah.*
>
> *G:* *I can arrange that. We'll set your bail high enough so he can't get you out.*

Douglas Carter is undoubtedly one of the few people in the annals of American penal history who requested to have his bail set at a level that he could not afford. Always interested in swelling the prison population, the judge complied, setting Douglas's bail at a quarter of a million dollars.

The boy's request sounded unbelievable to Detective Glaser, but he didn't know Brad Carter as Douglas did. It was not difficult for Douglas to predict how the forty-eight-year-old former weight lifter would react to the news. No only is it impossible to hide from your father that you have been arrested for hiring someone to kill him, but attempted patricide is just one of those crimes that would raise the ire of any father, especially Bradley Carter.

Carter Senior was definitely from the very old school of child rearing. Like Stanley Grant, Brad had raised Douglas and his older brother, Vincent, with two principles: he was their undisputed master, and their mission in life was to serve him. Physical punishment, humiliation, and subservience were the order of the day not only for the boys, but also for their mother, Elizabeth.

Best illustrating this was how he reacted to the child abuse investigators who had come to his home five years before the attempted murder plot, inquiring about the welts and bruises on Douglas's face, neck, and arms. Douglas was thirteen, in eventh grade at the time. Brad had severely beaten him because Douglas had visited a girl's house without his father's permission. The morning after the beating Douglas's home-room teacher noticed that, besides the marks on his body, the boy was deeply depressed. Yet he refused to tell his teacher what had happened to him.

Douglas was sent to the principal's office, and only after everal hours of cajoling did he agree to talk. Despite his leas that they not speak to his father, a school representative nd social service investigator appeared at his house the next fternoon.

"We've come to speak to you about your son," they told rad when he answered the door. He did not even let them .

With his two timid children standing behind him, he bel-wed, "You can't tell me what to do! This is my child. I ade him, and I can destroy him."

Brad then threatened to beat the two women unless they mediately got off his property. Before they even got in their r, Brad was pummeling his son in retaliation. The beating ade the previous one seem like a love tap.

The next day young Douglas was removed from the school, d two weeks later the family moved to another home. Nei-er the school nor the department of public social services lowed up. And not wanting to chance another visit from the authorities, Brad forbade Douglas to return to school. From then on Douglas worked in his father's grocery store.

Douglas and Vincent were the classic victims of extreme physical and psychological abuse. The battering began, as it often does, with their mother, Elizabeth, before the children were even born. Brad beat Elizabeth on their first date, and he continued to beat her throughout both pregnancies.

The boys' persecution began when they were still in diapers. In addition to the everyday punches and slaps, their punishments over the years included being burned with a cigarette to the palms of the hands, being whipped across the naked back, being bound with rope, handcuffs, and chains, and being threatened with guns.

Brad dominated his family so completely that he would mete out group punishment. As in an army barracks, if Brad thought one member of the family did something wrong, he punished the entire family.

One of Brad's most humiliating punishments in this regard was to force his wife and two sons to stand naked outside their home. When he was feeling more charitable, he allowed them to keep their underwear. When Douglas originally told Taylor about this punishment, he was so embarrassed that he could barely speak above a whisper: "Sometimes he used to make us all undress and put us out on the balcony. In the cold weather, in the winter, in the summer, in the rain, ever time. . . . When I was younger, I would get hit by myself but later [after the age of twelve] if I would do somethin wrong, we would all get hit. If I made a mistake, we'd all ge hit, and the same for my mom and brother. . . . When w were outside, he would just smoke and watch TV."

After three or four hours his father would go outside an say, "Okay, come on, everybody inside." The first thing Eliz abeth and her children would do was apologize, even if the hadn't done anything wrong, which was most of the time When he was asked why they apologized, Douglas responded "We didn't want to be hit no more."

One of the most devastating punishments Douglas remen bered occurred when he was about twelve and a half yea old. It was his responsibility to clean up after the family do and one day he forgot. Bradley flew into a rage when looked out into the backyard and noticed it had not been cleaned. Grabbing little Douglas by the collar, he threw him down, ripped his clothes off his body, and screamed, "Now it's your turn to stay there instead of the dogs." Brad took the dogs out of the doghouse and threw Douglas in. After about six hours sitting in the foul kennel, Douglas heard his father's footsteps. The door opened, but instead of releasing his son, Brad only put the dogs back inside. Douglas sat there from about three in the afternoon until his release the next morning, shivering and crying.

As repugnant as these acts of violence are, the problem is always corroboration. Though Douglas, like other abuse victims, appeared in all other respects to be telling the truth, a question remained about the accuracy of his accounts. As enlightened human beings, there are certain punishments that we refuse to believe any parent, even an abusive one, is capable of inflicting. In fact, this was a major problem in defending Byron and Cindy. Stanley, Byron's father, was undoubtedly a vicious man, but the death threats and threats against the sister (which were the key to Byron's defense) were only heard by Byron. Similarly, as in most cases of sexual abuse, the only witness to the sexual abuse was Cindy.

Luckily, in this case a witness came forward who backed up Douglas's allegations. Milos Ervin was a former neighbor and sometime employee of the Carter family. During Douglas's eventual trial, he would testify about what he saw. The questions were posed by Mel Taylor.

> *Q: Now did there ever come a time when you saw any of the family members outside of the home without clothes on?*
>
> *A: Yeah . . . it was Douglas, Vincent, and their mother. It happened in broad daylight. [It] must have been about twelve or one o'clock in the afternoon. . . . I was coming back from the corner store.*
>
> *Q: What door did they come out?*
>
> *A: The front door. . . . They had their undergarments, but it's still embarrassing to get thrown out of your house with your underwear on.*
>
> *Q: You say the mother was with them at the time?*

A: Yeah, the mother, she had like I guess a bra and panties on. . . . When they came out the front stairway, they ran down another entrance to the basement. . . .

Q: Did you see an incident while you were looking out your house window?

A: Yeah, I was taking a shower at the time and there was a lot of screaming coming from the house. I looked out the window and Brad had his sons like tied up. Douglas had on handcuffs, and Brad had a dog leash of some sort around Douglas's neck. He was like dragging him downstairs putting him in a little dog shed. . . . Brad left him there all night long.

Q: Did you hear anything else while that was happening?

A: I heard he was getting beat and stuff like that.

Q: Did you hear Douglas or Vincent saying anything?

A: They were just screaming.

Q: And do you recall if they had clothes on at the time?

A: No they didn't . . . they had underwear on. . . . [*Another*] time I was walking by the house. It was late at night. And there was screaming. I was curious. The dogs were locked up so I climbed over the fence and I went to the window. And I saw Douglas tied up over a table. He had like a multicolored rope around his wrist tied to his legs. . . . He was like arched over a table. His hands and legs were tied underneath like this so he couldn't move or flinch his body. . . . His father was hitting him with a stick of some sort. He was hitting him across his back, legs wherever he felt like.

Q: And you are certain you saw this?

A: Yeah, that's something you don't forget. . . .

Q: Did you make up these stories, these incidents?

A: You don't make up something like this.

Unfortunately, as in so many other cases we've seen, no one ever stood up for the boys. Elizabeth accepted her husband's word in all things as final. She took her marriage vows seriously, believing she was powerless to change her situation once she had said, "I do." Her predicament was compounded by the fact that being so chronically battered herself, she was unable to protect herself, let alone her sons. Elizabeth had no support system, except her frail, aged father. Though fifteen-year-old Douglas and seventeen-year-old Vincent learned over time to cope with their pain, they never got used to their mother's abuse. In fact as they got older, it became increasingly difficult to witness their father batter and humiliate their mother. And so, one Saturday evening after all three had spent several hours standing on the family porch in their underwear, the boys decided they had had enough.

After Brad went to sleep, the boys called a cab. Taking with her only a pocketbook containing several hundred dollars and a change of underwear, Elizabeth was ushered into the cab by her two sons. Because they only had enough cash for one airplane ticket, the boys stayed behind.

Though they professed ignorance of their mother's whereabouts the next morning, Brad knew the boys had to have been in on the escape. Consequently, the following weeks and months were the worst ever for them. Brad had let one member of his family get away; he wasn't about to allow the boys to escape, too.

They were only allowed out to go work at the grocery store, which was attached to the house. They worked sixteen hours a day, seven days a week. Several times a week Brad admonished his sons, "Remember, even though you're faster than me, if you try to get away, I'll track you down and kill you." Vincent was so intimidated that even after he turned eighteen, he remained at home. Both boys passively accepted their lot in life as indentured servants for Brad. Had Steven Ashton not come into their lives two years later, they would probably still be toiling for their father.

Brad hired Steven Ashton, a short, skinny, chain-smoking twenty-two-year-old with dull black eyes, to be a stock clerk at the store. Though Ashton was a drifter who often slept in the stockroom at night, Brad took an immediate liking to the young man, perhaps because he was a diligent worker and always treated Brad with the utmost respect. Since Ashton spent so much time around the family, it was impossible for him to ignore Brad's daily persecution of his sons. Ashton often tried to talk to the boys about their treatment, but it was to no avail. "That's just the way he is," was their stock response.

One afternoon about three months after he began work, Ashton saw Brad punch Vincent in the back of the head so hard that Vincent went flying into a wall. The reason for the assault: nineteen-year-old Vincent had forgotten to mop one corner of the store. Though the boys seemed to have an endless tolerance for the abuse, Ashton didn't.

After Brad had left the store, Steven angrily said to Douglas and Vincent, "If that was my father, I'd kill him for treating me like that." Though neither brother had ever even considered speaking back to their father, both, especially Douglas, became fascinated by Steven's idea.

Though he was the younger brother, Douglas was considered by all who knew the family to be brighter and more socially adept than Vincent. Just as George in Steinbeck's *Of Mice and Men* was dedicated to protecting Lenny, Douglas, from the age of five, had tried to protect his older brother. Sadly, he was not as successful as he would have liked to be. When Vincent was a toddler, his father frequently smacked him on the temple and threw him headfirst into walls. By the time Vincent was nineteen, the effects of these traumatic blows were tragically visible. Like those of a fighter who has been in the ring too long, Vincent's overall thought processes were impaired. His speech was slurred, and his logic and memory were poor. For some unknown reason, Douglas proved sturdier than his older brother.

Later that evening, Douglas met with Steven in the back of the store. He was by himself because he wanted to protect Vincent in case his plan went awry.

Douglas told Ashton he wanted his father killed, but he could never under any circumstances do it by himself. Steven, who had from time to time obviously earned his living in less than legal ways, told Douglas, "For three thousand dollars, I can find someone to take care of your problem. I'll take care of it all. . . . When he's dead, you give me the money." It seemed like the ideal plan, but Douglas wasn't sure if Steven, a person he barely knew, was capable of carrying it out. Douglas agreed to it, however, because he would have done anything to get away, short of killing his father himself.

Nothing happened for several days, with Ashton protesting that he was still looking for the right person for the hit. Since the idea had been planted in Douglas's mind, however, he could think of little else but his and Vincent's freedom. One afternoon, Douglas decided to stop waiting.

When Brad lay down for a nap, Douglas seized Brad's pistol from under the cash register and thrust it at Ashton, who was sweeping the floor.

"Just walk next door and shoot him while he's sleeping. We can make it look like a robbery."

Steven hesitated, but then took the gun. He had never said anything about doing the killing himself. For all his bravado, Steven had never killed anyone; more important, he was afraid of what his volatile boss would do to him if he woke up and saw Steven pointing a gun at him. His fear, however, took a back seat to the three thousand dollars. He fixed his finger on the trigger and quietly walked through the back of the store into the Carter residence.

Ashton stood in the doorway for several long moments watching Brad's silently heaving chest. He raised the revolver, but could not bring himself to pull the trigger.

Several minutes later Douglas reluctantly took the gun back and replaced it in its holster. Steven profusely apologized, telling Douglas that he could still be relied upon to get the job done.

Two days later at about nine in the morning, a scraggly teenager with a pimply face and short-cropped Mohawk hair-cut walked into the store. Brad was behind the cash register, Vincent was sweeping in the back, and Douglas was slicing some cold cuts.

The young man picked up a package of doughnuts, then went over to the magazine rack. He spent a sufficiently long enough time in front of the magazine rack to draw Brad's attention. The store had a "no browsing" policy that Brad strictly enforced. Brad walked briskly over to the teenager and told him that if he wasn't going to buy a magazine, then he should pay for the doughnuts and get the hell out of the store.

A shouting match ensued, which quickly degenerated into pushing and shoving. The shouts brought the two boys running to the front of the store. Neither attempted to intervene, thinking that their father could easily handle the young man. In a flash, however, the young man whipped out a six-inch switchblade and plunged it twice into Brad's belly.

The kid ran from the store, and Brad fell to the ground, cursing and clutching his profusely bleeding gut. Douglas raced to the phone to call the police, and Vincent gave chase. Vincent got within ten yards of his father's assailant and then stopped dead in his tracks when he saw the attacker jump into an idling car. Vincent was flabbergasted when he saw that it was Steven Ashton behind the wheel.

After speaking briefly with the police, Douglas and Vincent went to the hospital. On the way, Vincent said to Douglas, "What's going on here? You know who was driving that car?"

"We'll talk about it later," Douglas sternly told his brother. "Let's first see how Dad is doing."

Though the wounds were deep, the knife had not cut any major organs. The boys remained in the waiting room until their father's surgery was over. After Brad was moved to intensive care, the brothers drove back to the store. Almost as soon as they walked in the door, the phone rang. It was Steven, and he wanted them to meet him at a motel.

On the way to the motel, Douglas told his brother about his arrangement with Ashton. However, according to Douglas, he'd had no idea that the skinny kid was going to stab their father. Ashton had never told him where or when the hit was going to occur. Vincent was confused, but as he always had, he accepted whatever his brother told him.

At one of those sleazy adult motels that rented rooms by the hour, Ashton opened the door. The brothers saw the young man who had stabbed their father sitting on the bed. Next to him was a mousy-looking teenage girl with stringy, bleached-blond hair and a washed-out complexion. Ashton introduced them as Dennis Grady and Melissa Forchet.

Dennis, age nineteen, and his sixteen-year-old girlfriend were unemployed, homeless runaways who had just moved to the city from the Midwest. Steven had met them several weeks earlier at almost the moment they emerged from the downtown bus depot.

The brothers sat on the radiator in front of the window. Douglas of course did all the talking. "He's in critical condition, but he's not dead," he began testily.

Knowing that he would not be paid until Brad was dead, Ashton retorted, "It's okay, we'll do another hit." Douglas and Vincent passively listened.

Ashton's second plan was clearly more ambitious than the first: Melissa would dress up as a nurse and shoot a hypodermic syringe full of air into Brad's vein. After several minutes of discussion, however, Ashton changed his mind and decided that sulfuric acid—car-battery acid—would be more efficient. Melissa had never used a syringe in her life, but that didn't matter: Steven had experience with needles, and she herself was a devotee of "General Hospital."

The first stop for the five conspirators was an auto supply store. A twelve-volt car battery would provide more than enough acid for their purposes. The next stop was the hospital supply store located directly across the street from the municipal hospital where Brad was lying in the intensive care ward. There, they purchased a crisp, white nurse's uniform, matching stockings, shoes, and a name tag. Douglas made all the purchases with a stolen credit card Ashton had given him. Ashton also managed to find a syringe.

Ashton took Grady and Melissa back to the motel so that Melissa could practice with the syringe. The brothers went to the hospital to visit their father.

Brad was not only in great pain, he was also terrified. He cried when the boys walked in and took both of them to his chest. He was convinced that someone would try to kill him again. Not only was it the first time in their lives both had seen their father helpless, it was the first time they felt sorry for him. Douglas reassured Brad that he and his brother would take care of the store and would do everything possible to help the police in tracking down the attacker.

As the boys were preparing to leave, Brad begged them to spend the night with him in the room. "I'm so scared. Please stay and protect me." Ever the dutiful sons, Douglas slept curled up at the foot of his father's bed, and Vincent slept on the couch, an arrangement that continued for the next three nights.

Ashton and company spent three days planning the "hit." Ashton repeatedly drilled Melissa on appropriate injection techniques, impressing upon her the importance of inserting the syringe directly into the vein in Brad's forearm. This would insure a quick death, because the acid would go directly to his heart.

One other task remained before executing the assassination—finding a lookout. Brad would recognize Ashton and Grady, so it had to be a stranger. After several days, Ashton solved that problem by recruiting twenty-three-year-old Jack DeVonne. As could be expected, DeVonne's experience in these matters was as vast as Melissa's.

Ashton drove Melissa and Jack to the emergency room entrance and dropped them off, forgetting to give them one crucial piece of information—the location of Brad's room in the three-winged hospital. Aware that she would draw attention to herself if, as a nurse, she had to ask another hospital employee directions to a patient's room, Melissa and Jack roamed the hospital for about an hour and a half before finding Brad.

Jack stayed by the elevator, and Melissa went into the room. As soon as Melissa opened the door, she immediately saw another problem. Brad was not alone. Unbeknownst to his sons, Brad had hired two bodyguards, and they stood at either side of the bed to protect him from another attack.

Fearing that she would arouse suspicion by running out of the room, Melissa, using all the skills she had learned watching afternoon soap operas, confidently strode past the two beefy bodyguards. Later, during the trial, Melissa described what occurred next:

"I asked him how he was doing, because I was trying to make it seem like I was a real nurse.

" 'I have two injections for you—for your pains,' I told him. Then I went to inject him in the vein in the bend of his arm [so] that it would get into his heart quicker, but he pulled his arm away and said, 'Don't give it to me there, do it up here.'

"I said okay and gave him the shot. I injected all the battery acid in his upper arm. Then he said, 'It burns, it burns.'

"I said, 'I'll get a doctor.' "

With that assurance to Brad, Melissa fled to the elevator.

Had Melissa injected the acid into a vein, an expert later testified, Brad would have died a painful death in less than two minutes. But because she injected him in the fleshy part of his shoulder, the only effect was a reddened, sore arm.

By the time Melissa got back to the motel room, Douglas had already discovered that Brad was not dead. Needless to say, Douglas jumped on her and Ashton for what he viewed as sheer bumbling. Melissa, Grady, and Ashton screamed right back. They were upset that none of them had been paid. But Douglas held his ground. He wasn't paying any money until his father was killed.

After Melissa's attempt, Brad was placed under twenty-four-hour police protection. Three weeks after the stabbing, Brad was released from the hospital, but he was unable to go back to work. The boys took over the operation of the store, and each continued on as if nothing had happened. No one was ever paid, and Douglas gave up hope that he would ever be able to have his father killed. As Douglas later said, "I just didn't think it was possible to kill him."

Probably no one would ever have found out about the botched plots had Ashton not been arrested about a month later on a completely unrelated charge.

Following the last attempt on Brad's life, Steven had dropped out of sight for several weeks. During that time, as serendipity would have it, he was arrested for stealing a car. Not looking forward to an inevitable prison term, and being the resourceful fellow he was, Steven became a snitch. In return for immunity from prosecution, Ashton agreed to work with an undercover operative in setting up Douglas and Vincent.

The call to Douglas came six weeks after Brad was stabbed.

"I got another guy, and he's professional," Ashton said assuredly.

"Forget it, I'm not interested," Douglas said.

"No, come on, let's do it. This guy can do it," Ashton said, suddenly agitated.

"Forget it, I'm not interested," Douglas repeated.

After several minutes of cajoling, Douglas reluctantly agreed to meet Ashton and the new hit man. A meeting was set for later the next day.

Immediately prior to Steven's arrival, Douglas took ten dollars out of the cash register and gave it to Vincent.

"Go around the corner to a movie," he said. Vincent could tell that his brother was nervous.

"Anything wrong?" Vincent said.

"I'm okay. Just go, you need a break," Douglas said.

Douglas was worried about the meeting because Ashton

seemed so insistent. If something went wrong, he didn't want his brother to get in trouble.

Unlike the previous down-and-out pair, the undercover cop looked as if he'd been sent by central casting. He had dark, beady, furtive eyes and wore a small gold earring in his left ear. Under his sleek black leather jacket and tight-fitting black T-shirt, he also wore a wire to record everything. He walked into the back of the family's convenience store with an air of purpose. Before Douglas even had a chance to ask any questions, Ashton's hit man said, "Well, who is it that you want killed?"

Douglas felt something was wrong. He pulled Ashton aside and said, "Who is this guy? Is he a cop or something? He's acting strange."

"Are you crazy," Ashton nervously retorted. "He's a professional!"

Later, during Douglas's trial, the undercover agent explained to the jury what happened next:

> Douglas told me that he had a job for me to do for which he would pay me five thousand dollars if I went and took care of somebody for him. . . . We discussed the killing, and I told him it would be no problem, that was my job. He felt pretty comfortable with my answers. Then he gave me a picture of the person to be killed and showed me the weapon to use to kill the person. . . . Another person came in who I later found out to be Douglas's brother. . . . He just came in and asked Douglas what was going on, and Douglas told him he was conducting business with me. His brother then left us alone. . . . I then became curious and asked him who this person was that he wanted killed. He kept referring to this person as a friend that had done him wrong. . . . I kept asking him what kind of friend was this or what wrongdoing did he do. He finally told me it was a member of his family. That it was his dad.

Several minutes after the undercover officer walked out Detective Glaser and three other officers ran into the store

"I have some bad news for you, Doug. I'm placing you under arrest for the attempted murder of your father," Glase said. When Vincent returned from the movie, he, too, was arrested.

Both brothers were indicted on charges of attempted murder and soliciting murder. Dennis and Melissa were indicted for attempted murder, and Jack was indicted for being an accessory to murder. Steven, the mastermind of the murder plots, was not charged with anything; he walked away scot-free.

In exchange for her cooperation, Melissa pled guilty to attempted murder in juvenile court and was given five years in an institution for youthful offenders. No such deal was offered to her boyfriend. Because he was not directly involved in the various murder schemes, the district attorney allowed Vincent to plead guilty to attempted murder, with a recommendation of probation.

Though the district attorney, Robert Vasquez, was well aware of the allegations of abuse, he refused to discuss any plea for Douglas. He believed he had already shown leniency by allowing Vincent to plead guilty, but he wanted Douglas to serve the maximum prison term of thirteen years. Vasquez took the traditional prosecutorial position that there was absolutely nothing that justified a son's taking his father's life. The district attorney believed that if Douglas could ask a hit man for help, he should certainly have been able to seek assistance from the police or other social agency. And even if the system failed to assist them, the boys should have left home. There was, however, another element of the case that particularly bothered Vasquez. It was not just that Douglas had hired Ashton to kill Brad, it was that Douglas had tried so many times.

Had there been only one attempt on Brad's life, I believe the district attorney might not have felt such obvious antipathy for Douglas. Though Douglas admitted that he knew of the four attempts on his father's life—giving the gun to Ashton, the stabbing, the syringe of battery acid, and hiring the undercover cop—Detective Glaser believed that there were *at least* two other attempts. Douglas categorically denied all these allegations.

The police alleged that even before the stabbing, Douglas or Ashton tried to poison Brad by spiking his coffee with methamphetamine (speed). The only effect was that Brad became disoriented and nauseated for about a day.

The next attempt supposedly occurred the day before Melissa failed to kill Brad. After the knife attempt, Dennis Grady went to the hospital with a handgun, intent on shooting Brad. As soon as Grady appeared at the door of the hospital room, Brad screamed and Grady raced away.

While District Attorney Vasquez acknowledged that Brad was perhaps a strict father, he completely discounted the allegations of abuse. Rather, he insisted Douglas was primarily motivated by financial gain. And in this regard, Vasquez perceived Douglas Carter and Dennis Grady as merely two sides of the same coin. Both were avaricious teenagers who had no qualms about killing. Consequently, Vasquez (like the prosecutor in the Pierson case) steadfastly opposed separate trials for Douglas and Dennis. This decision was ultimately upheld by trial judge Anthony Hutton.

The first witness for the state was Detective Glaser. Typically, the lead investigator is used to establish the elements of the crime and to introduce the adolescent's confession into evidence. Though Vasquez had Glaser lay out in painstaking detail the various attempts on Brad's life, he was circumspect in his questions concerning Douglas's confession. Vasquez only asked Glaser about those parts of the confession where Douglas admitted to his involvement in the scheme to hire people to kill his father. Moreover, he purposely failed to move into evidence the tape recording of the confession. The logic of Vasquez's tactic became obvious when the entire tape was played during Glaser's cross-examination.

After Douglas waived his Miranda rights and agreed to speak without a lawyer present, Glaser confronted Douglas with all the police knew about Dennis, Melissa, and Steve and the various attempts and the fact that Douglas himself had a major role in the whole thing. After pausing a moment to let the enormity of the crimes sink in, Glaser said:

"I've already talked to your brother, and I understand that your dad used to beat you guys and beat your mother. And I understand that you were probably driven to do something, that you would normally not have done. After listening to what Vincent said about your childhood and how you were treated, personally, I couldn't have taken it so long."

". . . Nobody helped me out," Douglas responded. "I went to the child abuse authorities, and nobody helped me out. So we decided if nobody would help us out, we'd do it ourselves."

After the court ordered the entire tape played for the jury, Glaser explained that his expression of sympathy had been but an interrogation ploy. He was only trying to elicit a confession from Douglas, and he never for a minute believed Douglas's actions were justified.

Following Glaser and several other police officers, the state called Steve Ashton, then Melissa. A doctor also testified as to the gravity of the stab wound and to the fact that Brad would have died instantaneously if Melissa had stuck the needle in his vein. The final state witness was Brad himself. When he took the stand, it was the first time that Douglas and Vincent had seen their father since the night of their arrest. Brad stared at his son intently as Vasquez questioned him; Douglas, however, kept his eyes fixed on a yellow legal pad before him.

Through three days of direct and cross examination, Brad categorically denied he had ever abused his sons or even struck his wife. He portrayed himself as a kind, loving father. With tears in his eyes, he vehemently asserted that problems in his home were solved by discussion, not whips or handcuffs. Brad admitted hitting Douglas one time, because his then twelve-year-old son lied. He also stated he hit Vincent only *twice* in his life.

Brad testified he was at a loss as to why his sons would want to kill him. He told the court that he devoted his life to his sons and believed that it was their mother who pushed them to commit such a heinous act. His constant refrain throughout his testimony was, "I never tried to do any harm, my only purpose was to make them happy."

The primary defense witnesses were Milos Ervin and Barney Ellison. Ellison was another former employee at the grocery store. He now lived in another city and had only agreed to be a witness because he felt guilty that he hadn't helped the family earlier. The meek, balding thirty-year-old nervously told the court that he had once witnessed Brad mercilessly beat Douglas across the back with a stick.

"[After the beating] his whole body was black-and-blue. I told Douglas, 'I'm going to help you.'

" 'No. No, don't! If my father [finds out], he will kill me,' Douglas told me." Ellison testified that he persisted in trying to persuade Douglas to allow him to call the police, but the battered boy pleaded with Ellison to forget about the incident. Ellison complied. Several weeks later, Ellison told the court, he saw Vincent's head bleeding.

" 'What happened to your head?' I said.

" 'Don't ask me,' Vincent replied.

" 'Come on! Tell me!' I told him.

" 'My father did this, but please don't say anything.' "

Ellison told the court he gave up trying to help the boys and even lost interest in their plight because they refused help.

It was Ervin's testimony, however, that was by far the most compelling. In addition to witnessing the doghouse and outdoor-punishment incidents described earlier, Ervin gave the following account of the boys' lives:

"They weren't allowed to see anybody. They weren't allowed out of the house. . . . He liked hitting his boys. He would scream and yell a lot. . . . He threw things at them and hit them with whatever was convenient at the time. He used mostly a clenched fist. . . . They always had bruises and red marks around their necks. . . . I would talk to them, right and they said don't go to the police or anything because their father might kill them. Those are the words they always said."

Douglas was evaluated by a psychiatrist and a psychologist who both found that he suffered from chronic posttraumatic stress syndrome, the disorder suffered by most children who are successful in killing their parents. The psychiatrist explained his clinical diagnosis in simple, understandable language:

"The alleged offenses were the direct product of long-standing abuse suffered by the defendant and his brother at the hands of their father. . . . They have been threatened with death on numerous occasions. At least in part they seemed to have acted out of a fear that they would one day be killed by their father. They had been under severe, unrelenting stress for many years and finally reached the breaking point.

Douglas was the last witness to take the stand for the defense. In painstaking detail, he related incident after incident of abuse. No effort was made to deny the prosecutor's allegations that he plotted on at least four occasions to kill his father. Douglas testified that he was so desperate to get free from his father, he would have (and had) hired anyone who approached him. His fear was so great, he told the rapt jury, that even as he sat in the witness box, he was still afraid of his father.

Dennis Grady could not, of course, use the defense that he was abused. But he came remarkably close. Grady's attorney, Lois Kinston, did not contest the fact that her client was involved in a scheme to kill Brad. Instead she argued that Grady went to the store with the sole purpose of surveying the scene. After familiarizing himself with the grocery store, he was going to come back later that day to stab Brad. Grady was not told anything about Brad's personality. Upon entering the store he thought he'd find a harmless grocer. Instead he found a pugnacious brute.

Grady, his attorney argued, did not intend to speak to Brad, let alone confront him that morning. In fact, after Brad started screaming, Grady had tried to flee the store, but Brad blocked him, grabbing him around the neck and punching him in the face. Grady maintained that he pulled out his knife in self-defense only after it became clear Brad would not stop choking him.

The resolution of the trial proved to be as amazing as the descriptions of abuse and the murder plots. The jury found Douglas, the person who hired the assassins, not guilty, and found Dennis Grady, the hired assassin, guilty of attempted involuntary manslaughter. Douglas's verdict meant that the jury wholly accepted that he had acted in self-defense; and the verdict of involuntary manslaughter meant the jury believed Grady acted *almost* in self-defense. Grady's verdict, I later learned, actually reflected a compromise between those who believed he acted in self-defense and those who believed he intended to kill Brad. The verdicts moreover produced the anomalous circumstance of leaving Douglas free on the streets and putting all the people he hired behind bars. Even his own brother, who was at most a passive participant, was put on probation for several years.

As hideous as were the descriptions of torture, had Douglas's hirelings been successful, Douglas might not have been found innocent. In other words, the single most important witness for the defense had been Brad himself. One of the predominant defense problems in successful parricides is contending with the unspoken, but very real, feeling on the part of most jurors that the dead parent is not there to defend him or herself. Regardless of the unanimity of opinion among defense witnesses, not only are they like everyone else in that they don't like to hear bad things said about the dead, jurors also want to believe that no one could treat their child so heinously.

In this case, however, the parent had defended himself, but his outright denials were simply not believable. It was blindingly obvious to all twelve jurors that the other witnesses were telling the literal truth.

Following the verdicts, Douglas and his brother left the state to go live with their mother at an undisclosed location. Neither brother has heard from their father since the day Douglas was released from jail, and they don't want to.

Though on the surface, the cases of Cheryl Pierson and the Carter brothers appear to be fundamentally different from the other cases in this book, a close inspection of both reveals that they are quite similar. In virtually every one of my cases, the parent is killed when in his or her most defenseless position: sleeping, working over a desk, cooking dinner, or coming in the front door. I can only think of five cases over a five-year period in which the child killed his or her parent during an abusive episode.

My explanation of this behavior is that, as traumatized as these children are, their survival compasses are still functioning. They viscerally understand that they should strike only when they have the opportunity for maximum success. Under most circumstances and certainly in every case in this book, if the child attempted to kill the parent while the parent was being abusive or at the very least was aware that the child was about to harm him or her, the odds are good that the parent would have killed or gravely injured the child.

The other underlying explanation of the common modus operandi is that the children are incapable of directly challenging their parents about anything, even the fact that they are about to kill them. At least half of the children I have represented have told me that they could never have pulled the trigger if their parents were looking them in the eye.

One need only remember that when George (in Part I) was confronted by his stepmother after he shot his sleeping father, his finger actually froze on the trigger. He could not kill her, simply because she was looking at him.

Cheryl and Douglas were on the extreme end of the intimidation scale, so terrified by their parents that they were incapable of confronting them *at any time*. Technically, neither even came up with the original idea for the murder plots themselves. The idea of assassinating Jim Pierson arose as a result of a chance homeroom discussion about a newspaper story; the plot to kill Brad Carter was instigated by one of the family's employees. In the final analysis, Cheryl and Douglas employed only a slightly different tactic to insure the success of their attacks—they used another person's finger on the trigger.

Though I understand why Cheryl and Douglas went to the extremes they did in striking out, the motivations of those they hired remain unclear. I have been particularly interested in the question of what, if anything, was in the family histories and personalities of the "hitters" that made them so willing to become part of a plan to kill someone else's parent. For ethical reasons, I was never able to interview any of them, and therefore my conclusions are drawn merely from court records and newspaper accounts.

Many would argue that greed is one simple motivation for these hired killers. But looking at how the plans were executed and their outcomes, it is obvious that these young people were anything but shrewd entrepreneurs.

It appears that Sean got involved with Cheryl partly because he perceived himself as a latter-day knight in shining armor who was going to save a damsel in distress. Cheryl had never even spoken to Sean before soliciting his aid. She could have asked her older boyfriend, Rob, or any of her other high school friends to help, but instead she chose *him* to rescue her. Some boys try to impress potential girlfriends by doing charming things such as offering to carry the girl's books. Sean went a lot further to impress Cheryl: he killed her dad.

It is, however, equally plausible that Sean was an emotionally distraught boy who unconsciously confused his own dilemma with Cheryl's. Perhaps he perceived striking out at Mr. Pierson as an indirect way to get back at those who had abused him.

Cheryl promised Sean one thousand dollars, plus her dad's motorcycle and the right to live free in one of the family's rental homes. But for all his effort, Sean received just four hundred dollars and a long prison sentence.

And what about the conspirators in the Carter case? I know nothing about Steve Ashton's family, but I can only assume that Brad's treatment of his boys must have sparked some nightmares.

"If my dad did that to me, I'd kill him," Steven bitterly told Douglas. Perhaps Steven's dad had beaten him, and he had never been able to defend himself. Could the plans he hatched have been an indirect way to purge himself of his own ghosts?

All I know of the family histories of Melissa and Dennis Grady is that both were runaway teenagers. They had been in town no more than two weeks before they willingly agreed to kill another teenager's father. And what did they get for their efforts? Steven, Dennis, and Melissa were going to get paid three thousand dollars. None of them got a penny. All Steven received was a grant of immunity from prosecution; Dennis, Melissa, and Jack the lookout man were sent to prison for varying terms of two to six years.

The same question of hidden motivation must be asked of Melissa and Grady. Was their participation in such a ghoulish, harebrained scheme motivated by some unconscious desire to strike back against their parents? Or, asked the other way, if both came from loving, supportive environments, would they have become such eager participants?

Conclusion

Despite our increased awareness of and sensitivity to the problems of child abuse and family violence, the Tims and Cindys, the Stevens and Pattys, of this world remain pariahs, provoking intense anger and striking fear in most adults. What disturbs us is that parricide represents the ultimate defilement and repudiation of the most sacrosanct human relationship. It is the wisdom of centuries that, because they were given the gift of life, children should respect their parents, living life eternally grateful to them. There is, moreover, an unspoken expectation that, regardless of the depravity and violence visited upon a child, the child should still treat his or her parents with tolerance and understanding, compassion and love. The vast majority of abused children fulfill these expectations, going silently and "gently into that good night," treating their parents much better than their parents have ever treated them. This is obvious just from a comparison of national statistics on child abuse with those on parricide; parricide cases run in the low hundreds every year while approximately 2.5 *million* children are victims of serious abuse.

The normal response of a child to parental abuse is identical to that of an adult forced to endure oppressive and horrific treatment at the hands of another. Psychologists and psychiatrists have found, in fact, that individuals react in remarkably similar ways whether they are kidnapped, held hostage, or raped. Survival is the paramount concern; despair becomes the order of the day, and *they do not fight back.*

There is universal understanding and compassion for the rape victim who doesn't scream and the airplane passenger who doesn't attack his hijacker. And in those rare circumstances where the victim kills her persecutor, *no one* expects the victim to feel remorse; in fact, even to suggest such a thing would be regarded as utterly irrational.

In the aftermath of a parricide, the child experiences a range of intense emotions more perplexing and overwhelming than he has ever felt before or will probably experience again. As seen in most of the stories in this book, the youth initially becomes very depressed. And as the accounts of Tim, George, Cindy, and Steven reveal, oftentimes their despair leads them to thoughts of suicide. This emotional reaction we can at least rationally understand; their lack of remorse and guilt is much more disturbing to us.

These adolescents are simply unable to conceal their true feelings, or lack of them, for their parents. Because they were forced to numb their real emotions for so long, by the time of the parricide they have no tears. Some, such as George, are more honest (and uncomfortably so) than others. With a large part of his mind, George still loves his dad and is terribly sorry he killed him. But as he explained to me during our interview after his sentencing, "the moral of the story [is that] he should have left me *alone.*"

In discussing Cheryl Pierson's lack of remorse, Paul Gianelli expressed the sentiments of most children who kill their parents: "She felt she was right. And [i]t was very hard to show fake remorse for something that she felt was right to end the abuse."

That Gianelli understood is fairly unique, for defense attorneys are often disturbed by their clients' seemingly incomprehensible lack of contrition. In the privacy of their law offices, they comment to me, "No question the father tortured this kid. The son of a bitch deserved everything he got and more. But the kid doesn't seem to feel bad that he blew his old man away. He's totally without emotion, and I can't understand it for the life of me."

When children commit such grievous acts, adults expect them to fall apart, flagellating themselves and begging for forgiveness; to the outrage of many, however, this is a rare response. In fact, as Mike's case illustrated, the lack of repentance is one of the single biggest stumbling blocks to obtaining leniency from juries, prosecutors, and especially judges.

The plain fact is that the children I represent are not accorded the compassion of adult victims of violence. When a child kills his parents, understanding goes out the window, and the system comes back at the child with a vengeance. And as angered as I am by the child abuse, one of the most outlandish and insidious aspects of these cases is the mindless, insensitive, and morally bankrupt reaction of the legal system to the children's plight. The factors that were responsible for the homicide play themselves out with the same cruelty in the trial. With the help of the state, the parent reaches out from the grave to inflict one last act of abuse—the child's prosecution and imprisonment.

In protecting the interests of his client, the people of the state, the district attorney has a higher duty than merely prosecuting those who have broken the law. She must also "do justice." "Doing justice" is such a thoroughly elusive and controversial concept that there are about as many definitions as there are DAs. Essentially, however, the term means that, in advocating for the interests of the state, the prosecutor must consider the individual needs of the victim *and* the defendant. In theory, the decision to prosecute any case must be preceded by a conscientious balancing of these competing interests.

Most district attorneys interpret their roles narrowly in parricides. Ignoring the family dynamics that influenced the child, their knee-jerk reaction is to try the child as an adult, charge her with first-degree murder, and demand the maximum allowable penalty.

These are neat cases for the state, and the kids make them that way. There is almost always a complete taped confession including a recording of the 911 phone call. Or often the child has produced such a poorly conceived and botched alibi that his participation is obvious. Often plentiful are witnesses to whom the child has expressed his parricidal intentions, usually family and friends, as well as those to whom he has confessed. And the DA typically has all the inculpatory physical evidence she could want—the weapon with the kid's fingerprints, even handwritten notes or tape recordings explaining the child's actions. From cop to coroner, there is, moreover, voluminous documentation of the homicide—gruesome victim and crime-scene photos and a host of convincing scientific tests. But the strongest part of a prosecutor's case is in her effortless and convincing portrayal of the parent as the tragic *victim* of a senseless crime, as if the abuse had never happened. Taking advantage of our natural inclination never to speak ill of the dead, and even granting them absolution from their misdeeds, the DA starts the trial with a decided advantage.

The primary obstacle I face in defending these cases is that it is impossible to portray even a significant fraction of the sordid truth of the child's existence; for it is in the detail of these children's lives that the horror, and hence the defense, lies. Only in defending a parricide does one appreciate how perfect a crime child abuse really is.

Unlike the prosecution, the defense rarely has any hard corroborative evidence: there are no tape recordings of the screams and the daily denigration, no still photos of the bruises hidden beneath clothing, no videos of the beatings and rapes, and rarely any medical or other records documenting the abuse. Because most abuse occurs behind closed doors, and because both parents and children (for very different reasons) make conscious efforts to conceal it, jurors and judges typically have to rely only on a defense witness's unsupported statement.

What diminishes the impact and persuasiveness of even this meager body of evidence is that, for many reasons—the passage of time, embarrassment, anger, and fear—witnesses frequently leave out critical details and are not forthcoming with everything they know. More problematic is that the kids themselves are often unable or unwilling to talk about those specific events essential to their defense. Some of the abuse occurred too far in the past to be remembered, while other events are blocked out or repressed because they are so horrible. Repression and denial are the way these victims survived, numbing themselves to the pain, trying desperately to forget the present. Recapturing these memories with any clarity or specificity is, for many of them, an insurmountable and painful task.

The same deleterious factors that impair their memories

and hinder open discussion also alter their perceptions of reality, especially their judgment of subjective feelings of imminent, life-threatening danger, and their awareness of alternative strategies to escape that danger. Immobilized by fear and hopelessness, they believe neither they nor anyone else capable of securing their safety, let alone freedom. What they do have, however, is an acutely fine-tuned sense of their mortality.

Trial court judges, like prosecutors, have not been particularly sensitive to the unique problem of severely abused kids. Such judges peg the self-defense standard of reasonableness to that of a strong, healthy male, treating the child as if he killed a grocery clerk during an armed robbery. And the lower courts have for the most part been roundly supported by state appellate judges, whose rulings are cemented in fifteenth-century man-with-an-oaken-staff interpretations of self-defense. Expert witnesses, moreover, play no small role in perpetuating this revictimization of children in the courtroom. Because the short- and long-term effects of abuse and adolescent violence are still so poorly understood by the majority of psychiatrists and psychologists, even sympathetic juries and judges are deprived of a coherent explanation of parricide.

The most common outcome for the child after being caught in this legal quagmire shot through with ignorance, confusion, and intolerance is, in prison parlance, "long time." Verdicts of not guilty by reason of self-defense, like that received by Douglas Carter, are very rare. Manslaughter is a more frequent verdict, but by no means as common as a first- or second-degree murder conviction.

The sentences, moreover, are fairly arbitrary and capricious in that they vary widely depending on whether the child was transferred to adult court and the configuration of the state homicide statute. A child who is not transferred usually remains incarcerated until she reaches the age at which the juvenile court's jurisdiction ceases, usually eighteen or twenty-one. Allegedly, the opportunities for treatment are better in juvenile than adult court, but from what I know about reform schools, this notion is more theory than reality. If a child *is* tried as an adult, it is a foregone conclusion that he will receive no therapy, even in those states that find him guilty but mentally ill, a verdict that implies, falsely, the possibility of treatment. Though the actual number of years a child receives varies widely from state to state, in my experience the average sentence is between fifteen and twenty years.

One would think that children who have been ravaged by abuse and neglect would be accorded *more* understanding treatment by an enlightened society. Our myopic, mean-spirited treatment of these children, however, is not surprising, for it is inextricably tied to our dismal treatment of youth in general. Though they are our future, the reality is that we treat young people like some expendable commodity.

Kids are the poor stepchildren of the twentieth-century civil liberties and rights revolution, which humanized the nation's treatment of all its people, especially the disenfranchised. While things have improved since child labor laws were enacted in the early 1900s, people under eighteen have been playing catch-up ever since the days of the Massachusetts Stubborn Child laws of 1647, having the door of justice repeatedly slammed in their face. It was only in 1967, for example, that the U.S. Supreme Court ruled that an accused juvenile had the constitutional right to an attorney. Yet, soon after that, the same Court ruled that those juveniles do not have the right to trial by jury.

Both as a children's rights advocate and more recently as a father, I have observed that our nation does a great job of promoting its image as a youth culture and selling products to its young people, but an absolutely terrible job of protecting their lives, enriching their minds, and nurturing their souls. Huge sums are allocated to entice young minds to purchase everything from toys to video games to movie tickets; yet at the same time a disturbingly high number of these young consumers are illiterate, poorly nourished, and abused and neglected. Marketers are especially excited by the fact that by year 2000, half the world will be under twenty-five. Yet I, and many others, familiar with the desperate state of our children today, find this is a disquieting thought indeed.

When we do attempt to confront what we think are negative influences on our children, the last place we turn our attention is to what may be happening in our own homes. One glaring example of this is the recent press furor over the supposed connection between kids listening to heavy-metal rock music and then, inspired by the "satanic" lyrics, going out to do violence. In 1990, for example, fourteen-year-old Abigail Dartana, my youngest client, killed her savagely abusive father. While there was more than ample evidence of Mr. Dartana's physical and sexual abuse of Abigail, the prosecutor chose to focus his case on the supposition that her fascination with the heavy-metal group Motley Crue had inspired her to kill her father. Thankfully, the judge was not swayed by this specious argument and found her not guilty by reason of self-defense.

There was no legitimate research to support the prosecutor's position, just hysteria and ignorance. Americans have listened to songs containing disturbing, violent lyrics for generations, and it has never been proven that there is even a measurable relationship between hearing the lyrics and committing an act of violence. No one in the 1920s killed their lover just because he or she listened to the hit song "Frankie and Johnnie," nor forty years later when Jimi Hendrix sang "I Shot My Lady Down," did anyone go out and shoot their lover.

It's much easier for us to hear that our children's problems stem from the music they listen to than how we treat them. Though it is politically expedient to attribute the problems of kids to institutions outside the family, the reality is that the majority of a child's problems are caused by his own psychological makeup and his relationship with his parents. This obsessive fear of influences outside the family is not unlike our misconceptions about violence; any child is more likely to be harmed by someone in her family than by a stranger.

When Judge Harvey Sherman sentenced Cheryl Pierson, he newspaper *Newsday* reported that "though he received many letters, the case did not incite the outpouring of correspondence of another case five years ago," a case in which a man had been charged with cruelty to animals. " 'Would you believe there are more people concerned about dogs than there are about people?' he asked. Then he shook his head and concluded the interview."

It appears that, as we get older, our tolerance and understanding for youth diminishes. We tend to forget that, though many adolescents might look like us and can perform certain physical tasks as well or better than we can, *they are not adults*. They are constantly struggling with their identity, because for the first time they are experiencing themselves as individuals apart from the family unit. They fervently desire approval from their peers, yet they still need immense support from their parents. Child-development experts have found that adolescents are inherently more impulsive and moody than adults, yet it is these characteristics over which children have the least control that seem to irritate adults most.

I have been particularly amazed during jury selection at how much adults have forgotten about being a teenager. Frequently, jurors seem astonished that the defendant didn't report his parents or run away. They (along with many people I meet socially) appear to believe that the survival instinct supersedes the parental bond.

The reality is that even the average, well-adjusted child does not have the ability to turn in his parent or run away from home. For a severely abused child, these things are so immeasurably hard to do as to be inconceivable. When an indignant adult confronts me, asking why a child didn't report his parents, I often answer with the news story about the furor caused during the summer of 1987 by a child who turned in her drug-user parents to the police. While many applauded her initiative, a diverse chorus of adults decried the action comparing the child to the Hitler Youth who turned their "traitorous" parents in to the Third Reich.

"It would be easy for any one of us to state how we would have reacted and would have extricated ourselves," Tom Alan, Byron's attorney, wrote in his appeal brief, "but let us look at the facts. We are not Byron and thankfully never will be Byron. Those of us who were raised in even marginally normal homes will never know what it is like to be afraid every moment of one's life. We will not know what it is like to be threatened with specific descriptions of how we will be murdered. . . . We will not know what it is like to live in an insane environment where we are not only exposed to persons making such threats, but are also captives to the very person capable of making good on those threats. When one of us has the arrogance and audacity to say that we would have done such and such if we were Byron, we just plain have no damn bloody idea what we are talking about."

Fortunately for children and the rest of society, some of us are more honest than others about the past. After reading an article about one of my cases, the Reverend Jim Conn of the Ocean Park Community Church of Santa Monica, California, was moved to write an open letter to his parishioners. "I didn't kill my parents. But I wanted to. . . . I didn't strike back. I didn't kill them. I killed my feelings for them. I remember sitting on the cold porcelain of the bathroom of whatever house I lived in as a child fuming, helpless, unable to do a thing or say a word about it, forced finally to hug the very people who tormented me, convinced I deserved what I received, yet wanting to die, wanting to kill them, until deep inside I slipped my fingers around the neck of my feelings for them and squeezed until they were gone. Oedipus without blood."

Our pervasive and deeply ingrained prejudices about children are integral to shaping our judgments about the guilt and innocence of those who kill their parents. For, in apportioning guilt, we, along with our representatives in the courtroom, weigh not only the specific facts of the parricide, but also the broad questions of the moral rightness or wrongness of the homicide. Consciously or unconsciously each of us grapples with the dilemma of whether these kids are vigilantes taking the law into their own hands or victims escaping the only way they know. Or are they a little of both, living in that twilight world halfway between victim and perpetrator?

Your moral evaluation of parricide, I believe, is inextricably tied to the extent to which you understand abuse and appreciate its effects on a child. If you believe that abuse is no excuse, and that children who kill their parents consciously ignore alternative courses of action such as running away or reporting, then most likely you see them as lawless vigilantes. But if you believe as I do that they cannot fully appreciate or take advantage of the alternatives because they were abused, then they are victims acting to protect themselves.

There are, of course, other ways to apportion guilt or innocence, taking into account, for instance, the moral culpability of those, in and outside the family, who knew about the child's ordeal but fell silent; those who intervened inappropriately; those who didn't know but should have known, including those making the political decisions affecting programs that could help these kids. Obviously, the legal system is very imperfect in this sense, for it addresses only the person who pulled the trigger.

By holding these kids solely responsible, treating them like the bank robber who kills a teller, we clearly imply that all these other hidden actors in the wings are innocent, and that is morally reprehensible. Though they escape the arm of the law, there *are* others who have varying degrees of responsibility for the parricide.

The most culpable are those adult family members and close friends who knew about the torture, had the capacity to act, weren't intimidated by the parent, and yet consciously decided not to help. Equally culpable are the social workers, teachers, and law enforcement officers who acted negligently once they were apprised of the family situation.

The next level of blame belongs to those family and friends who heard the cries and saw the bruises but didn't act out of their own fear of, or intimidation by, the parent. It is understandable that someone would not want to confront a violent, aggressive individual, but such fear should not prevent an anonymous call to the school or department of social services.

It is the action and inaction of all these adults, I believe, that to one degree or another pressures the child to solve the "problem" herself. Mike, Byron, and Patty felt the passivity of others as a tightening of the noose that their parents had placed around their necks.

This discussion is not merely a philosophical musing; most or at least some of these homicides could have been prevented with appropriate intervention, and I do not mean just calling the police or department of social services. In George's case, if a single person who saw the tension building in him had then offered another place to stay or just had a heart-to-heart talk with him or Ken, things might have turned out differently. And had there been a conscientious monitoring of Patty's situation by the social services department, Deborah would probably be alive today.

While I believe family members, friends, and others share

some blame, the deceased parent also bears responsibility for the calamity. In court I invariably make the strategic decision to portray these parents as malevolent, showing little compassion for them. Regardless of the verdict, however, I leave the courtroom with a profound sense of sorrow for them because the hidden tragedy is that many of the parents were themselves victims of abuse. Most grappled throughout their adult lives with the effects of the gross mistreatment visited on them as children, never receiving the help they needed to ride out the storms that swept their lives. They traveled in life full circle, first a victim then a perpetrator, and ironically, finally a victim once more.

Some of these parents are so tortured by the ghosts of their past that I believe they unconsciously (and in some cases consciously) make their children the instruments of their own deaths. After being involved in so many of these cases, I have become convinced that many victims of parricide, especially the physically assaultive ones, carry with them the knowledge that every attack on their children is one more spin of the barrel in a lifelong game of Russian roulette.

Regardless of how you or a jury apportion guilt in these cases, all of these children have already been sentenced twice before they were even arrested: first when they were born into a pathologically abusive house and second when they killed. For all the anger these kids may engender in society and in the relatives and friends of the deceased parent, all can rest assured they suffer punishment the state could never impose.

The child enters the courtroom as a soul condemned to living the rest of her life with the terrible knowledge that she has killed the person who gave her life. Even the precious few who are found not guilty, or are mercifully sentenced, live their lives in a prison without bars. And the overwhelming majority who do go to prison spend their days in a cell within a cell.

Despite the apparently heinous nature of their crime, the majority of these kids pose no threat to society. If there is a risk, it is in incarcerating them in a prison where they will be re-abused by other inmates and deprived of therapy. Without counseling, many of these kids over time become confused about the circumstances that motivated them to kill. Principally, they have a tendency to rewrite history, downplaying the severity of the abuse, berating themselves for not trying other alternatives, and venting their anger and aggression on innocent people.

Depriving these adolescents of counseling is a further tragedy in that the problems they suffer are particularly amenable to treatment. One of the primary goals of therapy is to encourage the child to accept the reality of his family history and learn that the abuse was not his fault. This process involves reversing years of helplessness so that he regains control over his life. It is critical that he also realize his share of responsibility for the killing, but be made to understand that it resulted from events beyond his control.

Some of these children do mend, however, without therapy. As confused, angry, and distraught as they are after the homicide, many experience unprecedented feelings of exhilaration. In case after case, these kids say they feel freer after being arrested and incarcerated than at any previous time in their lives.

One paradoxical consequence of a parricide is that it often has a strangely positive and therapeutic effect on the relationship between the child and the surviving family members. It seems as if the patricide or matricide acts as a catalyst to restore safety, balance, and rationality to the family process.

Steven's case poignantly illustrates this positive but unexpected resolution. I asked him, in prison, how he now feels about his father.

"Now I call him Dad," he said matter-of-factly.

"But didn't you call him that before?" I asked incredulously.

"I mean, I called him Dad, but it didn't have any meaning. Now it has meaning," he said. Roger and his second wife echoed these sentiments, saying that they felt closer to Steven after the homicide than before.

Though his story was not included in this book, Seth, a fifteen-year-old boy who killed his father, has a better relationship with his mother than he did prior to the homicide, even though he is now in prison.

"We are seeing a lot more of each other now," he said with

a smile. "I can talk to her freely on the phone and stuff. . . In a sense it brought us back together."

"That's weird, isn't it?" I said.

"Yeah, before we were way far apart, and now we are real close; we're like a real family now."

Regardless of the sentence and the child's outward adjustment, however, the judge, defense lawyer, even prosecutor, should do everything possible to insure that the child gets therapy. Outside help is the best chance to insure that the cycle of violence is permanently broken.

Does a greater understanding of the legacy of violence inherited by these children—and a greater compassion for their plight—mean the onset of an open season on parents? Do not-guilty verdicts and lenient sentences amount to granting these kids a license to kill? Of course not. First, regardless of the depravity and violence you have just read about, the majority of children are raised by reasonable, caring parents. Most disputes between parents and their children do not represent abusive encounters, but are outgrowths of normal, healthy conflict.

It is, moreover, safe to say that as disturbing as these stories are, they are not part of any growing trend. Not only has the number of parricides remained fairly constant for the last ten years, but the motivations for these homicides have little to do with how a court later treats these children. If anything, children today have more reason to fear their parents than vice versa. "One of the most serious problems facing children and families and the nation," said U.S. Senator Christopher Dodd in 1987, "is the crisis presented by the growing number of child and youth deaths. . . . By conservative estimates, reports of child deaths from abuse or neglect jumped twenty-three percent nationwide between 1985 and 1986."

The first lesson a child should learn is that human life is sacred. Homicide, for any reason, is a blasphemy on the human soul. Yet I fervently believe that victims of child abuse are entitled to do anything necessary to free themselves from their tyranny. Murdering a parent is not an acceptable solution to child abuse; rather, it is one forced upon the child. For when a parent is killed, we must remember that beneath the surface there is, tragically, more than one finger on the trigger.

Children who have killed their abusive parents understand better than anybody else the critical necessity for developing effective programs to combat child abuse. Preparing for this book, I asked each of them, as well as their families and friends, if they had any advice to offer individuals or society. Sadly, the majority I interviewed, such as Patty, were not hopeful about the system's ability to help abused children. All Patty could say was, "If you're old enough, just leave. But if they're not old enough and not able to leave, just pray to the Good Lord that He will help you work your way out."

"Listen to your kids," George said. "Sit them down and talk to them, even if they don't want to talk. Try to get out what's bothering them . . . and [if he] asks for a gun, don't give it to him."

Barbara, George's mother, commented, "I'd like to have people stop and realize that kids are fragile, and they absorb feelings from the time that they are conceived. You have to be there to support them whether they're right or wrong, and you have to have open communication with them. Both parents need to be involved, 'cause a kid needs a balance of love from a man and a woman in order to be able to grow up to be healthy and have a strong life."

Tim had advice for both children and their parents. "If you

353

don't tell, it's going to hurt you more than it will help you. If you tell, it will help you because you can get therapy.

"For people that are doing this to their kids, seek help. I mean therapeutic help, you've got to talk to somebody, see a psychiatrist, a priest, or a doctor. It can be stopped," Tim said. "I think to a degree parents who sexually abuse their kids should be punished, but, you know, sex offenders are people, too. I think they should be helped. I mean with the proper care they could be normal again."

"What happens if they don't get help?" I asked.

"They're just going to keep on abusing and abusing and abusing. They're going to screw up a lot of people. . . . And then somebody like me is going to come along."

WHAT YOU CAN DO

A prevalent misconception that helps perpetuate abuse is that it is a problem that can only be solved by the government and social service organizations. This is wrong thinking, for every American can make a difference. Child abuse, in fact, is one area where the individual can actually accomplish much more than any federal, state, or local agency. And this involvement does not just apply to the obvious issue of not abusing your children. Where individuals can make a difference is in their relationships with extended-family members, friends, and neighbors.

While we all cherish our right to privacy, we should at the same time realize that our devotion to this cornerstone of democracy is strangling the lives of hundreds of thousands of children and youths every year. Abusive parents thrive on isolation and a perverted sense of privacy. Contrary to popular belief, by not intervening, relatives, friends, and neighbors are not "doing nothing"; to the contrary, they actively reinforce the offending parent's omnipotence as well as the abused child's helplessness.

Because children and most adolescents are unable to help themselves, it is incumbent upon adults who have even an inkling that abuse is occurring to be the child's voice. If calling the police or social services seems out of the question, an informal chat with the parent is better than nothing.

"You know, Jane, I think there's another way to discipline Billy other than by screaming at him or smacking him with a paddle. I know you're probably upset with him, but I just don't see the vile names and paddle doing too much good."

"This is difficult for me to say, Bill, but I think you've been acting kind of strange around your Jeanie. Jeanie told my boy that she plays pee pee games with you. I was wondering if there was anything going on between you two that shouldn't be. Because if there is, you really should get some help."

Some may cringe at imagining themselves speaking these words to a friend or relative. But as uncomfortable as it might be, think for a moment how difficult it is for a child to broach the subject with his or her parents.

If you are afraid to confront the parent directly or even to report them anonymously, another avenue is to approach other community members who have some relationship with the family: clergymen, teachers and principals, and pediatricians.

While an individual has a vital role to play in bettering the life of an abused child, preventing an abused child from killing a parent is a far more complex task. This is because parricide is such an infrequent occurrence that it is difficult to predict. There are, however, some warning signs that alone do not appear significant, but that together indicate a potentially lethal domestic situation.

Naturally, the first indication is the type of severe, long-term abuse in its various ugly forms seen throughout this book. Though some parents are skilled at concealing the abuse, especially those who sexually abuse their children, others are careless. It is especially important to be aware of those men and women who pride themselves on being stern disciplinarians—parents who boast they will go to any length to instill moral, religious, or other values in their children.

In the most common case, patricide by sons, the father will also abuse the other members of the family, but it will be the son who takes the brunt of the punishment. If the mother is present, she will undoubtedly play a subservient, nonsupportive role. Do not be misled by the apparent closeness between the parent and child or for that matter, by the child's courteous, deferential behavior. These are simply the insidious effects of abuse.

Adolescents are often pushed beyond the breaking poin by the failed attempts of private individuals or public agencie to intercede effectively on their behalf. The situation become particularly acute if the child herself instigated the interven tion; the effect of such a failure is a dramatic increase in he sense of hopelessness and despair.

With regard to a child's depression, it is important to tak suicide attempts, gestures, or even musings carefully. Suicid behavior should not be dismissed as being the mere result a generalized adolescent melancholy. In approximately ha of my cases, the teenager had attempted or spoken of suici within six months of killing a parent. Finally, though also obvious point, threats to kill parents should be taken ser ously. As George told me, "People thought it was a jok . . . My mom didn't believe me; neither did my aunt. Nobo thought I was serious."

Since the majority of parents are killed by their own wea ons or weapons they bought for their children, the presen of guns in any home should be cause for great alarm.

INFORMATION ON CHILD ABUSE

While your individual action can be crucial to helping pe petrators and victims of child abuse, its effectiveness depen on improving and in some instances totally revamping existi public- and private-sector efforts. The following suggestio are based upon my experience with parricide, but are app cable to the needs of all abused children and their famili I believe they represent a balance between the rights of p ents to raise their children according to their own perso beliefs and the rights of children to live as free individu and to grow into healthy adults.

Despite an immense increase in public awareness and infusion of tens of millions of dollars, a federally appoint child abuse commission noted as recently as 1990 that Americans should be outraged by child maltreatment. N only are child abuse and neglect wrong, but the nation's la of an effective response to them is also wrong. Neither be tolerated. Together, they constitute a moral disaster."

Because the majority of abuse victims still never seek he

more dynamic education efforts are vitally needed. We must first improve children's access to information.

The average child has an encyclopedic knowledge of toys and video games. She has no problem finding the closest McDonald's or locating the store that stocks the best selection of sneakers or skateboards. But ask these same kids where they would turn if they were abused, and you would get blank stares.

Though many social service agencies, schools, and communities have good outreach efforts, more are needed. Television is undoubtedly society's most effective educational tool, yet it is terribly underutilized in this area. Today, informational shows and public service announcements about child abuse tend not only to be poorly done, but are most often aired at times when virtually nobody is watching.

What is equally unfortunate is that even those shows marketed to children and youth—from Saturday-morning cartoons to the immensely popular Music Television (MTV)—lack child abuse information. Remarkably, not even the highly regarded "Sesame Street" has given any appreciable airtime to child abuse. "Sesame Street," like other educational children's shows, seems more comfortable warning children about the dangers of crossing the street than what might confront them in their own homes.

We also need to better our efforts at identifying and reporting abuse. More effective and rigorous training is critically needed for mandatory reporters. As the cases of Mike, Byron, and Patty poignantly demonstrate, teachers and school administrators—those who have the most contact with children besides their parents—are especially in need of help. Integral to assisting teachers in identifying abuse is training them how to understand and deal with the abused child or adolescent. Finally, these efforts must be directed not only to those in lower-income and middle-class schools as has been the tradition, but also to those who teach in affluent areas.

SHELTERS FOR ABUSED KIDS

Oftentimes abused children are compared to battered women. While they share certain psychological traits, there is one major difference: safe houses and shelters for abused wives are plentiful while unconditional safe havens for children are virtually nonexistent.

The prevailing national law enforcement policy is to return a runaway child to his parents because all fifty states decree that running away from home is a violation of the law.

Though no studies have been done on the subject, I am sure there are many more shelters for abused animals than abused children. Until shelter programs such as Children of the Night are offered to abused children, they will remain in their homes and we will see a perpetuation of abuse.

PARENTING

Parenting is without a doubt one of the most important and difficult jobs in society, yet it is one for which we receive little or no training. And tragically, the fact that 2.5 million kids are abused and neglected every year should tell us that something is wrong.

I have a fairly simple recommendation that might ameliorate the situation: just as we have driver's education, parenting classes should be made a mandatory part of junior and senior high curricula.

In view of the fact that physical abuse is at the heart of the majority of these parricides, it is critical that we learn as parents that physical punishment is simply not an acceptable way to discipline children. In making my recommendations here, I defer to family-violence specialist Murray Straus, who has developed a much deeper understanding of this problem. The following is excerpted from an interview I did with him for this book.

I want to see us have a national effort to help people avoid using physical punishment. In general parents don't want to hit their kids. Life is more fun with your kids if you're not hitting them. Sure there are some sadistic people who want to hit, but 99 percent of the physical punishment that goes on, parents don't want to hit their kids. They just feel it's necessary for their child's own good. They just want the kids to be properly behaved.

They don't really know about or have even thought through the alternatives. Even abusive parents by and large don't want to hit their kid. They just feel it's necessary, and in their case it has gotten out of hand.

The trouble with physical punishment is that it gets less effective over time until it finally gets to parents. And I've had lots who tell me this, you know, I just wish I could still put this kid over my knee—but he's too big.

In Sweden and several other countries . . . physical punishment is illegal. The way it works in Sweden is that there is no provision for punishment of people who violate the law. There's only a provision for getting them help. The assumption is that if they have to spank their kids, that means they're having trouble managing their children. They need some help in bringing up their kids in the way that they want to, and generally the way kids ought to be brought up. This law was treated with derision when it was first introduced. In 1979, three-quarters of the Swedish population were opposed to it. [Today] three-quarters are in favor of it.

A FINAL NOTE

Tim has been released on probation and is living on his own and working as a sales clerk. He continues his therapy and is dating a young woman.

Mike remains incarcerated in a youthful offender prison and will be eligible for parole in 1994.

George remains incarcerated in state prison and will not be eligible for parole until 2010.

Cindy continues to live in the small New England town where she moved after her release. She has not spoken with her mother or sisters since her sentencing.

Steven remains incarcerated in state prison and will not be eligible for release until sometime after 1998.

Patty remains incarcerated, but her case is now the subject of a pardon petition.

Byron remains incarcerated and will not be eligible for release until 2018.

The Carter brothers have not seen or heard from their father since the trial.